InstaEnglish

Student's Book and Workbook

2nd Edition

3

Patrick Howarth
Patricia Reilly
Olivia Johnston

macmillan education

InstaEnglish

Student's Book and Workbook **2nd Edition**

WALKTHROUGH

Check out how your combo edition of the **Student's Book and Workbook** is structured so you can make the most of it!

STUDENT'S BOOK

Your **Student's Book** is made up of a **Starter unit, 8 regular units,** 4 sets of **review activities,** plus 2 nifty sections: **Digital Literacy** after every 2 units, and **Global Citizenship** after every 4 units.

Starter unit

This two-page unit provides strategic language for you to kick off your studies!

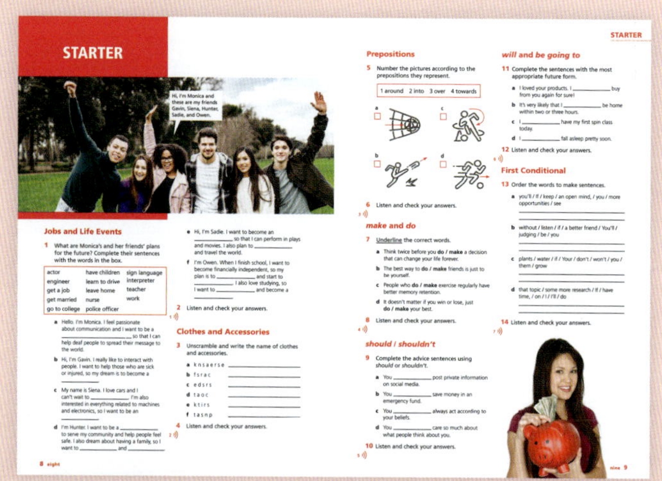

Opener

All regular units open with a visual treat to trigger your first thoughts on the main subject. What's the first thing that pops into your head when you look at it?

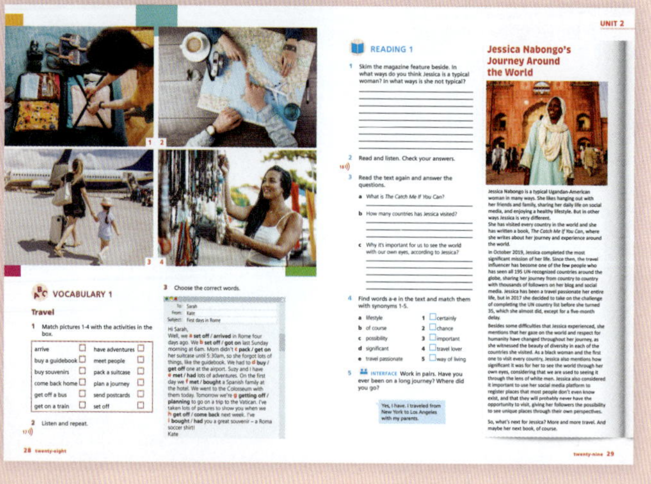

VOCABULARY 1

Here you will read, listen to, and look at pictures referring to words or phrases that will help you to explore the unit topic.

READING 1

Texts of multiple genres provide interesting content to practice your reading skills and introduce relevant language to be explored throughout the unit.

GRAMMAR 1

Grammar topics that were introduced in the reading text are systematically explored so you can easily work out all the rules and patterns.

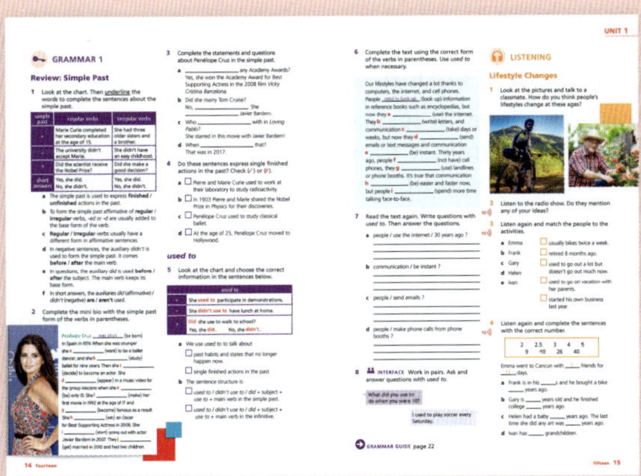

LISTENING

Learn and practice oral comprehension through engaging and contextualized oral texts.

SPEAKING

A clearly guided activity will help you practice your speaking skills using functional language in everyday situations. Throughout the levels, as you improve your ability to communicate orally, you will get increasing contact with real-life oral text genres.

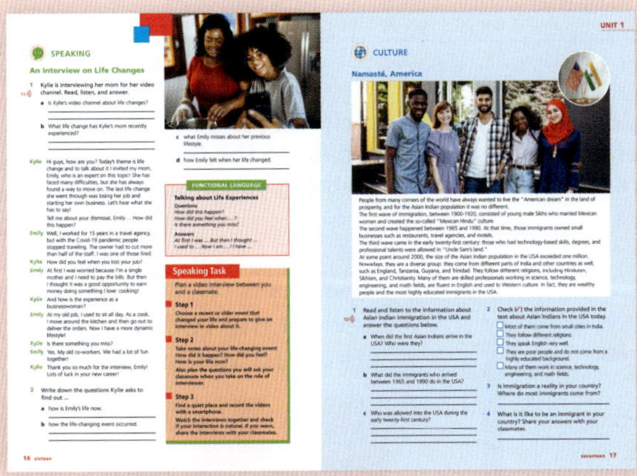

CULTURE

Discover cultural aspects of everyday life in English-speaking countries across the globe!

VOCABULARY 2

The second vocabulary set provides more words and phrases to allow you to go further into the unit topic.

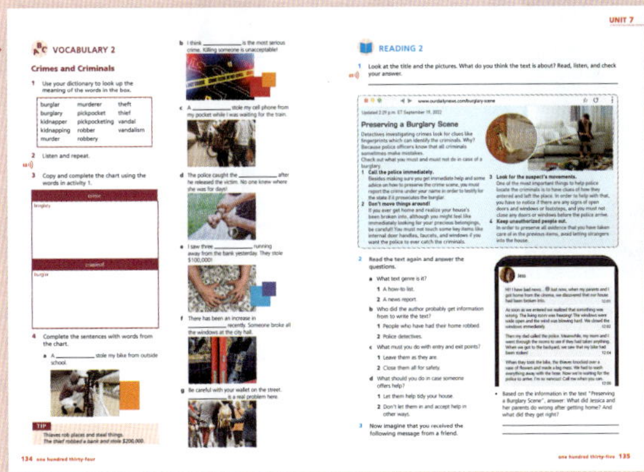

READING 2

The second reading text digs further into the main topic and provides more language to be explored.

GRAMMAR 2

A new grammar topic is introduced in the same contextualized and systematic way seen in **Grammar 1**.

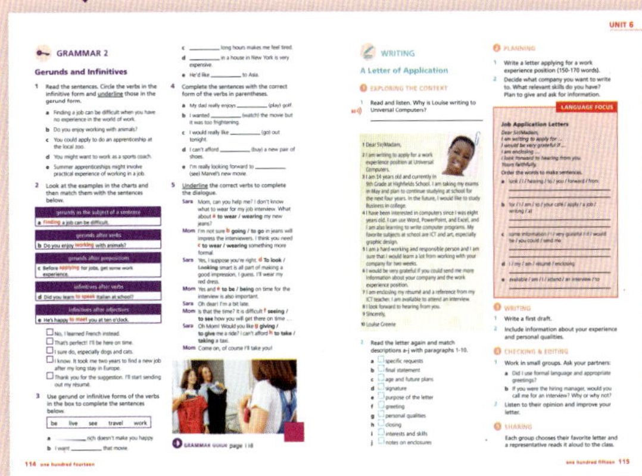

CLIL

In every odd-numbered unit, the **Grammar 2** section is accompanied by the **CLIL** section, for you to integrate your learning of the English language with other school subjects through fun texts and activities.

WRITING

In even-numbered units, the **Grammar 2** section is followed by the **Writing** section, where you are supported every step of the way to practice your writing skills in a range of text genres.

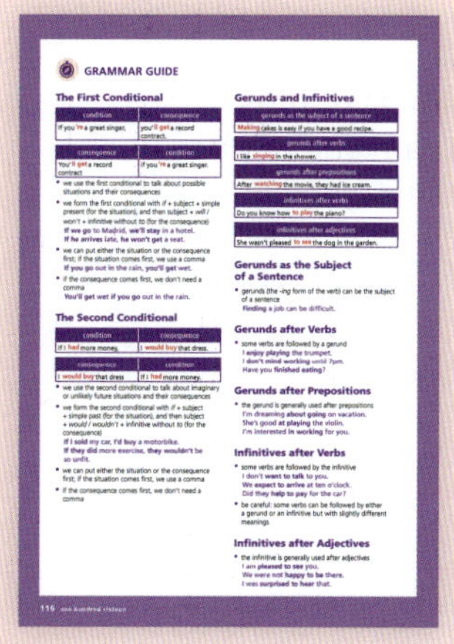

GRAMMAR GUIDE

This is a reference section for all the grammar topics explored in the unit.

VOCABULARY IN PICTURES

Have fun reviewing all the words and phrases learned in the **Vocabulary** sections, all richly illustrated!

PROGRESS CHECK

Once you complete the unit, cut this page out and close your book. Do the activities and check your overall progress. Then go back to the **Grammar Guide** and the **Vocabulary in Pictures** pages and revise anything you missed.

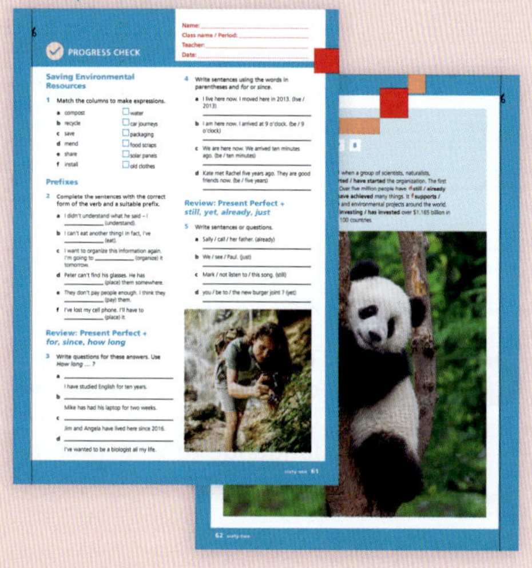

Review

Review the vocabulary and grammar from the previous two units starting with a game!

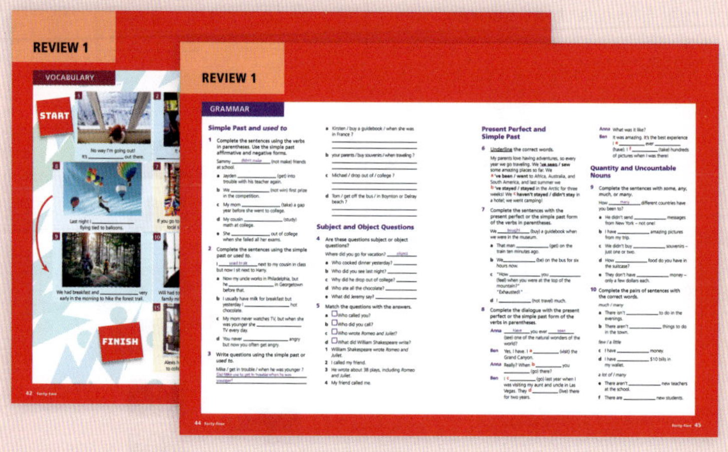

DIGITAL LITERACY

Do you think you use digital technology wisely? Follow siblings Lily and Daniel in a manga-style comic and see how they interact *with* and *through* the digital universe while reflecting about their (and your) relationship with the "digital."

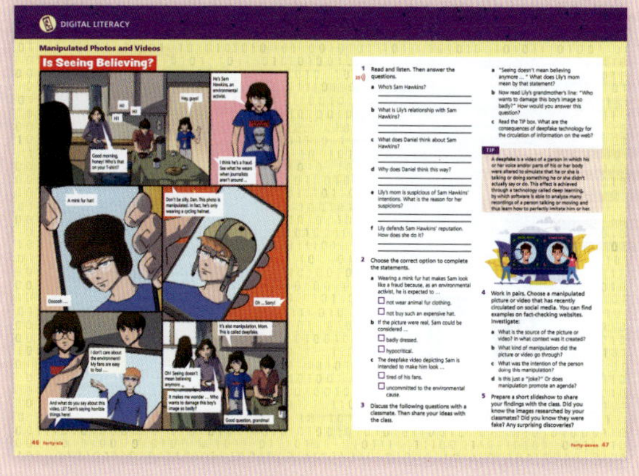

GLOBAL CITIZENSHIP

All of us need to nurture the perception that we are part of the same world. We need to build knowledge and develop skills to live together in the best possible way. That's what this section is all about!

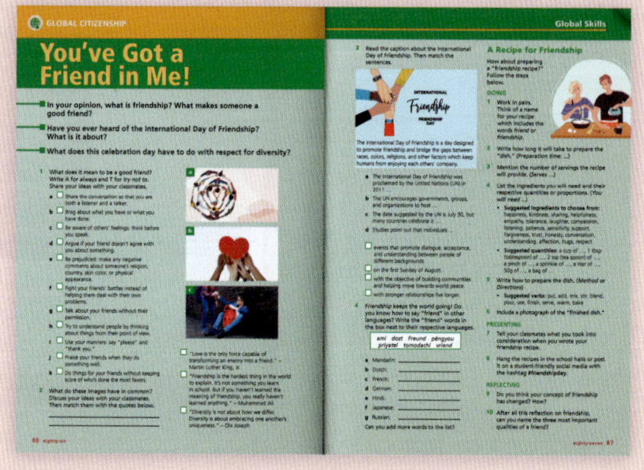

The **TIP, READING STRATEGY, PRONUNCIATION, CULTURAL FACT, FUNCTIONAL LANGUAGE, LANGUAGE FOCUS, CLASS VOTE,** and **INTERFACE** features will make your learning process more practical and effective.

WORKBOOK

The **Workbook** offers target-language practice and additional study material (consolidation and extension). It can be used as homework, independent study, or extra classroom practice. Some of the sections correspond to sections in the **Student's Book**:

VOCABULARY 1

GRAMMAR 1

GRAMMAR CHECK

A text with interesting and curious facts helps you check your reading and language skills.

VOCABULARY 2

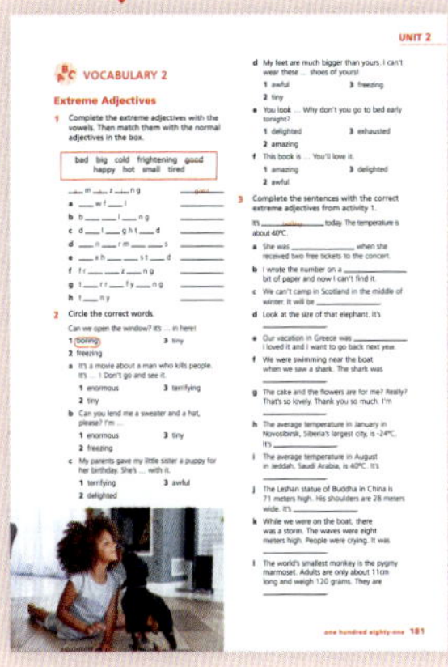

GRAMMAR 2

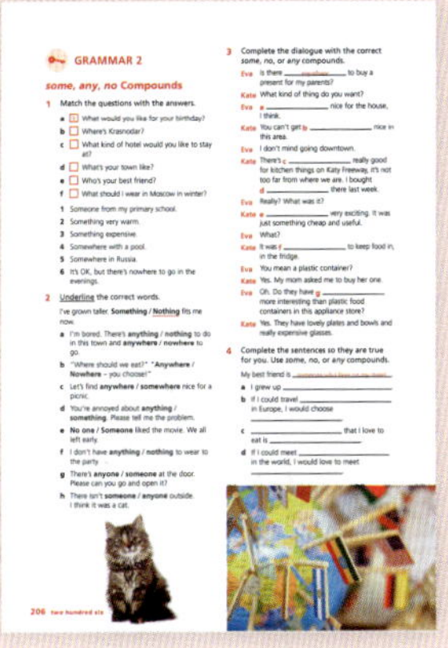

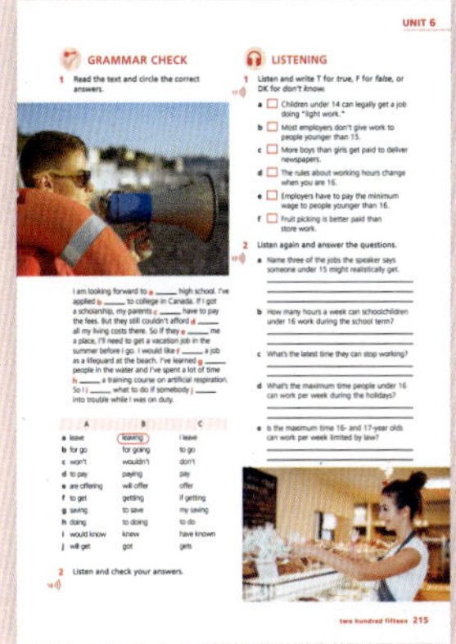

LISTENING

EXTENSION

This engaging section offers an extra challenge on grammar and vocabulary items.

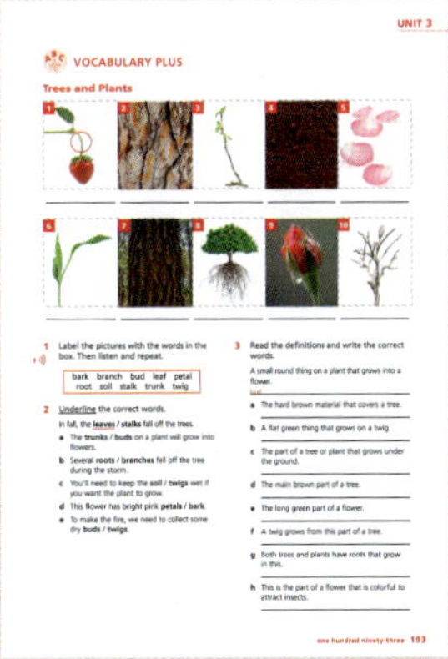

VOCABULARY PLUS

Learn more words related to the unit topic in a fun way! All words are illustrated.

Wordlist

This offers an alphabetical list of the key vocabulary in the **Student's Book** and from the **Vocabulary Plus** sections. It includes phonetic transcriptions and audio recordings.

DIGITAL OFFERINGS

InstaEnglish **2nd Edition** is a fully flexible course, which means you can study using your physical or your digital books and have access to the exact same content and activities. The digital books contain all the audio tracks and videos embedded. The digital offerings include the **On-the-go Practice** feature, for you to keep learning wherever you are!

CONTENTS

UNIT	VOCABULARY	GRAMMAR	READING
Starter **8**	Jobs and Life Events	Clothes and Accessories	Prepositions
 **1 CHANGING LIVES 10**	**1** Life-changing Events **12** **2** Verb + Preposition **18**	**1** Review: Simple Past / *used to* **14** **2** Subject and Object Questions **20**	**1** Awesome Women Who Have Changed the World. This Week meet ... Marie Curie! **12** **2** My New Life **18**
 **2 INCREDIBLE JOURNEYS 26**	**1** Travel **28** **2** Extreme Adjectives **34**	**1** Review: Present Perfect and Simple Past **30** **2** Review: Quantity and Uncountable Nouns **36**	**1** Jessica Nabongo's Journey Around the World **29** **2** Solo Sailor **35**
REVIEW 1 42			
 **3 THE WORLD AROUND US 48**	**1** Saving Environmental Resources **50** **2** Prefixes **56**	**1** Review: Present Perfect + *for, since, how long* **52** **2** Review: Present Perfect + *still, yet, already, just* **58**	**1** A Life without Trash **51** **2** Feeding Our Cities **56**
 **4 GOOD FRIENDS 64**	**1** Making Friends **66** **2** Verb and Noun Collocations **72**	**1** Obligation, No Obligation, Prohibition, Advice **68** **2** Second Conditional **74**	**1** Making Friends at Home and Abroad **67** **2** Questionnaire **73**
REVIEW 2 80			
GLOBAL CITIZENSHIP – YOU'VE GOT A FRIEND IN ME! 86			
 **5 FOLLOWERS OF FASHION 88**	**1** Style Adjectives **90** **2** Phrasal Verbs: Clothes **96**	**1** Relative Pronouns **92** **2** *some, any, no* Compounds **98**	**1** An article **91** **2** What is Happening on Saturday Evening? **96**
 **6 WORK AND MONEY 104**	**1** The World of Work **106** **2** Work Verbs **112**	**1** First and Second Conditionals **108** **2** Gerunds and Infinitives **114**	**1** The BEST Job in the World **107** **2** Try an Apprenticeship **113**
REVIEW 3 120			
 **7 CRIME DOESN'T PAY 126**	**1** Crime Verbs **128** **2** Crimes and Criminals **134**	**1** Modals of Deduction and Possibility **130** **2** Review: *must / must not* **136**	**1** Watch Out for Animal Smugglers! **129** **2** Preserving a Burglary Scene **135**
 **8 COMMUNICATE 142**	**1** The Written Word **144** **2** Adjectives with *-able* and *-ible* **150**	**1** Tense and Form Review: The Present; The Past; The Future **146** **2** Tense and Form Review: Questions **152**	**1** Text Genres **145** **2** The Man Behind the Chickens **150**
REVIEW 4 158			
GLOBAL CITIZENSHIP – A BETTER ME EVERY DAY 164			
IRREGULAR VERBS 166			
WORKBOOK 167			
WORDLIST 234			

LISTENING	SPEAKING	CULTURE	CLIL	WRITING
make and *do*	*should* / *shouldn't*	*will* and *be going to*	First Conditional	
Lifestyle Changes **15**	An Interview on Life Changes **16**	Namasté, America **17**	Science: Animal Migration **21**	
Dream Vacations **31**	The Trip of a Lifetime! **32**	David Livingstone and his Journey in Africa **33**		A Travel Journal Entry **36**
DIGITAL LITERACY – MANIPULATED PHOTOS AND VIDEOS 46				
Buy Nothing Day (BND) **53**	A News Podcast **54**	Electric Cars in Canada **55**	Art: Contemporary Protest Songs **59**	
My Gang **69**	An Advice Video **70**	Being Friendly or Being Friends? **71**		A Letter of Recommendation **74**
DIGITAL LITERACY – CYBERBULLYING 84				
A Famous Designer **93**	Prom Night **94**	Fashion Revolution in South Africa **95**	Art: The Victoria and Albert Museum **99**	
Part-time Jobs **109**	A Job Interview **110**	Working Teenagers in the US **111**		A Letter of Application **115**
DIGITAL LITERACY – PHISHING 124				
Crime News **131**	Witnessing a Crime **132**	Cybercrime in India **133**	Art: Graffiti – Inside or Outside the Law? **137**	
Communication Quiz **147**	Good News **148**	American Sign Language **149**		A Comment on a Blog Post **152**
DIGITAL LITERACY – CLICKBAIT 162				

STARTER

Jobs and Life Events

1 What are Monica's and her friends' plans for the future? Complete their sentences with the words in the box.

actor	have children	sign language interpreter
engineer	learn to drive	teacher
get a job	leave home	work
get married	nurse	
go to college	police officer	

a Hello. I'm Monica. I feel passionate about communication and I want to be a ______________ so that I can help deaf people to spread their message to the world.

b Hi, I'm Gavin. I really like to interact with people. I want to help those who are sick or injured, so my dream is to become a ______________.

c My name is Siena. I love cars and I can't wait to ______________. I'm also interested in everything related to machines and electronics, so I want to be an ______________.

d I'm Hunter. I want to be a ______________ to serve my community and help people feel safe. I also dream about having a family, so I want to ______________ and ______________.

e Hi, I'm Sadie. I want to become an ______________ so that I can perform in plays and movies. I also plan to ______________ and travel the world.

f I'm Owen. When I finish school, I want to become financially independent, so my plan is to ______________ and start to ______________. I also love studying, so I want to ______________ and become a ______________.

2 Listen and check your answers.

1

Clothes and Accessories

3 Unscramble and write the name of clothes and accessories.

a k n s a e r s e ______________

b f s r a c ______________

c e d s r s ______________

d t a o c ______________

e k t i r s ______________

f t a s n p ______________

4 Listen and check your answers.

2

Prepositions

5 Number the pictures according to the prepositions they represent.

1 around 2 into 3 over 4 towards

a ☐

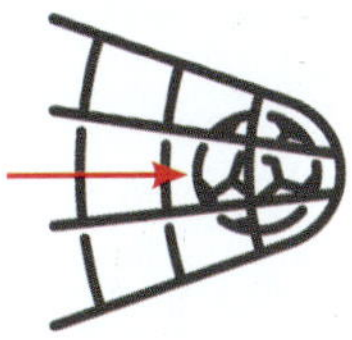

c ☐

b ☐

d ☐

6 Listen and check your answers.

3

make and *do*

7 Underline the correct words.

a Think twice before you **do / make** a decision that can change your life forever.

b The best way to **do / make** friends is just to be yourself.

c People who **do / make** exercise regularly have better memory retention.

d It doesn't matter if you win or lose, just **do / make** your best.

8 Listen and check your answers.

4

should / shouldn't

9 Complete the advice sentences using *should* or *shouldn't*.

a You ______________ post private information on social media.

b You ______________ save money in an emergency fund.

c You ______________ always act according to your beliefs.

d You ______________ care so much about what people think about you.

10 Listen and check your answers.

5

will and *be going to*

11 Complete the sentences with the most appropriate future form.

a I loved your products. I ______________ buy from you again for sure!

b It's very likely that I ______________ be home within two or three hours.

c I ______________ have my first spin class today.

d I ______________ fall asleep pretty soon.

12 Listen and check your answers.

6

First Conditional

13 Order the words to make sentences.

a you'll / If / keep / an open mind, / you / more opportunities / see

____

____

b without / listen / if / a better friend / You'll / judging / be / you

____

____

c plants / water / if / Your / don't / won't / you / them / grow

____

____

d that topic / some more research / If / have time, / on / I / I'll / do

____

____

14 Listen and check your answers.

7

1

CHANGING LIVES

Marie with her husband Pierre Curie on their honeymoon.

Marie in New York with her daughters and journalist Mrs. William B. Maloney. In the picture, Marie is the third from left to right.

VOCABULARY 1

Life-changing Events

1 Use your dictionary to check the meaning of the words in the box.

be widowed	go abroad	retire
become rich	go for a job interview	settle down
change schools	have an accident	start your own business
drop out of college	make new friends	take a gap year
get into trouble	move	win an award

2 Listen and repeat.

8

3 Choose the correct answers.

a Are your parents bored of working for someone else? They should think about **starting their own business / winning an award**.

b Tom **retired / had an accident** last year. Now that he isn't working he has more time to see his grandchildren.

c My older brother **moved / got into trouble** from Charleston to Boston. He **dropped out / made new friends** quickly and he's even **settled down / won an award** with his wife.

d Amy **had an accident / went abroad** yesterday – she broke her leg.

e A few years ago, Mark **retired / got into trouble** because he bullied some other students. He **changed schools / had an accident** and he's much happier now.

f Lucy **dropped out of college / moved house** because she didn't like studying math. She **settled down / went for a job interview** last month and now she's working as a chef.

g My older brother **took a gap year / became rich** before he started college. He **retired / went abroad** and worked as a volunteer in a school in Africa.

h My uncle **was widowed / changed schools** two years ago. To forget how much he missed my aunt, he began to paint canvases. He became such a good painter that he **had an accident / won an award** in a national art contest.

4 INTERFACE Work in pairs. Ask and answer the question.

What event has changed your life most?

READING 1

1 Look at the photographs that show different moments in Marie Curie's life. When do you think these pictures were taken?

a In the 18th century.

b Between the end of the 19th century and the beginning of the 20th century.

c In the second half of the 20th century.

2 Number the photographs in the order you think they were taken.

3 Read and listen to Marie Curie's mini biography on page 13. Then check your answers in activities 1 and 2.

9

Maria Sklodowska (later Marie Curie) in Warsaw with her brothers and sisters. In the picture, Marie is the third from left to right.

1

Marie and Pierre in their laboratory while first experimenting into the radio-activity of radium.

www.awesomewomen.com

Awesome Women Who Have Changed the World
This week meet ... Marie Curie!

Maria Salomea Sklodowska, later known as Marie Curie, was born on November 7, 1867, in Warsaw, the capital of present-day Poland. The youngest of five children, she had three older sisters and a brother. Her parents ensured that their girls were educated as well as their son.

At the age of 15, Maria completed her secondary education, graduating first in her class. She and her sister Bronislawa wished to pursue a higher education, but the University of Warsaw did not accept women. Bronislawa was the first to leave their country, going to study at a medical school in France. In 1891, it was Maria's turn to move to Paris, where she studied physics and math at the Sorbonne. By that time, she began to call herself "Marie" to seem more French.

In the spring of 1894 she met Pierre Curie, who was completing his doctorate of science. The couple were married in the next year and she took her husband's surname, becoming Marie Curie. Pierre and Marie would have two daughters, Irène and Eve.

In 1896, a French chemist named Henri Becquerel discovered that uranium emitted energy and subatomic particles. In their laboratory, Pierre and Marie studied this phenomenon, which they called radioactivity. Together, they discovered two new radioactive elements, radium and polonium, the last named after Marie's native Poland.

In 1903, Pierre and Marie shared the Nobel Prize in Physics for their discoveries. At first, the French Academy of Science had nominated only Pierre, but he insisted that they should be considered for the prize together. Three years later Marie was widowed – Pierre died in a traffic accident.

Marie assumed Pierre's chair at the Sorbonne and dedicated all her energy to completing the scientific work they had started together. In 1911 she was awarded the Nobel Prize in Chemistry for isolating pure radium.

From the beginning of the World War I, Marie studied the medical applications of radium. She made a conscious decision, however, not to patent the substance. As the price of radium soared, she could not afford to buy enough for her research. Fortunately, an American journalist, Mrs. W. B. Meloney, campaigned for USA women to fund Marie Curie's research. In 1921, Marie was in the United States with her daughters to receive the donation and also met with President Warren Harding at the White House. Marie Curie died of leukemia in France on July 4, 1934 after exposure to radioactive elements.

READING STRATEGY

False friends are words with a similar spelling but different meaning in another language. *Parents* can be a false friend as it looks similar to some words in Latin languages but can have different meanings. Check for the possibility of different meanings.

4 Read the text again and answer the questions.

a Why couldn't Maria and Bronislawa attend the University of Warsaw?

____

b What happened in Marie's life in 1895?

____

c What were Pierre and Marie researching together?

____

d How many Nobel Prizes has Marie received in total?

____

e Why did Marie find it difficult to continue her research into the medical applications of radium?

____

f Who helped Marie Curie to continue her research?

____

5 CLASS VOTE Do you know other "awesome women who have changed the world?" Name one of them.

GRAMMAR 1

Review: Simple Past

1 Look at the chart. Then underline the words to complete the sentences about the simple past.

simple past	regular verbs	irregular verbs
+	Marie Curie completed her secondary education at the age of 15.	She had three older sisters and a brother.
–	The university didn't accept Marie.	She didn't have an easy childhood.
?	Did the scientist receive the Nobel Prize?	Did she make a good decision?
short answers	Yes, she did. No, she didn't.	Yes, she did. No, she didn't.

a The simple past is used to express **finished** / **unfinished** actions in the past.

b To form the simple past affirmative of **regular** / **irregular** verbs, *-ed* or *-d* are usually added to the base form of the verb.

c **Regular** / **Irregular** verbs usually have a different form in affirmative sentences.

d In negative sentences, the auxiliary *didn't* is used to form the simple past. It comes **before** / **after** the main verb.

e In questions, the auxiliary *did* is used **before** / **after** the subject. The main verb keeps its base form.

f In short answers, the auxiliaries *did* (affirmative) / *didn't* (negative) **are** / **aren't** used.

2 Complete the mini bio with the simple past form of the verbs in parentheses.

Penélope Cruz ___was born___ (be born) in Spain in 1974. When she was younger she **a** ____________ (want) to be a ballet dancer, and she **b** ____________ (study) ballet for nine years. Then she **c** ____________ (decide) to become an actor. She **d** ____________ (appear) in a music video for the group Mecano when she **e** ____________ (be) only 15. She **f** ____________ (make) her first movie in 1992 at the age of 17 and **g** ____________ (become) famous as a result. She **h** ____________ (win) an Oscar for Best Supporting Actress in 2008. She **i** ____________ (start) going out with actor Javier Bardem in 2007. They **j** ____________ (get) married in 2010 and had two children.

3 Complete the statements and questions about Penélope Cruz in the simple past.

a ________________ any Academy Awards?
Yes, she won the Academy Award for Best Supporting Actress in the 2008 film *Vicky Cristina Barcelona*.

b Did she marry Tom Cruise?
No, ________________. She ________________ Javier Bardem.

c Who ________________ with in *Loving Pablo*?
She starred in this movie with Javier Bardem!

d When ________________ that?
That was in 2017.

4 Do these sentences express single finished actions in the past? Check (✓) or (✗).

a ☐ Pierre and Marie Curie used to work at their laboratory to study radioactivity.

b ☐ In 1903 Pierre and Marie shared the Nobel Prize in Physics for their discoveries.

c ☐ Penélope Cruz used to study classical ballet.

d ☐ At the age of 25, Penélope Cruz moved to Hollywood.

used to

5 Look at the chart and choose the correct information in the sentences below.

	used to
+	She **used to** participate in demonstrations.
–	She **didn't use to** have lunch at home.
?	**Did** she use to walk to school? Yes, she **did**. No, she **didn't**.

a We use *used to* to talk about
☐ past habits and states that no longer happen now.
☐ single finished actions in the past.

b The sentence structure is:
☐ *used to* / *didn't use to* / *did* + subject + *use to* + main verb in the simple past.
☐ *used to* / *didn't use to* / *did* + subject + *use to* + main verb in the infinitive.

6 Complete the text using the correct form of the verbs in parentheses. Use *used to* when necessary.

Our lifestyles have changed a lot thanks to computers, the internet, and cell phones. People __used to look up__ (look up) information in reference books such as encyclopedias, but now they **a** ____________ (use) the internet. They **b** ____________ (write) letters, and communication **c** ____________ (take) days or weeks, but now they **d** ____________ (send) emails or text messages and communication **e** ____________ (be) instant. Thirty years ago, people **f** ____________ (not have) cell phones, they **g** ____________ (use) landlines or phone booths. It's true that communication **h** ____________ (be) easier and faster now, but people **i** ____________ (spend) more time talking face-to-face.

7 Read the text again. Write questions with *used to*. Then answer the questions.

a people / use the internet / 30 years ago ?

____

____

____

b communication / be instant ?

____

____

____

c people / send emails ?

____

____

____

d people / make phone calls from phone booths ?

____

____

____

8 INTERFACE Work in pairs. Ask and answer questions with *used to*.

What did you use to do when you were 10?

I used to play soccer every Saturday.

GRAMMAR GUIDE page 22

LISTENING

Lifestyle Changes

1 Look at the pictures and talk to a classmate. How do you think people's lifestyles change at these ages?

2 10 Listen to the radio show. Do they mention any of your ideas?

3 10 Listen again and match the people to the activities.

a Emma
b Frank
c Gary
d Helen
e Ivan

☐ usually bikes twice a week.
☐ retired 8 months ago.
☐ used to go out a lot but doesn't go out much now.
☐ used to go on vacation with her parents.
☐ started his own business last year.

4 10 Listen again and complete the sentences with the correct number.

2	2.5	3	4	~~5~~
9	~~10~~	26	40	

Emma went to Cancun with __5__ friends for __10__ days.

a Frank is in his ______s and he bought a bike ______ years ago.

b Gary is ______ years old and he finished college ______ years ago.

c Helen had a baby ______ years ago. The last time she did any art was ______ years ago.

d Ivan has ______ grandchildren.

SPEAKING

An Interview on Life Changes

1 Kylie is interviewing her mom for her video channel. Read, listen, and answer.
11

a Is Kylie's video channel about life changes?

____

b What life change has Kylie's mom recently experienced?

____

Kylie Hi guys, how are you? Today's theme is life change and to talk about it I invited my mom, Emily, who is an expert on this topic! She has faced many difficulties, but she has always found a way to move on. The last life change she went through was losing her job and starting her own business. Let's hear what she has to say!

Tell me about your dismissal, Emily ... How did this happen?

Emily Well, I worked for 15 years in a travel agency, but with the Covid-19 pandemic people stopped traveling. The owner had to cut more than half of the staff. I was one of those fired.

Kylie How did you feel when you lost your job?

Emily At first I was worried because I'm a single mother and I need to pay the bills. But then I thought it was a good opportunity to earn money doing something I love: cooking!

Kylie And how is the experience as a businesswoman?

Emily At my old job, I used to sit all day. As a cook, I move around the kitchen and then go out to deliver the orders. Now I have a more dynamic lifestyle!

Kylie Is there something you miss?

Emily Yes. My old co-workers. We had a lot of fun together!

Kylie Thank you so much for the interview, Emily! Lots of luck in your new career!

2 Write down the questions Kylie asks to find out ...

a how is Emily's life now.

____

b how the life-changing event occurred.

____

c what Emily misses about her previous lifestyle.

____

d how Emily felt when her life changed.

____

FUNCTIONAL LANGUAGE

Talking about Life Experiences

Questions

How did this happen?
How did you feel when ... ?
Is there something you miss?

Answers

At first I was ... But then I thought ...
I used to ... Now I am ... / I have ...

Speaking Task

Plan a video interview between you and a classmate.

Step 1

Choose a recent or older event that changed your life and prepare to give an interview in video about it.

Step 2

Take notes about your life-changing event: How did it happen? How did you feel? How is your life now?

Also plan the questions you will ask your classmate when you take on the role of interviewer.

Step 3

Find a quiet place and record the videos with a smartphone.

Watch the interviews together and check if your interaction is natural. If you want, share the interviews with your classmates.

CULTURE

Namasté, America

People from many corners of the world have always wanted to live the "American dream" in the land of prosperity, and for the Asian Indian population it was no different.

The first wave of immigration, between 1900-1920, consisted of young male Sikhs who married Mexican women and created the so-called "Mexican Hindu" culture.

The second wave happened between 1965 and 1990. At that time, those immigrants owned small businesses such as restaurants, travel agencies, and motels.

The third wave came in the early twenty-first century: those who had technology-based skills, degrees, and professional talents were allowed in "Uncle Sam's land."

At some point around 2000, the size of the Asian Indian population in the USA exceeded one million. Nowadays, they are a diverse group: they come from different parts of India and other countries as well, such as England, Tanzania, Guyana, and Trinidad. They follow different religions, including Hinduism, Sikhism, and Christianity. Many of them are skilled professionals working in science, technology, engineering, and math fields, are fluent in English and used to Western culture. In fact, they are wealthy people and the most highly educated immigrants in the USA.

1 Read and listen to the information about Asian Indian immigration in the USA and answer the questions below. 12

a When did the first Asian Indians arrive in the USA? Who were they?

____

____

____

b What did the immigrants who arrived between 1965 and 1990 do in the USA?

____

____

____

c Who was allowed into the USA during the early twenty-first century?

____

____

____

2 Check (✓) the information provided in the text about Asian Indians in the USA today.

- ☐ Most of them come from small cities in India.
- ☐ They follow different religions.
- ☐ They speak English very well.
- ☐ They are poor people and do not come from a highly educated background.
- ☐ Many of them work in science, technology, engineering, and math fields.

3 Is immigration a reality in your country? Where do most immigrants come from?

____

4 What is it like to be an immigrant in your country? Share your answers with your classmates.

____

VOCABULARY 2

Verb + Preposition

1 Look at the verbs in the box. Use your dictionary to look up the meaning of any unknown words. How do you say these words in your language?

agree about	depend on	participate in
agree with	dream about	talk to
argue about	listen to	wait for
argue with	look forward to	worry about

2 Listen and repeat.

13

3 Complete the questions with the correct prepositions.

What music do you like listening ___to___?

a Who do you talk ________ when you have problems?

b What do you dream ________ doing in the future?

c Do you usually agree ________ your friends?

d Do you often participate ________ activities in class?

e Which things do you argue ________?

f Do you and your best friend agree ________ anything?

g Can your friends depend ________ you?

4 INTERFACE Work in pairs. Ask and answer the questions in activity 3.

What music do you like listening to?

I like listening to jazz and hip-hop. How about you?

5 Choose the correct answers.

a My brother and I have different opinions about everything. I often **argue with / argue about** him.

b I'm at the train station. I'm **waiting for / looking forward to** a train.

c Who's on the phone? Who are you **talking to / participating in**?

d Pete is a nervous person. He **depends on / worries about** absolutely everything.

PRONUNCIATION

Sentence Stress

1 Listen to the sentences and underline the most stressed syllables.

14

Do you dream about traveling the world?

a We're looking forward to the party.

b She used to participate in demonstrations.

c She didn't have an easy childhood.

2 Listen again and repeat the sentences, emphasizing the stressed syllables.

14

READING 2

1 Look at the pictures and the title of the text on page 19. Which life change do you think the text describes?

a changing jobs **b** going abroad

2 What kind of text is it?

a a fact file **b** a personal account

3 Read and listen. Check your answers.

15

My New Life

My name is Aminata and I'm 14 years old. I live in Chicago in the USA. I used to live in Senegal in Africa but I moved here three years ago with my family. When I was younger, I used to dream about living in America, so when my parents told me we were moving I was really looking forward to it.

I thought everything would be easy here and that everyone would be kind and I'd have a good time. I didn't realize how wrong I was. When I started school, some of the other students were really awful to me. They said things like, "Why don't you go back to where you came from?" I was shocked and upset, but I didn't listen to them.

I realized that most of the students at my school were ignorant about other countries and cultures, but that isn't an excuse for treating others badly. Diversity makes the world an interesting place and we can all learn a lot from each other.

It was really hard at first because I missed my friends from Senegal, but I was lucky – I made some new friends and they helped me a lot. We started a diversity club at school to embrace the differences between others and ourselves. Being an immigrant is hard, but now I know that you should respect other people's differences.

I've also had some great experiences since I moved to the USA. The school system here is good and teenagers can be very independent. It's fun getting to know new people who enjoy my company because of who I am.

4 Read the text again and complete the statements.

- **a** Aminata used to live in ________________ in Africa.
- **b** Now she lives in ________________ in the USA.
- **c** She has lived in her new country since she was ________________ years old.
- **d** Before moving, Aminata thought it would be ________________ to live in the USA.
- **e** When Aminata started school, some of the students were ________________ to her.
- **f** Aminata started a ________________ with her friends.

Cultural fact

Diversity groups promote the equality of people from minority groups of all kinds, including race, gender, disability, and religion. They exist in some schools and communities in the USA.

5 Answer the questions.

- **a** How did Aminata feel when her classmates treated her badly?

  ____

  ____

- **b** In Aminata's opinion, why were her classmates hostile to her?

  ____

  ____

- **c** Why does Aminata consider herself lucky?

  ____

  ____

- **d** What advantages does Aminata see in living in the USA?

  ____

  ____

6 Discuss the following questions with a classmate. Then share your ideas with the class.

- **a** In your opinion, why did Aminata dream of living in America?
- **b** According to Aminata, ignorance of other cultures "isn't an excuse to treat others badly." In your opinion, how should we act when we meet a person from another country or another culture?

7 INTERFACE Work in pairs. Have you ever had a foreign classmate? Share your experience.

> I had a Bolivian classmate when I was in 4th grade. He taught me some Spanish words.

GRAMMAR 2

Subject and Object Questions

1 Read the questions below. Underline the verbal structures and circle the question words.

a Who helped Aminata?

b What happened when she started school?

c Who did Aminata miss?

d What did Aminata and her new friends start at school?

2 Look at the rules below. Complete the chart with the words in the box.

did … miss	did … start
happened	helped

a Sometimes question words carry no auxiliary verb and the order in the question is not inverted. In this case, they are the subject of sentences that are called *subject questions*.

b The answer of a subject question will be the subject.

c When the question word is followed by auxiliary + subject + main verb in the base form, that is an *object question*. The answer in object questions will come after the verb, in the object.

subject questions
Who ___________ Aminata? *Her new friends helped her.* **What** ___________ when she started school? *Some students were awful to her.*
object questions
Who ___________ Aminata ___________? *She missed her friends from Senegal.* **What** ___________ Aminata and her new friends ___________ at school? *They started a diversity group.*

3 Read the questions and answers. Which one is an *object question* (O) and which is a *subject question* (S)?

a What did you do yesterday?

☐ *I went to the movies.*

b What happened at the movies?

☐ *All the tickets were sold out.*

4 Look at the diagram. Match the questions with the answers.

a Who did Andy write to?

b Who wrote to Andy?

c Who did Wessam write to?

d Who wrote to Wessam?

☐ Ava wrote to him.

☐ Mari wrote to him.

☐ He wrote to Ava.

☐ He wrote to Mari.

GRAMMAR GUIDE page 22

CLIL

SCIENCE

Animal Migration

Many species in the animal kingdom migrate, including birds, fish, mammals, and reptiles. They often travel great distances to reach another part of the world. Humpback whales swim more than 5,000 miles in one direction, while one species of bird flies 7,000 miles non-stop in just eight days. Animals migrate because they need to find food (some plants or animals may only be available in a certain area at particular times of the year), a better climate (the winter may be very cold) or the best place to reproduce.

The migration cycle may happen every time the seasons change, once a year, or perhaps just once in the animal's lifetime. For example, Scottish salmon are born in freshwater rivers. Then they swim thousands of miles north to find food in the Atlantic Ocean. When it's time for the salmon to reproduce, it swims back to the river where it was born. After it lays its eggs there, it dies.

1 Read and listen. Answer the question.

16 Why do Scottish salmon migrate?

____

____

2 Find and circle four types of animals that migrate.

reptilesadmfishscmabirdsfimammalses

3 Complete the sentences with the words in the box.

climate distances food lifetime miles reasons year

a When animals migrate they often travel great __________.

b Humpback whales swim more than 5,000 __________ in one direction.

c Animals migrate for many different __________.

d They often migrate at a particular time of the __________.

e Some animals migrate in order to find __________.

f When they migrate, some animals are looking for a better __________ or a place to reproduce.

g Some animals migrate every year and some only once in a __________.

GRAMMAR GUIDE

Review: Simple Past

+	I / You	**moved**.
	He / She / It	**moved**.
	We / You / They	**moved**.
–	I / You	**didn't move**.
	He / She / It	**didn't move**.
	We / You / They	**didn't move**.
?	**Did** you **move**? Yes, I **did**. No, I **didn't**.	

- we use the simple past to talk about events in the past, especially if we express a definite point in past
  I **played** tennis yesterday.
- we form negative sentences with *didn't* + the base form of the verb
  They **didn't walk** to school.
- we form questions in the past with *did* + base form of the verb. In short answers, we don't repeat the main verb
  Did he **buy** a car? Yes, he **did**.

used to

+	She **used to** participate in demonstrations.
–	She **didn't use** to have food at home.
?	**Did** she **use to** travel abroad? Yes, she **did**. No, she **didn't**.

- we use *used to* + base form of the verb to talk about past habits and situations. We use it to talk about things that people did regularly in the past but that they don't do now
  They **used to** live in Chicago, but now they live in Boston.
  He **used to** ride his bike to work, but now he takes the bus.

Subject and Object Questions

subject questions
Who went to the movies yesterday? Joe went to the movies yesterday.
object questions
What did Joe **do** yesterday? He went to the movies.

- question words can be either the subject or the object of the verb
- if the question word is the subject of the question, we don't use an auxiliary verb
  Who made the cake? **Jenny** made the cake.
- if the question word is the object of the question, we use an auxiliary verb (*do*, *does*, or *did*)
  What did Jenny make? She made a **cake**.

Name: ______________________

Class name / Period: ______________________

Teacher: ______________________

Date: ______________________

PROGRESS CHECK

Life-changing Events

1 Match a-d with 1-4 to make sentences.

a ☐ Dan and Mandy moved

b ☐ They decided to start

c ☐ Mike made

d ☐ Kathy said that she wanted to take

1 their own business.

2 a gap year before college.

3 last year.

4 new friends after he changed schools.

Verb + Preposition

2 Complete the expressions with the correct prepositions.

a agree ________ someone

b agree ________ something

c look forward ________ something

d depend ________ someone

e participate ________ something

Simple Past and *used to*

3 Choose the correct answers.

a I **used to move / moved** to France three years ago.

b I **used to go / went** hiking twice a month when I was younger.

c Last weekend I **used to go / went** shopping, but I **didn't use to buy / didn't buy** anything.

d What **did you use to do / did you do** on weekends when you were 10?

e Peter **used to get / got** married last week.

4 Complete the questions and answers with the correct form of the verbs in parentheses.

a Did you ________ to ________ (live) in a different town or city?

Yes, I ________ (live) in Albuquerque, but I ________ (live) in Miami now. I ________ (move) here two months ago.

b ________________ (Sue / like) vegetables?

No, she ____________ (not like) them, but now she ________ (be) a vegetarian. She ________ (stop) eating meat last year.

c What ________________ (Tony / do) every Saturday?

He ________ (go) swimming, but last year he ________ (start) playing football. He ________ (not go) swimming now.

Subject and Object Questions

5 Write subject or object questions with *who* or *what* for the information in bold. Then answer the questions.

Sally went shopping **with her friends**.

Who did Sally go shopping with?

She went shopping with her friends.

a **Sally** went shopping with her friends.

____

____

b Mike visited **the new museum**.

____

____

c **Mike** visited the new museum.

____

____

Grammar Buildup 1

1 2 3 4 5 6 7 8

6 Choose the correct answers.

Nick **a used to win / won** the lottery ten years ago and he **b used to change / changed** his life. Before, he **c got up / used to get up** early, but then he **d used to start getting up / started getting up** very late, like 12 o'clock! In his old life, he **e was working / used to work** very hard, but he **f stopped working / didn't use to stop working** after the lottery. To get to work he **g was catching / used to catch** the bus, but he **h used to buy / bought** a new car and he **i traveled / used to travel** everywhere in his car for about three years. Nick **j didn't use to go / didn't go** to dinner parties or travel abroad, but since winning the lottery he's done that many times!

VOCABULARY IN PICTURES

Life-changing Events

be widowed

become rich

change schools

drop out of college

get into trouble

go abroad

go for a job interview

have an accident

make new friends

move

retire

settle down

start your own business

take a gap year

win an award

Verb + Preposition

agree about / agree with

argue about / argue with

depend on

dream about

listen to

look forward to

participate in

talk to

wait for

worry about

2

INCREDIBLE JOURNEYS

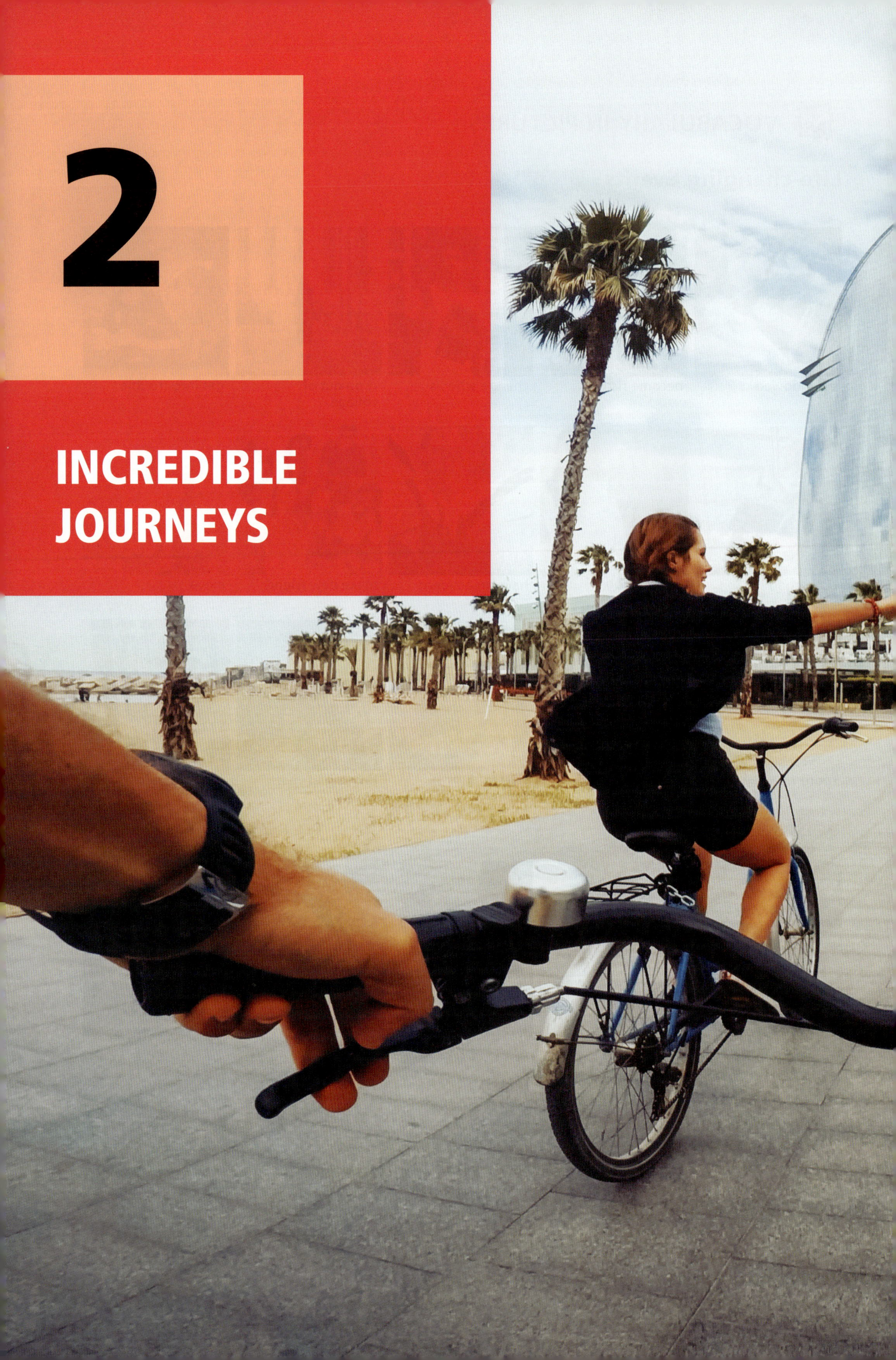

1

2

3

4

VOCABULARY 1

Travel

1 Match pictures 1-4 with the activities in the box.

arrive	☐	have adventures	☐
buy a guidebook	☐	meet people	☐
buy souvenirs	☐	pack a suitcase	☐
come back home	☐	plan a journey	☐
get off a bus	☐	send postcards	☐
get on a train	☐	set off	☐

2 Listen and repeat.

17

3 Choose the correct words.

To: Sarah
From: Kate
Subject: First days in Rome

Hi Sarah,
Well, we **a set off** / **arrived** in Rome four days ago. We **b set off** / **got on** last Sunday morning at 6am. Mom didn't **c pack** / **get on** her suitcase until 5:30am, so she forgot lots of things, like the guidebook. We had to **d buy** / **get off** one at the airport. Suzy and I have **e met** / **had** lots of adventures. On the first day we **f met** / **bought** a Spanish family at the hotel. We went to the Colosseum with them today. Tomorrow we're **g getting off** / **planning** to go on a trip to the Vatican. I've taken lots of pictures to show you when we **h get off** / **come back** next week. I've **i bought** / **had** you a great souvenir – a Roma soccer shirt!
Kate

READING 1

1 Skim the magazine feature beside. In what ways do you think Jessica is a typical woman? In what ways is she not typical?

2 Read and listen. Check your answers.

18

3 Read the text again and answer the questions.

a What is *The Catch Me If You Can*?

b How many countries has Jessica visited?

c Why it's important for us to see the world with our own eyes, according to Jessica?

4 Find words a-e in the text and match them with synonyms 1-5.

a	lifestyle	1	certainly
b	of course	2	chance
c	possibility	3	important
d	significant	4	travel lover
e	travel passionate	5	way of living

5 INTERFACE Work in pairs. Have you ever been on a long journey? Where did you go?

Yes, I have. I traveled from New York to Los Angeles with my parents.

Jessica Nabongo's Journey Around the World

Jessica Nabongo is a typical Ugandan-American woman in many ways. She likes hanging out with her friends and family, sharing her daily life on social media, and enjoying a healthy lifestyle. But in other ways Jessica is very different.
She has visited every country in the world and she has written a book, *The Catch Me If You Can*, where she writes about her journey and experience around the world.

In October 2019, Jessica completed the most significant mission of her life. Since then, the travel influencer has become one of the few people who has seen all 195 UN-recognized countries around the globe, sharing her journey from country to country with thousands of followers on her blog and social media. Jessica has been a travel passionate her entire life, but in 2017 she decided to take on the challenge of completing the UN country list before she turned 35, which she almost did, except for a five-month delay.

Besides some difficulties that Jessica experienced, she mentions that her gaze on the world and respect for humanity have changed throughout her journey, as she witnessed the beauty of diversity in each of the countries she visited. As a black woman and the first one to visit every country, Jessica also mentions how significant it was for her to see the world through her own eyes, considering that we are used to seeing it through the lens of white men. Jessica also considered it important to use her social media platform to register places that most people don't even know exist, and that they will probably never have the opportunity to visit, giving her followers the possibility to see unique places through their own perspectives.

So, what's next for Jessica? More and more travel. And maybe her next book, of course.

GRAMMAR 1

Review: Present Perfect and Simple Past

1 Look at the following sentences. Underline the verb forms.

a She has traveled to England.

b He has written four books.

c I have lost my cell phone.

d We haven't seen her at the hotel.

2 Read the rules below and complete the chart with the verb forms in the box.

a The present perfect is formed from the verb *have* (*have*, *has*) + the past participle of the main verb.

b Negative sentences in the present perfect need *haven't* or *hasn't*.

c Questions follow the structure: *have / has* + subject + main verb in the past participle.

d The past participle of regular verbs usually take *-d / -ed*.

e Irregular verbs have different past participle forms.

f The present perfect is used to talk about past actions or experiences without saying when they happened.

g The simple past is used to talk about completed actions at a definite time in the past.

completed decided has been
has visited has written

present perfect	simple past
Jessica ______________ every country in the world.	In October 2019, Jessica ______________ the most significant mission of her life.
She ______________ a book.	In 2017 she ______________ to take on the challenge of completing the UN country list before she turned 35.
Jessica ______________ a travel passionate her entire life.	

3 Write sentences using the present perfect.

a Chimamanda Ngozi Adichie / have / an influence / all over the world.

____

____

b Many people / read / books / written by her.

____

____

c She / win / many awards and honors / throughout her life.

____

____

4 Fill in the blanks with the verb forms in the box below.

has happened has taken
have adopted have you got
haven't been

a ______________ more time than money?

b Backpackers in South Africa ______________ a "kikoi" (sarong-like piece of clothing). It's usually boiling hot all year long and kikois are comfortable for long walks.

c Quite a lot ______________ in South Africa in the past 20 years. The country ______________ lots of good steps forward.

d Race relations ______________ so difficult.

5 Read this testimonial of a backpacker in India and fill in the blanks with the present perfect or simple past of the verbs in parentheses.

"The first time I **a** ______________ (be) in India, I **b** ______________ (not have) a good experience. I **c** ______________ (try) to see the whole country in just one month – I **d** ______________ (travel) quickly and I **e** ______________ (get) sick because I **f** ______________ (eat) lots of spicy food. The good thing was that I **g** ______________ (travel) with a friend so I **h** ______________ (enjoy) it more.
After that trip, I **i** ______________ (be) back 5 more times. I **j** ______________ (travel) with friends, on tours, and, sometimes, alone.
I **k** ______________ (also meet) people from all over the world!"

6 Underline the correct verb forms to complete the dialogue below.

Jed What are you reading?
Beth I'm reading *Around the World in 80 Days*. **a Have you read / Do you read** it?
Jed No. Is it good?
Beth Yeah. I **b did read / have read** it before, I really liked it.
Jed Who's it by?
Beth Jules Verne. He **c has written / wrote** it in 1873.
Jed Oh, I know him. I **d have read / read** *Two Years' Vacation* a few years ago.
Beth I **e have saw / have seen** the animation based on that book. **f Did you like / Have you liked** the book?
Jed Yes, it **g was / were** great. You should read it. I **h have seen / saw** an old TV show called *Around the World in 80 Days* last year.
Beth With Michael Palin? Yes, I remember you mentioned it. He **i has made / has make** lots of travel shows, right?
Jed Yes, they're really good. Michael is really lucky that they could travel to a lot of foreign countries. I **j haven't been / have been** to any.
Beth Haven't you? I **k have been / has been** to lots. Last year I **l have gone / went** to Greece with my family.
Jed Lucky you!

GRAMMAR GUIDE page 38

LISTENING

Dream Vacations

1 Look at the pictures. What type of vacations do they show?

____

2 Listen to the advertisements and number the journeys. 19

a ☐ A family adventure vacation
b ☐ The Trans-Mongolian Express
c ☐ A Mediterranean cruise

3 Listen again. Then write T for *true* or F for *false*. 19

a ☐ On a cruise you travel by ship.
b ☐ The cruise takes you to France.
c ☐ The Trans-Mongolian is a train journey.
d ☐ The Trans-Mongolian goes from Moscow to Beijing.
e ☐ On the family adventure you travel by plane.
f ☐ The family adventure vacation is in India.

4 Listen again and underline the correct answers. 19

a How many countries does the cruise visit?
1 ten **2** three **3** six

b How can you get information about the cruise?
1 online **2** by phone **3** both

c Which other country does the train go through?
1 Thailand **2** Mongolia **3** Kazakhstan

d What can you visit in India?
1 elephant safari **2** camping safari **3** tiger safari

e Where can you stay for two nights in India?
1 a hotel **2** a palace **3** the Taj Mahal

5 INTERFACE Work in pairs.

Which journey do you think is the most interesting?

And you? Which is the most interesting in your opinion?

SPEAKING

The Trip of a Lifetime!

20 Jack and Ron are talking about Ron's adventure in New Zealand. Listen and complete the dialogue.

How **a** ____________ your trip to New Zealand, Ron?

It **b** ____________ such an adventure. New Zealand is an incredible country! Anyone who loves being active and outdoors will feel at home there.

So, tell me, what **c** ____________?

So many things ... I **d** ____________ to Wai-O-Tapu Thermal Wonderland. The geothermal pools and volcanic acidic lakes are awesome! This natural attraction **e** ____________ called one of the twenty most surreal areas in the world!

Cool! How about Zorbing? **f** ____________ it?

You bet! Rolling down a hill on a plastic ball was so much fun! High adrenaline!

What **g** ____________ best there?

Actually, I **h** ____________ the Tamaki Maori Village. I was welcomed by the Powhiri – It's a formal welcoming ceremony; the Maori **i** ____________ war dances and **j** ____________ ... a real blast!

Yeah, an excellent way to learn about local culture.

Absolutely! A must-see.

FUNCTIONAL LANGUAGE

Describing a Journey

How was it? / What was it like?
Where did you go?
Have you tried ... ?
What did you like best?

Speaking Task

Plan a dialogue between you and a classmate about an incredible journey.

Step 1
Choose an incredible journey you've recently taken abroad or in your own country.

Step 2
Think about the places you've visited / things you've seen and how you liked it.

Step 3
Work with your partner. Follow the conversation above as a guide. Take turns practicing your dialogue.

CULTURE

David Livingstone and his Journey in Africa

THE MEETING AT UJIJI. *From a Sketch by Stanley.*

David Livingstone was a Scottish doctor, famous missionary, and abolitionist who crossed Africa in the mid-19th century. During his travels, he witnessed the horrors of the African slave trade. He believed in the dignity of Africans and he spoke out in favor of commercial enterprises for the continent. He was devastated when, in the village of Nyangwe, he saw Arabic slave traders killing hundreds of people.

Livingstone wrote and published *Narrative of an Expedition to the Zambesi and Its Tributaries* in 1865 and *Missionary Travels and Researches in South Africa* in 1857. In the first book, he described his use of quinine for malaria and the connection between malaria and mosquitoes.

Livingstone took many journeys in Africa and came across a wonderful waterfall on the Zambezi River on the border between Zambia and Zimbabwe. He named it Victoria Falls. In the local language, it is called Mosi-oa-Tunya – "The Smoke that Thunders." Despite his empathic anti-slavery defense, he named it Victoria Falls after the British monarch at the time, demonstrating his contradictory imperialist aspirations.

Livingstone married Mary Moffat, had several children and died from dysentery and malaria in 1873, at the age of 60, in a small village in Zambia (called Northern Rhodesia at the time).

DR. LIVINGSTONE READING THE BIBLE TO HIS MEN
DRAWN FROM DATA FURNISHED BY MR. H. M. STANLEY

1 21 **Read and listen to the information about David Livingstone. Then write T for *true* or F for *false*.**

a ☐ David Livingstone was born and lived all his life in Africa.

b ☐ He was a doctor, missionary, and abolitionist.

c ☐ In his book *Missionary Travels and Researches in South Africa*, he described his use of quinine for malaria and the connection between malaria and mosquitoes.

d ☐ Livingstone took many journeys in Africa and came across a wonderful waterfall on the Zambezi River, which he named Niagara Falls.

2 **INTERFACE** Join a classmate and research the definition of *missionary*. Then discuss as a class: How do you think the work of missionaries impacted local cultures?

VOCABULARY 2

Extreme Adjectives

1 Match the extreme adjectives with the adjectives below.

a

amazing

b

awful

c

boiling

d

delighted

e

enormous

f

exhausted

g

freezing

h

terrifying

i

tiny

☐ frightening	☐ tired	☐ bad
☐ good	☐ happy	☐ cold
☐ big	☐ small	☐ hot

2 Listen, check, and repeat.

22

3 Write the extreme adjective for each sentence.

I don't like flying. It's frightening. ___terrifying___

a The journey was really bad. ______________

b I love Greek food. It's good. ______________

c My sister was tired when she came back home from New York. ______________

d Mark was happy when he saw his hotel room. ______________

e It's hot on this bus. Can I open a window? ______________

f There were 300 people on our flight. The plane was big. ______________

4 Choose the correct words.

a I really enjoyed my vacation. Athens was **amazing / delighted / enormous**.

b I'm **tiny / exhausted / freezing**. I'm going to bed early.

c Oh no, I haven't drunk my coffee and now it's **boiling / freezing / terrifying**.

d Julie was **delighted / tiny / exhausted** with the souvenir I gave her.

READING 2

1 Look at the picture and the title of the text. What do you think the news article is about?

____

2 Read and listen. Check your answer.

23

SOLO SAILOR

Mike Perham didn't have much time to celebrate his 17th birthday. Not because he had exams or was working, but because he was in the middle of the Indian Ocean. In 2009 Mike became the youngest person to sail around the world solo. His amazing journey took him nine months and he sailed over 30,000 miles on his 50ft yacht, called totallymoney.com.

Mike had a lot of adventures on his trip. Sailing conditions in the Indian Ocean were wonderful, but he had to sail through enormous 50ft waves in the South Pacific after leaving New Zealand. He didn't have many problems with his boat. However, he had to stop in the Canary Islands, Portugal, and Cape Town to repair his auto-pilot, the machine that sailed the boat while Mike slept. Fortunately, he didn't meet any whales or sharks!

Mike returned home to the UK exhausted but ecstatic to be a world record holder. What was the first thing he wanted? Some steak and chips! Mike didn't have any fresh food on the boat, so he didn't eat a lot of fruit or vegetables while he was sailing.

In 2010 Mikes' record was broken by a New Zealand-born Dutch sailor, Laura Dekker, when she was 16. Both Mike and Laura had amazing adventures and are true inspirations!

3 Read the text again. Answer the questions.

a Where did Mike celebrate his 17th birthday?

____

b What world record did Mike set?

____

c How big were the waves in the South Pacific?

____

d Why did Mike stop in the Canary Islands?

____

4 Find the adjective *ecstatic* in the text. What do you think it means?

a extremely tired

b extremely emotional

c extremely happy

5 Read this excerpt again and answer the questions.

> Mike Perham didn't have much time to celebrate his 17th birthday. Not because he had exams or was working, but because he was in the middle of the Indian Ocean.

a What does the underlined passage refer to?

☐ To the reasons why Mike couldn't celebrate his birthday in previous years.

☐ To common reasons why a 17-year-old would fail to celebrate his birthday.

b Why did the journalist include this underlined passage?

☐ To emphasize how surprising the real reason is: Mike was in the middle of the ocean.

☐ To emphasize how important study and work are in the lives of ordinary young people.

6 Talk to a classmate, then share your ideas with the class.

a There was no fresh food on board Mike's yacht. What foods would you take on a long sailing journey?

b What emotional skills does a person need to sail alone for long periods?

c Do you think Mike was too young to sail around the world alone? Why or why not?

GRAMMAR 2

Review: Quantity and Uncountable Nouns

1 Look at the chart. Circle the quantifiers and underline the countable and uncountable nouns.

countable nouns	uncountable nouns
how many …?	**how much …?**
a He saw a lot of whales.	**b** He had a lot of fresh food.

c He saw some / a few whales.	**d** He had some / a little fresh food.

e He didn't see many whales.	**f** He didn't have much fresh food.

g He didn't see any whales.	**h** He didn't have any fresh food.

2 Look at the sentences in activity 1 and complete the rules with the words and phrases in the box.

> *a lot of* (2x) can't be *many* *much*
> one by one plural (2x) *some* or *any* (2x)

a Countable nouns can be counted __________ and can be made __________. To indicate large quantities, countable nouns can be preceded by __________ or __________. To refer to an indefinite quantity, they can be preceded by __________.

b Uncountable nouns __________ counted one by one, nor can they be made __________. To indicate large amounts, uncountable nouns can be preceded by __________ or __________. To refer to an indefinite amount, they can be preceded by __________.

3 Complete the questions with *How much* or *How many*.

a __________ is a trip to Australia?

b __________ countries would you like to visit?

4 Choose the correct words.

Dear Parents,

Next week is the school camp for 9th graders.

All students will need to bring **a some / much** warm clothes, but they don't need **b many / much** because the camp only lasts for three days. Please pack **c a few / a little** extra socks because the camp is cold at night. Students do not need to bring **d any / many** food.

The camp provides all meals with **e a lot of / much** fresh fruit and vegetables.

They can bring **f a little / a few** money but not too **g much / many**. See you next week!

The Teachers

TIP

How many and *How much* are used to ask about quantities and amounts.
How many + countable noun in the plural
How much + uncountable noun

How much is also used to ask about prices:
How much did that trip cost?

GRAMMAR GUIDE page 38

WRITING

A Travel Journal Entry

1 EXPLORING THE CONTEXT

1 Skim the text on page 37 quickly. What is a travel journal for?

a Documenting travel experiencies.

b Helping other travelers plan their trips.

2 Read, listen, and check your answer. 24

04-24-2023

From London to New York

We've arrived in New York – at last! What a journey! It was a nightmare!

The plane left London on time. The food was OK and the in-flight movies were excellent. I watched "Morbius." It's great.

But when we were only 30 minutes from New York, there was a disaster! We couldn't land because of bad weather. First, we had to fly to Washington, DC. Then we had to wait for three and a half hours to get off the plane. We waited for an hour in line at the immigration desk. Next, we lined up for another two hours for a hotel. After that we waited 45 minutes for the shuttle bus to the hotel. We finally arrived at the hotel at midnight – eight hours after landing! And the restaurant was closed, so there was no food!

We're going to New York this morning, I hope!

3 Identify the false statement about the journal entry.

- **a** The word *nightmare* makes it clear that the author's experience was bad.
- **b** Specifying the amount of time spent at each stage reinforces how tiring the trip was.
- **c** The text is subjective. The author expresses her feelings and opinions on the facts.
- **d** Without the picture you could not understand the written text.
- **e** The journal entry has title and date.

4 Read the journal entry again and order the events.

- **a** ☐ had to fly to Washington
- **b** ☐ arrived at the hotel
- **c** ☐ waited at the immigration desk
- **d** ☐ the plane left London
- **e** ☐ waited for a shuttle bus
- **f** ☐ lined up for a hotel

2 PLANNING

1 Imagine that you also have a travel journal.

2 Think about the journey you will report and make notes. Where were you going? Was it a good or bad journey? What happened?

LANGUAGE FOCUS

Linkers

First*, we had to fly to Washington, DC.*
Then *we had to wait for three and a half hours.*
Next*, we lined up for two hours for a hotel.*
After that *we waited 45 minutes for the bus shuttle.*
We ***finally*** *arrived at the hotel at midnight.*

1 Look at the sentences above. Complete the following rules with the words in bold.

- **a** We use ____________ to indicate what happened before in a sequence of events.
- **b** We use ____________, ____________, and ____________ to indicate the order of events.
- **c** We use ____________ to indicate the last event in a sequence.

2 Choose the correct words.

We went on a sightseeing bus tour in New York last year. We set off from Broadway and **a** **next / first** we went to Times Square, in the center of Manhattan. **b** **Then / Finally**, we drove up one side of Central Park and saw the Museum of Natural History. **c** **After / Next**, we went to Harlem and saw the Apollo Theater. **d** **After that / First**, we drove down Park Avenue. Lots of famous people live there. **e** **Then / Finally**, we got off the bus by the Guggenheim Museum. It was wonderful!

3 WRITING

1 Write your first draft. Express your emotions and opinions about the journey.

2 Use linkers to show the order of events.

3 Choose images related to your experience.

4 CHECKING & EDITING

1 Ask a classmate to read your draft and ask:

- Can you identify the sequence of events?
- Can you recognize the emotions that the events provoked in me?

2 Consider your classmate's opinions and enhance your text. Make a final copy of your work on a separate sheet.

5 SHARING

1 Work in groups of 3-4 students. Read each other's journals and talk about them.

2 If you want, continue your travel journal. Record not only trips but also tours and interesting events you attend.

GRAMMAR GUIDE

Review: Present Perfect and Simple Past

- we use the present perfect to talk about experiences in the past when we don't know or don't mention the exact time

  They **have been** to the USA.
- we never use the present perfect for something that happened at a specific time in the past, we use the simple past in this case

  We **went** to the movies **last Saturday**.
- we use the simple past to talk about completed actions at a definite time in the past

  They **went** to the USA in 2009.
- we use the present perfect to ask questions about experiences in the past

  Have you ever **been** to the USA?
- we use simple past questions to ask for more information about the experience

  When **did** you **go** to the USA?

time expressions	
present perfect	**simple past**
this week in the last weeks never recently	yesterday last year when I was young in 2009

Review: Quantity and Uncountable Nouns

	countable nouns	uncountable nouns
+	He had **a lot of** apples. He had **some / a few** apples.	He had **a lot of** money. He had **some / a little** money.
–	He didn't have **many** apples. He didn't have **any** apples.	He didn't have **much** money. He didn't have **any** money.
?	How **many** apples did he have? Did he have **any** apples? Yes, he did. / No, he didn't.	How **much** money did he have? Did he have **any** money? Yes, he did. / No, he didn't.

uncountable nouns	
food fruit information milk money	music rice space tea water

- we use *some*, *any*, *a lot of*, *a few*, *a little*, *much*, and *many* to talk about quantities of things
- we use *a lot of* with plural countable nouns and uncountable nouns to talk about a large quantity

  They eat **a lot of** fruit and vegetables.
- we use *some* in affirmative sentences with plural countable nouns and uncountable nouns to talk about a medium quantity

  All students will need to bring **some** warm clothes.
- we use *a few* in affirmative sentences with plural countable nouns to talk about a small quantity

  Please pack **a few** extra socks as the camp is cold at night.
- we use *a little* in affirmative sentences with uncountable nouns to talk about a small quantity

  You can bring **a little** money.
- we use *many* in negative sentences with plural countable nouns to talk about a small quantity

  I don't have **many** friends.
- we use *many* in formal affirmative sentences with plural countable nouns to talk about a big quantity

  I have **many** co-workers.
- we use *much* in negative sentences with uncountable nouns to talk about a small quantity

  She doesn't have **much** time.
- we often use *much* associated with words like *too* in affirmative sentences with uncountable nouns to talk about a big quantity

  They spent **too much** time standing in line.
- we use *any* in negative sentences with plural countable nouns and uncountable nouns to talk about zero quantity

  Students don't need to bring **any** food.
- we use *How many …?* with plural countable nouns and *How much …?* with uncountable nouns to ask questions about quantity

  How many friends do you have?
  How much fruit have you eaten today?

6

PROGRESS CHECK

Name: ____________________
Class name / Period: ____________________
Teacher: ____________________
Date: ____________________

Travel

1 Complete the sentences with the words in the box.

adventures	home	journey
postcard	souvenir	suitcase

a You haven't packed your ______________. You're going to be late!

b My mom bought me a ______________ T-shirt in Venice.

c Paul sent me a ______________ from Australia.

d I planned a ______________ with my guidebook.

e Lucy had lots of ______________ when she went to Japan.

f I had such a great vacation that I didn't want to come back ______________!

Extreme Adjectives

2 Match adjectives a-f with extreme adjectives 1-6.

a ☐ big — **1** awful
b ☐ small — **2** enormous
c ☐ cold — **3** exhausted
d ☐ tired — **4** amazing
e ☐ good — **5** tiny
f ☐ bad — **6** freezing

Review: Present Perfect and Simple Past

3 Complete the sentences with the present perfect or simple past form of the verbs in parentheses.

a ______________ you ______________ (be) to Tunisia?

Yes, I have. I ______________ (go) there in 2012. It was great.

b ______________ you ever ______________ (read) a *Diary of a Wimpy Kid* book?

Yes, I have. I ______________ (not like) it.

c ______________ you ______________ (send) your dad a postcard?

Yes. I ______________ (send) it yesterday.

d ______________ your brother ______________ (go) to Australia?

Yes, he has. He ______________ (set off) two days ago.

Review: Quantity and Uncountable Nouns

4 Choose the correct words.

a I haven't packed **any / much** socks.

b Nick's bought **much / a lot of** souvenirs.

c I don't have **many / much** time.

d Did you meet **many / much** people while you were traveling?

e I only spent **a little / a few** money on vacation.

Grammar Buildup 2

1 2 3 4 5 6 7 8

5 Choose the correct answers.

Alice **a** ______ to Morocco, Mark?
Mark Yes, I have. It's **b** ______ country I've ever been to.
Alice When **c** ______?
Mark Two years ago.
Alice Did you eat **d** ______ snails?
Mark Yes, I did. They were awful. I **e** ______ them.
Alice And did you buy **f** ______ souvenirs?
Mark No, they were **g** ______ expensive. So, have you ever visited Marrakech?
Alice No, I've never been abroad.

a	**1** Do you go	**2** Did you go	**3** Have you ever been
b	**1** better	**2** the best	**3** best
c	**1** did you go	**2** have you gone	**3** were you going
d	**1** much	**2** any	**3** a little
e	**1** didn't like	**2** haven't liked	**3** am not liking
f	**1** any	**2** much	**3** a little
g	**1** enough	**2** too	**3** not enough

VOCABULARY IN PICTURES

Travel

arrive

buy a guidebook

buy souvenirs

come back home

get off a bus

get on a train

have adventures

meet people

pack a suitcase

plan a journey

send postcards

set off

Extreme Adjectives

big / enormous

small / tiny

good / amazing

bad / awful

frightening / terrifying

tired / exhausted

happy / delighted

cold / freezing

hot / boiling

REVIEW 1

VOCABULARY

START

1

No way I'm going out!
It's ______________ out there.

2

It didn't take long for me to ______________ when I moved to France.

8

Last night I ______________ flying tied to balloons.

7

If you go to the Andes, don't forget to visit the local shops to ______________.

9

We had breakfast and ______________ very early in the morning to hike the forest trail.

10

Will had to ______________ because his family moved to the other side of the city.

15

Alexis has just heard she was admitted to college. She's ______________!

FINISH

3

________ that bus now, because it leaves in five minutes!

4

She has gotten married, moved to a new house, and finally ________.

6

My cousins took a ________ to study cooking and hike mountains.

5

This *Little Prince* miniature is so cute! The pieces are very delicate and ________.

11

My aunt always rolls her clothes when she ________ her suitcase.

12

My friend ________ her team's performance in the championship.

14

Lots of students ________ the protest against the closing of public schools.

13

Laura ________ by the war.

REVIEW 1

GRAMMAR

Simple Past and *used to*

1 Complete the sentences using the verbs in parentheses. Use the simple past affirmative and negative forms.

Sammy ___didn't make___ (not make) friends at school.

a Jayden ________________ (get) into trouble with his teacher again.

b We ________________ (not win) first prize in the competition.

c My mom ________________ (take) a gap year before she went to college.

d My cousin ________________ (study) math at college.

e She ________________ out of college when she failed all her exams.

2 Complete the sentences using the simple past or *used to*.

I ___used to sit___ next to my cousin in class but now I sit next to Harry.

a Now my uncle works in Philadelphia, but he ________________ in Georgetown before that.

b I usually have milk for breakfast but yesterday I ________________ hot chocolate.

c My mom never watches TV, but when she was younger she ________________ TV every day.

d You never ________________ angry but now you often get angry.

3 Write questions using the simple past or *used to*.

Mike / get in trouble / when he was younger ?
Did Mike use to get in trouble when he was younger?

a Kirsten / buy a guidebook / when she was in France ?
____
____

b your parents / buy souvenirs / when traveling ?
____
____

c Michael / drop out of / college ?
____
____

d Tom / get off the bus / in Boynton or Delray beach ?
____
____

Subject and Object Questions

4 Are these questions subject or object questions?

Where did you go for vacation? ___object___

a Who cooked dinner yesterday? ________

b Who did you see last night? ________

c Why did he drop out of college? ________

d Who ate all the chocolate? ________

e What did Jeremy say? ________

5 Match the questions with the answers.

a ☐ Who called you?

b ☐ Who did you call?

c ☐ Who wrote *Romeo and Juliet*?

d ☐ What did William Shakespeare write?

1 William Shakespeare wrote *Romeo and Juliet*.

2 I called my friend.

3 He wrote about 38 plays, including *Romeo and Juliet*.

4 My friend called me.

Present Perfect and Simple Past

6 Underline the correct words.

My parents love having adventures, so every year we go traveling. We **'ve seen / saw** some amazing places so far. We **a 've been / went** to Africa, Australia, and South America, and last summer we **b 've stayed / stayed** in the Arctic for three weeks! We **c haven't stayed / didn't stay** in a hotel; we went camping!

7 Complete the sentences with the present perfect or the simple past form of the verbs in parentheses.

We ___bought___ (buy) a guidebook when we were in the museum.

a That man ______________ (get) on the train ten minutes ago.

b We______________ (be) on the bus for six hours now.

c "How ______________ you ______________ (feel) when you were at the top of the mountain?"
"Exhausted!"

d I ______________ (not travel) much.

8 Complete the dialogue with the present perfect or the simple past form of the verbs in parentheses.

Anna ___Have___ you ever ___seen___ (see) one of the natural wonders of the world?

Ben Yes, I have. I **a** ___________ (visit) the Grand Canyon.

Anna Really? When **b** ___________ you ___________ (go) there?

Ben I **c** ___________ (go) last year when I was visiting my aunt and uncle in Las Vegas. They **d** ___________ (live) there for two years.

Anna What was it like?

Ben It was amazing. It's the best experience I **e** ___________ ever ___________ (have). I **f** ___________ (take) hundreds of pictures when I was there!

Quantity and Uncountable Nouns

9 Complete the sentences with *some*, *any*, *much*, or *many*.

How ___many___ different countries have you been to?

a He didn't send ______________ messages from New York – not one!

b I have ______________ amazing pictures from my trip.

c We didn't buy ______________ souvenirs – just one or two.

d How ______________ food do you have in the suitcase?

e They don't have ______________ money – only a few dollars each.

10 Complete the pairs of sentences with the correct words.

much / many

a There isn't ______________ to do in the evenings.

b There aren't ______________ things to do in the town.

few / a little

c I have ______________ money.

d I have ______________ $10 bills in my wallet.

a lot of / many

e There aren't ______________ new teachers at the school.

f There are ______________ new students.

Manipulated Photos and Videos

Is Seeing Believing?

1 25 **Read and listen. Then answer the questions.**

a Who's Sam Hawkins?

b What is Lily's relationship with Sam Hawkins?

c What does Daniel think about Sam Hawkins?

d Why does Daniel think this way?

e Lily's mom is suspicious of Sam Hawkins' intentions. What is the reason for her suspicions?

f Lily defends Sam Hawkins' reputation. How does she do it?

2 **Choose the correct option to complete the statements.**

a Wearing a mink fur hat makes Sam look like a fraud because, as an environmental activist, he is expected to …

☐ not wear animal fur clothing.

☐ not buy such an expensive hat.

b If the picture were real, Sam could be considered …

☐ badly dressed.

☐ hypocritical.

c The deepfake video depicting Sam is intended to make him look …

☐ tired of his fans.

☐ uncommitted to the environmental cause.

3 **Discuss the following questions with a classmate. Then share your ideas with the class.**

a "Seeing doesn't mean believing anymore … " What does Lily's mom mean by that statement?

b Now read Lily's grandmother's line: "Who wants to damage this boy's image so badly?" How would you answer this question?

c Read the TIP box. What are the consequences of deepfake technology for the circulation of information on the web?

TIP

A **deepfake** is a video of a person in which his or her voice and/or parts of his or her body were altered to simulate that he or she is talking or doing something he or she didn't actually say or do. This effect is achieved through a technology called deep learning, by which software is able to analyze many recordings of a person talking or moving and thus learn how to perfectly imitate him or her.

4 **Work in pairs. Choose a manipulated picture or video that has recently circulated on social media. You can find examples on fact-checking websites. Investigate:**

a What is the source of the picture or video? In what context was it created?

b What kind of manipulation did the picture or video go through?

c What was the intention of the person doing this manipulation?

d Is this just a "joke?" Or does manipulation promote an agenda?

5 **Prepare a short slideshow to share your findings with the class. Did you know the images researched by your classmates? Did you know they were fake? Any surprising discoveries?**

3

THE WORLD AROUND US

1

2

3

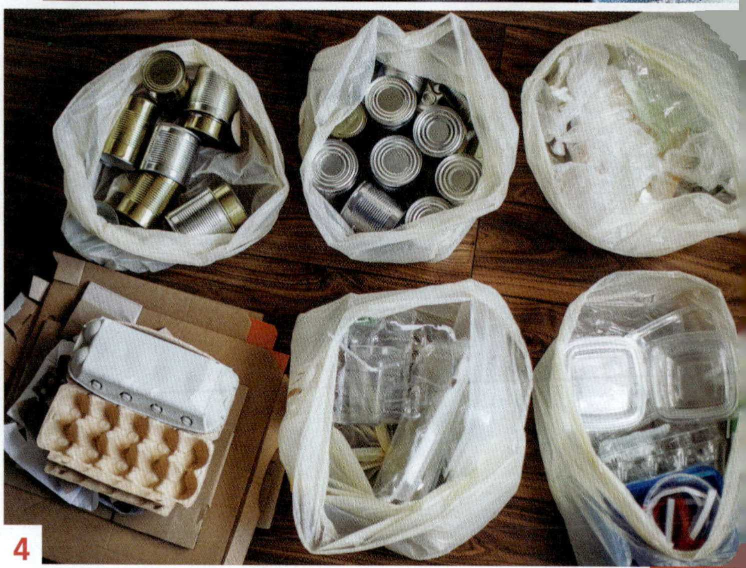
4

VOCABULARY 1

Saving Environmental Resources

1 Look up the meaning of the phrases in the box in a dictionary. Then listen and repeat.
26

compost food scraps	save water
install solar panels	share car journeys
insulate windows	travel by public transportation
mend old clothes	turn off lights
recycle packaging	use rechargeable batteries
ride a bike	

2 Write the phrases from the box in activity 1 that correspond to pictures 1-4.

1 ____________________

2 ____________________

3 ____________________

4 ____________________

3 Complete the quiz with phrases from activity 1. Then answer the questions.

QUIZ!

A Sharing car journeys is cheaper than having your own car. How much money can you save every year?

1 $50 **2** $2,000 **3** $3,000

B Which type of packaging is it most difficult to ____________?

1 plastic **2** paper **3** aluminum

C How many people ____________ to work every day in New York?

1 200 **2** 50,000 **3** 1 million

D Installing ____________ is an environmentally friendly way to generate energy. How many square meters of them are there in the world?

1 4 million **2** 90 million **3** 180 million

READING 1

1 Do you think it's possible to live trash-free? Why (not)?

____

A Life without Trash

How much trash do you throw away every day? Go on, be honest! If you're like most people, then you probably don't recycle that much.
But could you imagine not producing any trash at all? Impossible? The Reid family – Michael and his wife Amanda and their daughter Natalie (14) and son Ryan (10) – decided to prove it was possible.
Like most people, the Reids didn't use to recycle much. Then, last January they decided to go trash-free for a year. Since then, they've reduced their waste to a minimum and Natalie is posting pictures and videos on Instagram to share their experience.
They've recycled as much as possible for the past few months. The town's garbage service collects paper, cans, and plastic bottles and the Reids take glass, aluminum, and cartons to a drop-off location. They compost vegetable waste too.
They've started growing a lot of their own fruits and vegetables. They've learned new skills too – Natalie now makes her own soap, toothpaste, and cheese.
Michael and Amanda have just taken a course to learn about repurposing things, or making new things from old items. Michael's already made a lamp from pieces of old metal and Amanda is making a chair for her bedroom from a bike.
They've also started mending their old clothes instead of buying new ones.
"Getting new things is complicated," explains Ryan. "All my friends buy new cell phones and electronic gadgets, but they all have a lot of packaging." Both Natalie and Ryan now download all their music and movies from the internet and they're members of Freecycle.* "I got my cell phone from there," says Natalie. "It's really cool. I also swap computer games with my friends. It's a good idea because we all have fun and we spend less." For Ryan the hardest thing was not eating fast food. "My friends go to burger joints a lot, but fast food has so much packaging!"
Both the kids think it's possible to live a greener life and still have fun. "With a bit of planning, you can do it," they say.
The Reids are optimistic about the future.
Since they started on January 6th, they've reduced their trash dramatically. They only have one small box of garbage. "I think we're going to continue even after the year finishes," says Michael. "We're making a difference and that's a fabulous feeling."

*Freecycle = an online organization where people offer things they don't use anymore to other members.

Amanda in the Reids' vegetable garden. The Reids have started growing their own fruits and vegetables.

2 Read and listen. Put the information in the order that it appears in the text. 27

a ☐ Natalie got her cell phone from Freecycle.
b ☐ Natalie makes her own soap.
c ☐ The Reids went trash-free.
d ☐ The family compost vegetable waste.
e ☐ They only have one box of garbage.

3 What kind of text is it?

a a human interest feature
b a tabloid article
c a letter to the editor

4 Read the text again. Then write T for *true* or F for *false*. Correct the false sentences.

a ☐ Natalie is writing a diary about their experience.
____
b ☐ The town's garbage service collects paper, cans, and plastic bottles.
____
c ☐ Michael has made a table from old metal.
____
d ☐ Ryan goes to burger joints.
____
e ☐ They think they'll continue the project.
____

GRAMMAR 1

Review: Present Perfect + *for, since, how long*

1 Read the sentences below. Write (P) if the sentence indicates the *period of time of an action*; (PT) if the sentence describes *an action from one point in time until the present*; and (AT) if it asks about the *amount of time of an action*.

a ☐ How long have the Reids lived trash-free?

b ☐ They've reduced their garbage to a minimum since last year.

c ☐ They've recycled as much as possible for the past few months.

2 Look at the chart below. Check (✓) the correct information.

present perfect + *for, since, how long …?*
They'**ve recycled** as much as possible **for** the past few months. **Since** January, they **have reduced** their garbage dramatically. **How long have** they **lived** trash-free?

a *How long* + *present perfect* asks about:

☐ the duration of a state or an activity.

☐ when in the past something happened.

b The *present perfect* with *since* or *for* talks about:

☐ a situation that started and finished in the past.

☐ a situation that started in the past and is still going on in the present.

c The *present perfect* + *for* talks about:

☐ a period of time.

☐ a point in past time.

d The *present perfect* + *since* talks about:

☐ a period of time.

☐ a period after a specific point in past time.

TIP

We can use *since* before a sentence in the simple past that refers to a point in time.
I've learned a lot since I started this course.
Since I left school, I've worked in an office.

3 Write questions for the answers below. Use *how long* + present perfect.

a ______________________________
Jack has used solar panels in his house since he moved in.

b ______________________________
We have recycled packaging for two years now.

c ______________________________
The Reids have grown their own food since the beginning of this year.

4 Insert the time expressions from activity 3 in the chart below. Then include the following:

100 years 1995 20 minutes a long time I was born Monday nine o'clock three days

for	*since*
a period of time	a point in time

5 Complete the sentences with *for* or *since*. Underline the present perfect structure.

We've had our blog ___for___ six months.

a I have learned a lot ________ I started this project in May.

b They have grown their own vegetables ________ two years.

c Anna has tried to recycle more ________ last month.

d I've biked to school ________ January.

6 Look at the sentences in the chart below. Circle the verb forms and underline the time expressions.

present perfect and simple past
a My neighbor recycled for three months last year.
b My neighbor has recycled for three years.
c How long have the Reids lived without trash?
d How long did the course about recycling take?

7 Notice that *how long* and *for* can be used with the present perfect and the simple past. Match the rules with the sentences from activity 6.

☐ *How long* + *present perfect* asks about the duration of an action that started in the past and continues up to the present.

☐ *How long* + *simple past* asks about the duration of an action in the past. This action is no longer happening.

☐ *for* + *present perfect* describes the amount of time an action which started in the past is still in course.

☐ *for* + *simple past* describes how long the action lasted in the past.

8 Complete the text with the correct form of the verbs in parentheses. Use the simple past or the present perfect.

My friend Suzy is really green. She __has recycled__ (recycle) as much as possible for years. Last year she **a** ________________ (write) a great article for the school magazine about recycling. Since then, the students **b** ________________ (try) to recycle all the paper and plastic we use at school. We **c** ________________ (not throw away) any paper since then!
For the past year, Suzy **d** ________________ (buy) green presents for everyone. For my last birthday she **e** ________________ (buy) me some organic chocolate and a Fairtrade T-shirt. The chocolate **f** ________________ (be) delicious and I **g** ________________ (wear) the T-shirt often for a long time. Unfortunately, it **h** ________________ (shrink) when I **i** ________________ (wash) it last week.
Well, I'm going to try to be greener like Suzy! How about you? Will you be green-friendly this year?

9 INTERFACE Ask and answer questions about green habits. Use *how long*, *for*, or *since*.

> How long have you used recycled paper?

> I've used it since the 5th grade.

GRAMMAR GUIDE page 60

LISTENING

Buy Nothing Day (BND)

1 Look at the pictures. What do you think Buy Nothing Day is?

a An event which highlights the environmental consequences of shopping.

b An event which encourages people to stop shopping completely.

2 Listen and check your answers. 28

3 Listen again. Then write T for *true* or F for *false*. Correct the false sentences. 28

a ☐ If you participate in Buy Nothing Day, you don't buy anything for 12 hours.
____

b ☐ Buy Nothing Day is on the same day as Black Friday.
____

c ☐ Buy Nothing Day is an international event that happens in many countries.
____

d ☐ At swap days, people sell items that they don't use.
____

e ☐ At workshops, people learned to make presents from old items.
____

f ☐ On Buy Nothing Day some participants write to supermarkets to ask them to use less packaging.
____

SPEAKING

A News Podcast

1 Jessica and Eric are podcasters. Below is the transcript of an episode of their podcast. Read the first two lines and answer: *What is The Earth News podcast about?*

a News articles on environmental issues.

b How technology can help the environment.

2 Read and listen to the podcast episode and check your answer.

29

Jessica: Good evening! My name's Jessica Wu and this is *The Earth News*, the podcast that comments on articles related to environmental issues. And here beside me is Eric Muller. Hi, Eric! What will we talk about today?

Eric: Hello, Jess! Hello, listeners! Today we'll talk about an article published in the prestigious *Time* magazine. It's an article about how technology can help the environment.

Jessica: Interesting! And what does it say exactly?

Eric: It says that technological innovations may harm the environment if not used wisely, but they can certainly help solve some ecological problems we have created.

Jessica: I bet renewable energy is an example, isn't it?

Eric: Yes, you're right. Recently, some eco-friendly tech advancements have taken place in the clean energy field, such as solar panels.

Jessica: What about the shift from print to digital? I imagine this has also benefited the environment ...

Eric: Absolutely. The article reminds us that, in the past twenty years, we have used smartphones to take notes, companies have sent bills, newsletters, etc. over email; files have been stored in the cloud ... Less paper has been used, which means fewer trees have been cut down and the result is: rainfall won't be affected and the atmosphere won't be unstable ...

Jessica: Technology has allowed people to move in a more environmentally friendly way. Thank you for introducing us to such a cool article, Eric! See you again tomorrow?!

Eric: Sure, Jess. Thank you and good evening to all our listeners!

3 Discuss the following questions with a classmate. Then share your ideas with the class.

a Some podcasters present their show in pairs, as Jessica and Eric do. What are the advantages of this format?

b Do you think the questions and answers were pre-arranged by Jessica and Eric? Why (not)?

FUNCTIONAL LANGUAGE

Discussing and Commenting on Articles

It's an article about ...
What does it say (exactly)?
It says ... / mentions ...
What about ... ?
Have you read / heard about ... ?
Have you noticed ... ?

Speaking Task

Work in pairs. Record a podcast episode commenting on an article on environmental issues.

Step 1

Browse news websites and choose an article on an environmental topic.

Step 2

Read the article and underline the main information.

Write a script to work as a guideline for the podcast. Give it a creative name.

Rehearse and record a first version of the episode leaving room for improvisation. Show it to another pair and ask them to evaluate it.

Step 3

Record a final version of your work and share it with the class.

CULTURE

Electric Cars in Canada

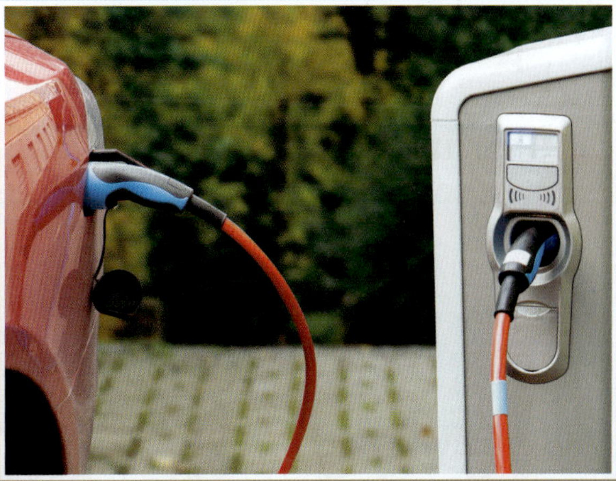

Electric cars, or EVs, are a fast-growing alternative to gas everywhere in Canada as they run on electricity and have zero tailpipe emissions. These cars can be charged at public charging stations (some of them are free to use) or in the comfort of your home, after work, while doing something else. Many Canadians have reported saving a lot of money as the maintenance cost of these cars is low: the engine needs no lubrification, for instance.

Studies in Canada show that EVs produce much fewer polluting emissions and can be a great way to reduce your carbon footprint. The Ministry of Environment and Climate Change in Canada points out that electric cars are becoming cheaper and a very good solution to fight climate change. The country plans to invest in more charging stations to make electric cars a more and more viable choice for Canadians. Supporting clean technology investments, in their view, will not only reduce GHG emissions but will also be fundamental for economic growth, the creation of new jobs and the possibility of taking Canadian businesses to the forefront of the clean-energy revolution.

However, some electric cars require an enormous charge to function properly. So, when purchasing an electric car, Canadians must consider all the options to not make an unwise investment which will show up on their monthly electricity bill. Some electric cars are still very expensive, especially because of the technology used to develop them.

In spite of that, using electricity to power an EV in Canada can reduce greenhouse-gas emissions a lot: around 60-90% per vehicle, making it competitive worldwide in the near future.

1 Read and listen to the information about electric cars and complete the chart below.

30

electric vehicles (EV) in Canada	
advantages	**disadvantages**

2 How popular are electric cars in your country?

____

____

3 What is being done in your country to produce clean and green energy? Share your findings with your friends.

____

____

VOCABULARY 2

Prefixes

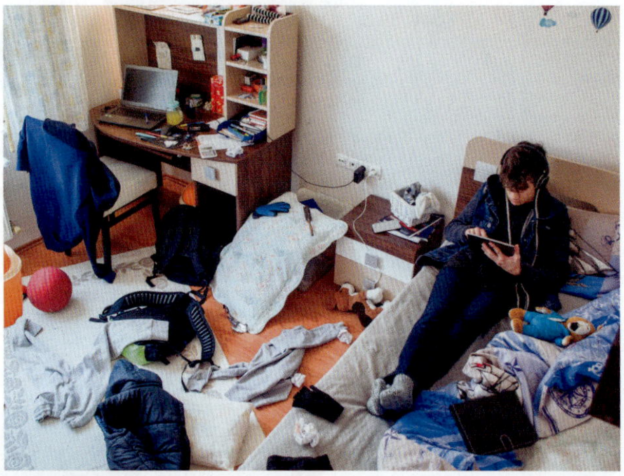

I need to reorganize!

I think I misunderstood.

I've overeaten!

Oh no! It's undercooked!

1 Look at the pictures. Then match the prefixes to the meanings.

a re-
b mis-
c over-
d under-

☐ do something to excess
☐ do something again
☐ do something less than necessary
☐ do something incorrectly

2 Look at the verbs in the box. Use your dictionary to check the meaning of any unknown words.

misinform	overpopulate	undercook
misplace	recycle	underestimate
misunderstand	reorganize	underpay
overcrowd	replace	underuse
overeat	replay	

3 Listen and repeat.

31

4 Underline the correct words to complete the sentences.

a The smartphone is broken. We need to **replace / misplace** it.

b There were too many people at the store, it was **overpopulated / overcrowded**.

c I have **replaced / misplaced** my wallet. I can't find it anywhere.

d Don't **underestimate / misinform** Simon, he's more intelligent than he appears to be.

READING 2

1 Look at the picture and the title of the text on page 57. What do you think this structure is for?

a Providing more places to live.

b Producing food for city inhabitants.

FEEDING OUR CITIES

Our cities are overcrowded places. They are ecological nightmares because they use huge amounts of resources. Nowadays, more people live in cities than in the country, so one of the biggest problems is providing food. As food isn't grown in cities, it must be transported over long distances. Scientists have been aware of the problem for years, but they still haven't found an effective solution.

In the late 1990s, now-retired Columbia University professor Dickson Despommier was convinced that farms in skyscrapers could be the solution.

"In many cities, people have already built vertical gardens – gardens that grow up walls. I think we can take this idea one step further: we can replace traditional skyscrapers with special skyscrapers that contain farms," Despommier proposed. The farms would produce crops, chicken, and fish in a controlled environment using existing technology. Not only that, they could recycle the water that people use. Solar power could provide all the heat and electricity.

This means that everyone in cities could get enough food and safe, clean water. Vertical farms could also be built in countries that don't have a lot of room for agriculture, such as Iceland, and countries with big populations, such as India and China. "I believe that at the moment technology is underused and we could make our cities more environmentally friendly and greener places to live," the professor said.

Despommier went on to write a book describing his idea, *The Vertical Farm: Feeding the World in the 21st Century,* in 2010. Two years later, the world's first commercial vertical farm opened in Singapore. Since then, similar structures have been built in several countries around the world.

Unfortunately, however, vertical farming isn't a global solution. Powering LED lights, software, and the sophisticated growing systems it demands is expensive, and the poorest countries have not yet been able to afford these costs. Despite this, the vertical farming market is growing and is expected to be a $10 billion-a-year industry worldwide by 2026.

2 Read and listen. Check your answer.

32

3 Read the text again and answer the questions.

a Do more people live in cities or in the country?

____

b Why does food have to be transported to cities?

____

c What did Despommier propose as a solution?

____

d When and where was the world's first vertical farm opened?

____

e Why are vertical farms not a global solution?

____

____

4 Complete the mind map with information from the article you read.

Problem: Many people live in cities and **a** ______________.
Food isn't grown in cities.
Professor Dickson **Despommier's proposal:** To produce crops, chickens, and fish in **b** ______________.

How?
Replacing traditional skyscrapers with **c** ______________.

Additional advantages
- Farms would recycle **d** ______________ ______________.
- Energy would be **e** ______________ (no pollution).
- Countries with little room for agriculture / **f** ______________ could also use them.

g ______________
Singapore, 2012

Trend
Expanding market – $10 billion a year by **h** ______________.

Obstacle to global expansion
i ______________

READING STRATEGY

A mind map is a useful tool for deepening the understanding of informative texts. Write the main idea in the center and complement it with the secondary ideas.

GRAMMAR 2

Review: Present Perfect + *still, yet, already, just*

1 Look at the sentences in the chart. Underline the correct words to complete the rules below.

present perfect + *still, yet, already, just*
In many cities, people have **already** built vertical gardens.
Despommier has designed a prototype, but he hasn't been able to build a vertical farm **yet**.
Unfortunately, he **still** hasn't built the vertical farm.
Have scientists found a solution to the problem **yet**?
Despommier has **just** had a great idea which he plans to put into practice in no time!

a We use **yet / already** in affirmative sentences. It goes before the main verb.

b We use **yet / already** in negative sentences and questions. It always goes at the end of the sentence.

c We use **still / already** in negative sentences. It goes before the auxiliary verb.

d We use **just / still** between the auxiliary and the main verb. It means "a short time ago."

e We use **yet / just** to talk about something expected to happen. It means "any time until now."

f We use **already / still** to talk about something that hasn't happened / finished.

g We use **already / still** to talk about something that happened before we expected.

2 Complete the sentences below with *still*, *yet*, *already*, or *just*.

a We have ________ taken 50 kilos of glass for recycling this year.

b Have you built the vertical garden ________?

c Peter ________ hasn't decided what to do with all that garbage.

d They haven't come to a decision ________. That should happen soon.

e They have ________ talked to the mayor about the Food Empowerment Project. Five minutes ago, in fact.

3 Look at Jack's list and write questions. Then answer the questions using the words in parentheses.

Has he joined Freecycle yet?

(already) Yes, he has already joined Freecycle.

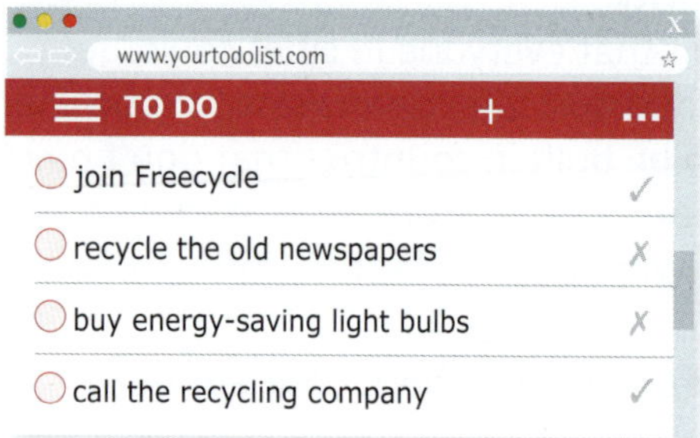

a ________________________

____

(still) ________________________

____

b ________________________

____

(yet) ________________________

____

c ________________________

____

(already) ________________________

____

TIP

Use the present perfect to ask for new information:
***Have** you **talked** to your teacher about the solar panel project yet?*
Use the simple past to mention when the action occurred in the past:
*Yes, I've already talked to him. We **discussed** it last week.*

GRAMMAR GUIDE page 60

Contemporary Protest Songs

Folk music is the traditional music of a country, region, or community. Traditional folk music is played on local instruments, such as the bagpipes in Scotland or the *sitar* in India. However, in the 1960s, so-called "contemporary" folk singers like Bob Dylan, Joni Mitchell, and Joan Baez appeared in the USA. These folk musicians played guitars and sang about personal subjects like love and marriage, or about more social and political concerns, like war and work. When Bob Dylan released the song "Blowin' in the Wind" in 1963, it soon became the anthem for the very active American Civil Rights Movement and the anti-war demonstrations taking place in the USA at the time. In the song, Dylan asks questions about war, peace, and freedom. He sings that the answers to all our questions are "blowing in the wind." But who can catch the wind to find the answer?

Cover of a compilation album of songs by protest singers Bob Dylan and Joan Baez.

Front cover of *Blue* (1971), considered one of the greatest albums by Joni Mitchell.

1 **Read and listen. Answer the question.**

33

What things does Bob Dylan ask about in his song "Blowin' in the Wind"?

____

____

2 **Read the questions and choose the correct answers.**

a What did the folk singers mentioned in the article sing about?

1 love and politics

2 nature and the environment

b What instrument did these folk musicians play?

1 guitar

2 saxophone

c When was "Blowin' in the Wind" released?

1 1943

2 1963

d What did this song become the anthem for?

1 The American Civil Rights Movement

2 The American Space Program

GRAMMAR GUIDE

Present Perfect

+	I / You	have ridden	a bike.
	He / She / It	has ridden	
	We / You / They	have ridden	
–	I / You	haven't ridden	a bike.
	He / She / It	hasn't ridden	
	We / You / They	haven't ridden	
?	Have you ridden a bike? Yes, I have. No, I haven't.		

for, since, how long

How long have you lived in Boston?
I've lived in Boston **for** two years.
I've lived in Boston **since** 2015.

- we use *how long … ?* to ask about the duration of an event or situation
- we use *for* with a period of time
- we use *since* with a point in time

for	*since*
five minutes	2015
five hours	5pm
three days	January
three weeks	this afternoon
a month	I was born
a year	Friday
a long time	last week

still, yet, already, just

I **still haven't recycled** the plastic bottles.
He **hasn't mended** his shoes **yet**.
Has he **mended** his shoes **yet**?
We**'ve already bought** rechargeable batteries.
Paul **has just left** the house.

- we use *still* and *yet* in negative sentences to talk about things we haven't done
- we also use *yet* in questions to ask if something has been done
- we use *just* to talk about something we've done a short time before the moment of speaking
- we use *already* in affirmative sentences to talk about things we have done

6

✓ PROGRESS CHECK

Name: ____________________
Class name / Period: ____________________
Teacher: ____________________
Date: ____________________

Saving Environmental Resources

1 Match the columns to make expressions.

a	compost	☐	water
b	recycle	☐	car journeys
c	save	☐	packaging
d	mend	☐	food scraps
e	share	☐	solar panels
f	install	☐	old clothes

Prefixes

2 Complete the sentences with the correct form of the verb and a suitable prefix.

a I didn't understand what he said – I ______________ (understand).

b I can't eat another thing! In fact, I've ______________ (eat).

c I want to organize this information again. I'm going to ______________ (organize) it tomorrow.

d Peter can't find his glasses. He has ______________ (place) them somewhere.

e They don't pay people enough. I think they ______________ (pay) them.

f I've lost my cell phone. I'll have to ______________ (place) it.

Review: Present Perfect + *for, since, how long*

3 Write questions for these answers. Use *How long ... ?*

a ____

I have studied English for ten years.

b ____

Mike has had his laptop for two weeks.

c ____

Jim and Angela have lived here since 2016.

d ____

I've wanted to be a biologist all my life.

4 Write sentences using the words in parentheses and *for* or *since*.

a I live here now. I moved here in 2013. (live / 2013)

____

b I am here now. I arrived at 9 o'clock. (be / 9 o'clock)

____

c We are here now. We arrived ten minutes ago. (be / ten minutes)

____

d Kate met Rachel five years ago. They are good friends now. (be / five years)

____

Review: Present Perfect + *still, yet, already, just*

5 Write sentences or questions.

a Sally / call / her father. (already)

____

b We / see / Paul. (just)

____

c Mark / not listen to / this song. (still)

____

d you / be to / the new burger joint ? (yet)

____

Grammar Buildup 3

1 2 3 4 5 6 7 8

6 Choose the correct answers.

The WWF has existed **a since / for** 1961 when a group of scientists, naturalists, businessmen, and political leaders **b started / have started** the organization. The first office **c was / has been** in Switzerland. Over five million people have **d still / already** joined and together they **e achieved / have achieved** many things. It **f supports / is supporting** about 1,300 conservation and environmental projects around the world. In fact, **g for / since** 1985 WWF **h was investing / has invested** over $1.165 billion in more than 11,000 projects in more than 100 countries.

VOCABULARY IN PICTURES

Saving Environmental Resources

compost food scraps

install solar panels

insulate windows

mend old clothes

recycle packaging

ride a bike

save water

share car journeys

travel by public transportation

turn off lights

use rechargeable batteries

Prefixes

misinform

misplace

misunderstand

overcrowd

overeat

overpopulate

recycle

reorganize

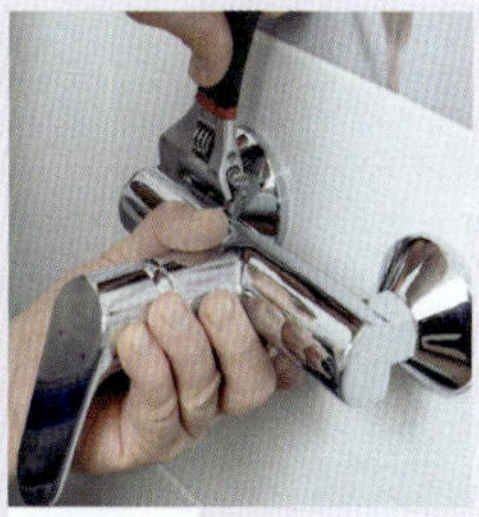
replace

replay

undercook

underestimate

underpay

underuse

4

GOOD FRIENDS

1

2

3

4

5

6

VOCABULARY 1

Making Friends

1 Match six of the phrases to the pictures. How do you say them in your language?

arrive early	☐	jump a line	☐
be late	☐	point at someone	☐
be polite	☐	shake hands	☐
be rude	☐	snap your fingers	☐
bring a present	☐	take off your shoes	☐
interrupt a conversation	☐	tell jokes	☐

2 Listen and repeat.

34

3 Which of the actions in activity 1 have you done today?

____

4 Choose the correct options.

a I **was late / interrupted their conversation / kissed my mother** because I woke up late.

b He asked me to **tell a joke / take off my shoes / jump the line** because they were dirty.

c I **arrived early / shook hands with / was rude to** Lionel Messi. He was really friendly.

d I **told a joke / took off my shoes / clicked my fingers**, but nobody laughed.

e He **was late / brought a present / arrived early**, so he helped us cook dinner.

f My teachers were talking so I couldn't **take off my shoes / be polite / interrupt their conversation**.

g Don't **tell a joke to / snap your fingers at / shake hands with** the waiter. It's very rude.

h He **jumped the line / told a joke / pointed at her** because he wanted to get on the bus first.

READING 1

1 Read and listen to the blog post on the right. Match headings a-d with paragraphs 1-4.
35

a ☐ Chatting
b ☐ Visiting someone's house
c ☐ Having a meal
d ☐ Meeting people

2 Read the blog post again and answer the questions.

a What should you do when you meet someone for the first time in the UK?

b In which region is it mandatory to take our shoes off when we arrive?

c In which country is it acceptable to burp?

d Can you interrupt a conversation in the USA?

3 INTERFACE Work in pairs. What other cultural rules do you know?

In India, you should only eat with your right hand.

In Italy, you shouldn't cut your pasta with a knife. A fork is the only utensil that should touch your pasta.

Cultural fact

In some countries it is polite to burp after a meal. Is it polite in your country?

www.blogger.com/cultural-roles

Patrick Johnson Follow
August 15 • 3 min read

Making Friends at Home and Abroad

Are you going on an exchange this year? Are you going to stay with a host family? Do you want to make new friends?

Then you need to know how to be polite, because being polite is different in different countries.

1

When you meet new people in Spain or France, you usually kiss women twice on the cheek. Men shake hands. People in the UK are more formal, so you should shake hands when you meet a stranger.

2

In the UK you don't have to bring a present, like flowers or chocolates, but people will think you are very polite if you do. In Germany, Austria and the UK you must not be late. It's very rude. In Mexico you should be late – it's normal. In the USA you must not arrive early. In central and eastern Europe and Scandinavia, you must take your shoes off when you arrive, so always wear clean socks.

3

In China you must never snap your fingers anywhere – it's very rude. However, it's OK to burp in China, in fact it's polite, but in most European countries you must not. In France you shouldn't tell jokes at dinner. The French take eating seriously.

4

In some countries it's OK to interrupt a conversation, but you shouldn't in the UK or the USA. You should wait until the other speakers have finished, especially if they are older than you.

Wherever you go, have fun. And remember: if you want to make friends, be polite!

GRAMMAR 1

Obligation, No Obligation, Prohibition, Advice

1 Complete the chart with the sentences below, according to what they express: obligation, no obligation, prohibition, or advice.

a You should shake hands when you meet a stranger.

b You must not be late.

c You must be polite everywhere.

d In the UK you don't have to bring a present, like flowers or chocolates.

obligation	no obligation
prohibition	**advice**

2 Complete the rules below.

a We use ______________ to show **obligation**.

b We use ______________ to show there is **no obligation**.

c We use ______________ to show **prohibition**.

d We use ______________ to suggest something, to give **advice**.

3 Choose the correct options.

RULES FOR SUMMER CAMP

a You **don't have to / must** be polite to the counselors.

b You **must not / don't have to** talk in bed. People need to sleep.

c You **must not / don't have to** make your bed. You can choose.

d You **have to / don't have to** look after the key to your room.

e You **must / must not** be late. Activities start at 8:30am.

4 Complete the dialogue using *must, have to, don't have to* or *must not*.

Jim: Can I go to the mall this weekend?
Mom: Yes, but there are some rules. You **a** ______________ stay with your friends. You **b** ______________ go anywhere on your own.
Jim: Right, Mom.
Mom: And you **c** ______________ ride your bicycle into town, because there aren't any buses on Saturday.
Jim: Yes, Mom.
Mom: And you **d** ______________ lose your keys or your new jacket.
Jim: Yes, Mom.
Mom: And you **e** ______________ call me when you arrive.
Jim: OK, Mom.
Mom: But you **f** ______________ buy me a present – only if you want to!
Jim: Thanks, Mom!

5 Underline the correct words to complete the text.

My Sister and My Best Friend

I'm really lucky because I **a shouldn't / don't have to** wait to talk to my best friend at school. My best friend is my older sister, Karen, and we share a bedroom. However, we do have some rules. For example, there are borrowing rules. I **b must not / don't have to** borrow her clothes and she **c has to / doesn't have to** ask me when she wants to use my smartphone. We also **d have to / should** follow other rules in our bedroom. We both **e must not / have to** keep our stuff tidy. We have one more rule. Because Karen's older than me, she **f doesn't have to / must not** go to bed when I do, but when she comes to bed, she **g doesn't have to / must not** wake me up if I'm asleep! Luckily she's really kind, so she never does. I **h should / don't have to** be more like her!

6 Look at the question and answers in the chart. Check (✓) the correct information.

obligation – question and short answers
Do I **have to** bring a present? Yes, you do. / No, you don't.

In questions, *have to* is used instead of *must* and it indicates that …

☐ the obligation comes from somebody else and can't be changed.

☐ the obligation comes from somebody else but can be changed.

7 Write questions using *have to*.

young people / be / polite?
Do young people have to be polite?

a you / be home / before midnight?

______

b do / your homework / tonight?

______

c your dad / get up early / on Saturday mornings?

______

d visitors / bring presents / in your country?

______

8 INTERFACE Work in pairs. Ask and answer the questions in activity 7.

Do young people have to be polite?

Yes, they have to be polite.

TIP

For obligation (*have to* or *must*) in the past, always use *had to*.
I had to take off my shoes.
Did you have to do your homework?

9 Read about Joan and match the phrases.

When I was a child, …

a I had to help mom with household chores.
b I had to wake up at 6am to go to school.
c I had to do my homework in the afternoon.
d I had to walk my dog everyday.

☐ Now, I don't have a pet.

☐ Now, I live in my own apartment and do all the chores.

☐ Now, I wake up at 7am to go to work.

☐ Now, I have to work full-time and go to college in the evening.

GRAMMAR GUIDE page 76

LISTENING

My Gang

1 Listen and choose the correct words.

36

a Harry has **a best friend / a group of friends**.

b Maria has **a best friend / lots of different friends**.

2 Listen again and choose the correct answers.

36

a Harry and his friends like **going to parties / playing basketball / drawing and painting**.

b Alex is **approachable and sociable / funny / quiet and creative**.

c To join Harry's group of friends you must **love soccer / support Los Angeles FC / support LA Galaxy**.

d Harry and his friends like **dance music / hip hop / fast guitar music**.

e Maria has lots of friends from **secondary school / different places / primary school.**

f Marcus and Amelia are Maria's friends from **school / the beach / her neighborhood**.

g Maria believes friends **have to / should / don't have to** see each other every day.

h For Maria, it is important that her friends are **creative / funny / honest**.

3 CLASS VOTE Is it important that your friends like the same things as you?

SPEAKING

An Advice Video

1 Aunt Jo has a relationship advice channel. Read and listen to her video. Then answer: *Who's asking Aunt Jo for advice? Why?*

37

Good evening, my dear nieces and nephews! Welcome to the channel *1 Minute with Aunt Jo*. As always, let's read a message from one of our subscribers.

Hello, Aunt Jo! I'm a 15-year-old student and I never miss the videos on your channel! I'd like some advice on how to act with my friend Jim. He's a good friend, passionate, and loyal, but he's always getting in trouble and it's up to me to help him. The last straw was last Saturday ... Jim called me from the mall saying he had spent all his money shopping and had no way to get home. His parents cut off his credit card because he always spends too much money. So he asked me to go over there and lend him some money. I took a bus to the mall and left $20 with him. I wasted my entire Saturday afternoon and felt like an idiot. Help me, Aunt Jo! What should I do to maintain my friendship with Jim but not get involved in his troubles? Signed: Angry Friend.

Hello, Angry Friend! First of all, thank you for watching. The situation you are experiencing is delicate. I think you should support Jim, as a good friend would, but you shouldn't do everything he asks. Last Saturday, for example, you should have used your credit card to call a taxi to pick up Jim at the mall and take him home. Then you should have sent the taxi bill to his parents. This way, you would help your friend, but without wasting your time or money ... What do you think of this suggestion, Angry Friend? Answer in the comments!

And you who are watching this video now ... Do you also want some advice about relationships? Send your message and Aunt Jo will respond! Bye!

2 Read the video transcript again. Choose the correct options.

a Jim needed help because he had **lost his wallet / spent all his money**.

b Jim doesn't have a credit card because his parents **won't let him use it / can't afford it**.

c Jim returned home with the money that **his parents gave him / Angry Friend lent him**.

d Aunt Jo thinks Angry Friend should have **taken a taxi to the mall / called a taxi for Jim**.

e She also thinks he should **send the taxi bill to Jim's parents. / make Jim pay for the taxi**.

FUNCTIONAL LANGUAGE

Asking for / Giving advice

Questions
What should I do to ... ? / What do you think?
I'd like some advice on ...

Answers
You should / shouldn't ...

Speaking Task

Plan an advice video with your classmates.

Step 1

Work with one or two partners. Each one of you writes a message to the *1 Minute with Aunt Jo* channel asking for advice on relationships.

Exchange messages so that each one can play Aunt Jo and record a video to respond another partner's message.

Step 2

Firstly plan your message to ask for advice. Then write it.

What problem are you experiencing? With whom?

When you record the video to reply a partner's question, read the message you received and plan how you will respond.

What do you think your groupmate should / shouldn't do? Why?

Record the video. Greet the audience, read the message, and then give your advice. In the end, say goodbye.

Step 3

With your teacher's help, create a video channel for the class and upload the videos.

Like and comment on your classmates' videos.

CULTURE

Being **Friendly** or Being **Friends**?

That is a tough question to answer, depending on where you are from. Western Indians believe real friends should be there for one another, for better or for worse. You will never be alone, you will have at least 10 offers from friends to join you in anything you do. Eventually, you will understand that you must go to your coleague's son's 1st birthday or his or her mother-in-law's 70th birthday. You must find no excuses not to join them for lunch or *chai* even after having just had a big meal (you don't have to call in advance) and you have to try to help your friend's brother's niece get a job wherever you work.

Something you shouldn't expect from your Indian friends is the use of "please" and "thank you." For them, doing so means you are treating them as a business acquaintance, which is something they dislike. After all, you are friends! You shouldn't feel they are not treating you well because they do not use the so called "magic words" of Western etiquette.
The expectations friends have about one another do not rest only on the small things. Should you have an emergency, Indians feel it's quite appropriate to order you around. It may sound inconvenient, but, for them, that is loyalty.
Although our culture may affect the way we see the world, it is fundamental to learn to separate the wheat from the chaff. In this sense, Indians are kind, empathetic, welcoming, passionate, and extremely giving people, that is, friends.

1 Read and listen to the information. Then write T for *true* or F for *false*. 38

- **a** ☐ Western Indians think friends don't have to be there for one another.
- **b** ☐ In India, you are invited to lots of social gatherings.
- **c** ☐ Indians use "please" and "thank you" all the time, especially among friends.
- **d** ☐ In India, the expectations friends have about one another are very high.
- **e** ☐ Indians are kind, empathetic, welcoming, passionate, and extremely giving people.

2 What is it like to "be friends" in your country?

____

____

____

____

3 What do you think about saying "please" and "thank you" between friends? Do you feel it is necessary? Why or why not?

____

____

____

____

VOCABULARY 2

Verb and Noun Collocations

1

2

3

4

5

6

1 Match the expressions in the box with the pictures. Check if some expressions can match with more than one picture.

give advice	☐	receive praise	☐
give praise	☐	receive presents	☐
give presents	☐	spend money	☐
have an argument	☐	spend time	☐
have fun	☐	tell lies	☐
receive advice	☐	tell the truth	☐

2 Listen and repeat.

39

3 Choose the correct words.

a I love spending **money on / time with** my neighbor. We always have **an argument / fun**.

b I've tried to give my sister **presents / advice**, but she never listens to me.

c My cousin always tells me **the truth / lies**. She's extremely honest.

d John spent a lot of **money / time** on my birthday present. He's very generous.

e My mom always gives **praise / advice** to her co-workers. She says they are competent and reliable.

f My brother told me **a lie / the truth** last night and we had a terrible **fun / argument**.

g He got a great **advice / present** from his uncle – a leather jacket.

4 Complete the sentences with verbs from activity 1.

Do you ever ___give___ advice to your friends? What about?

a When did you last __________ an argument with a friend?

b Is it ever OK to __________ a lie?

c How much time do you __________ with your parents on the weekends?

d What presents did you __________ for your last birthday?

e What are you going to do to __________ fun this weekend?

f Do you feel embarrassed when you __________ praise?

5 INTERFACE Work in small groups. Ask and answer the questions in activity 4.

READING 2

1 Read and listen to the questionnaire. Choose the best title.
40

a Friends or Family – What's More Important?

b You Must Not Tell Lies

c Friends – What Would You Do?

Questionnaire

a If you wanted to make friends with a new student in class, would you …

1 give praise to him or her all the time?

2 invite him or her to join in your study group?

3 organize a welcome party for him or her?

b If it were your best friend's birthday, would you …

1 give him or her an expensive present?

2 make him or her a cake?

3 sing "happy birthday to you" in the classroom for him or her?

c If you didn't like your friend's brother / sister, would you …

1 do nothing, because they're family?

2 avoid being with your friend when his or her brother / sister is around?

3 ask your friend to stop spending time with his or her brother / sister?

d If your friend told you a lie, would you …

1 do nothing, because it's not important?

2 ask him or her to tell you the truth?

3 wait for him or her to apologize?

e If you had an argument with your best friend, would you …

1 apologize immediately?

2 try to talk to him or her when you are cool-headed?

3 tell other friends how cruel he or she was to you?

2 Read the questionnaire again and choose the best answers for you.

3 Work in small groups.

a From the answers given, we can outline three types of friend. Read the description of the second type, corresponding to people who answered mostly 2.

b Then read all the 1 answers and discuss: What kind of friend is the person who answered mostly 1?

c Write the description of this type of friend in the space provided.

d Repeat the procedure with 3.

What kind of friend are you?	
Mostly 1s	______________________
Mostly 2s	You are an honest and balanced friend. You show consideration for your partners, but you know how to preserve your own space as well as theirs.
Mostly 3s	______________________

4 CLASS VOTE Do you like to answer this type of questionnaire? Do you think it can help us get to know ourselves better?

GRAMMAR 2

Second Conditional

1 Look at the following sentences. Circle the clause which indicates a *condition* and underline the one which indicates the *consequence* in case that condition becomes a fact.

a If I had an argument with a friend, I would apologize.

b If a friend told me a lie, I would be very upset.

c If I didn't like my friend's sister, I would avoid talking to her.

2 Complete the chart with the clauses. Then choose the correct information as to the rules of the second conditional.

if clause	consequence

a The second conditional is used to express a particular condition in the future.

☐ There is NOT a real likelihood for this condition to happen.

☐ There is a real likelihood for this condition to happen.

b The structure of the second conditional is:

☐ if + simple present (condition) – will + verb base form (consequence).

☐ if + simple past (condition) – would + verb base form (consequence).

3 Choose the correct words.

a What **would / did** you say if your best friend **were / would be** late to meet you?

b Robert **would go / went** to the movies with Mike if he **wouldn't / didn't** play soccer all the time.

c If he **told / would tell** me a lie, I **wouldn't be / wasn't** happy.

d **Would you tell / Did you tell** the truth if you **didn't / wouldn't** like a friend's sister?

4 Complete the sentences using the second conditional.

a I'm going to Paris this summer, but if I ________________ (go) to London, I ________________ (visit) my English friend.

b If Mike ________________ (not have) a lot of homework, he ________________ (go) out.

c If she ________________ (have) more money, she ________________ (buy) some new shoes.

d If we ________________ (go) to the swimming pool instead of the movies, we ________________ (have) more fun.

GRAMMAR GUIDE page 76

WRITING

A Letter of Recommendation

1 EXPLORING THE CONTEXT

1 Do you know what a letter of recommendation is? Read the definition.

A **letter of recommendation** is a document in which the writer attests to someone's academic or professional qualifications. Typically, the letter is about a candidate for a job, a scholarship, or an award. It's written by a former employer, a teacher, or a classmate / co-worker of the candidate.

2 Now infer: To whom is a letter of recommendation addressed?

a To the candidate for a job, scholarship, or award.

b To the person(s) responsible for giving the job, scholarship, or award.

3 41 Read and listen to the letter of recommendation on page 75. Answer the questions.

a What is Jemima being recommended for?

____

b Who is recommending her?

____

Young Achievers
514 S. Magnolia St.
Orlando, FL 32806

123 6th St.
Melbourne, FL 32904
12 April

Dear Sir/Madam,
I am writing to nominate my friend Jemima Downside for a Young Achievers Award.
Although Jemima is only 13, she has achieved a lot. Her father is ill and cannot work, so Jemima has to look after him while her mother is at work. She does the shopping and the cooking for her whole family as well as her homework every night. However, she never complains and is always happy and cheerful.
Furthermore, Jemima has raised over $3,500 for Cancer Research by doing sponsored swims. In addition, she plays the drums in a local band and always gets excellent grades at school. Most importantly, however, Jemima is a fantastic friend. She is funny, thoughtful, loyal, and trustworthy.
For all these reasons I think you should make Jemima a Young Achiever.
Yours faithfully,
Damien Rogers

4 Read the letter again and underline parts where Damien ...

- **a** identifies Jemima.
- **b** talks about Jemima's achievements.
- **c** mentions positive things about Jemima.
- **d** writes what he is recommending Jemima for.

5 What examples of formal language does Damien use?

____

2 PLANNING

1 Write a formal letter (120-150 words) recommending a friend to be a Young Achiever. Make notes:

- **a** Who do you want to recommend?
- **b** What are his or her achievements?
- **c** What is he or she like?

LANGUAGE FOCUS

Linkers of Addition and Contrast

Although *Jemima is only 13, she has achieved a lot.*
However*, she never complains.*
Furthermore*, Jemima has raised over $3,500.*
In addition*, she plays the drums* ***and*** *always gets excellent grades at school.*

1 Look at the sentences above and complete the rules with the words in bold.

- **a** We use ___________ and ___________ to show contrast.
- **b** We use ___________, ___________, and ___________ to show addition.

2 Rewrite the sentences in your notebook using linkers.

- **a** Tom is a bit eccentric. He's very approachable.
- **b** She's very thoughtful. She's not very reliable.
- **c** My sister is good at sports. She's very clever.
- **d** John can speak five languages. He's now learning Arabic.

3 WRITING

Write a first draft. Divide your letter into four paragraphs. Use linkers.

4 CHECKING & EDITING

1 Ask a classmate to read your letter. Ask them to check:

- Is the information indicated in activity 4 of Step 1 present? Are linkers used correctly?

2 Use your classmate's suggestions to prepare the final version of your letter. If possible, include a picture of your friend.

5 SHARING

1 Work in groups of 6-7 students.

- **a** Three students from the group will form a jury to elect a Young Achiever. They read the letters and elect the Young Achiever, considering the qualities pointed out.
- **b** The group's students then switch roles: those who were judges now submit their recommendations to the new jury, and that new jury chooses another Young Achiever. This way, there will be two winners for each group (or only one, if the same person was chosen both times).
- **c** When all groups have done their readings and votes, the groups share their results.

GRAMMAR GUIDE

Obligation

I / You He / She / It We / You / They	**must** be polite. **have / has to** be polite.

- we use *must* and *have to* to show obligation
- in questions about obligation we only use *have to*
  Do I **have to** do my homework?

No Obligation

I / You	**don't have to** come.
He / She / It	**doesn't have to** come.
We / You / They	**don't have to** come.

- we use *don't have to* to show there is no obligation or that something isn't necessary
  She **doesn't have to** prepare dinner tonight.

Prohibition

I / You / He / She / It / We / You / They	**must not** be late.

- we use *must not* to show prohibition. It does not mean the same as *don't have to*
  You **must not** be late for school.

Advice

+	I / You	**should** go.
	He / She / It	
	We / You / They	
–	I / You	**shouldn't** go.
	He / She / It	
	We / You / They	
?	**Should** I / you **go**? Yes, I **should**. No, I **shouldn't**.	
	Should he / she / it **go**? Yes, he **should**. No, he **shouldn't**.	
	Should we / you / they **go**? Yes, we **should**. No, we **shouldn't**.	
?	**Do** I / you **have to** bring a present? Yes, I **do**. No, I **don't**.	
	Does he / she / it **have to** bring a present? Yes, he **does**. No, he **doesn't**.	
	Do we / you / they **have to** bring a present? Yes, we **do**. No, we **don't**.	

- we use *should / shouldn't* to give advice
  You **should** eat more fruit.

Second Conditional

if clause	consequence
If he told a lie,	what would you do?
If he told a lie,	I'd be angry.
consequence	***if* clause**
What would you do	if he told a lie?
I'd be angry	if he told a lie.

- we use the second conditional to talk about events in the present and future that are unlikely to happen
- to form second conditional sentences we use *if* + subject + simple past (for the situation), subject + *would / wouldn't* + infinitive without *to* (for the consequence)
- when the situation comes first, we use a comma
  If I **were** famous, **I'd** buy a big house.
- we don't use a comma if the consequence comes first
  Len **would be** sad **if** I **didn't tell** the truth.
- we form questions with (question word) + *would* + subject + infinitive without *to* + *if* + subject + simple past
  What **would** you **do if** you **had** an argument with your best friend?
- in the *if* clause, the verb *be* usually takes the form *were* for the first and the third persons
  If I **were** you, I wouldn't be rude to your friend.
- however, the form *was* is also used in everyday speech.
  If she **was** my friend, I would give her some advice.

6

PROGRESS CHECK

Name: ____________________
Class name / Period: ____________________
Teacher: ____________________
Date: ____________________

Making Friends

1 Complete the text with the correct form of the verbs in the box.

bring	shake	snap	take	tell off

WHEN YOU MEET YOUR HOST FAMILY, REMEMBER THIS ADVICE!

1 **a** ____________ hands with the parents.

2 It's a good idea to **b** ____________ a present for the mother of the family.

3 Look at what your exchange partner does. If he **c** ____________ his shoes, you should too.

4 It's OK to **d** ____________ jokes to your host family.

5 When you're in a restaurant it is rude to **e** ____________ your fingers at the waiter.

Verb and Noun Collocations

2 Match verbs a-e with nouns 1-5.

a ☐ give
b ☐ tell
c ☐ spend
d ☐ receive
e ☐ have

1 an argument with / fun with
2 advice from / a present from
3 advice to / a present to
4 money on / time with
5 lies to / the truth to

Obligation, No Obligation, Prohibition Advice

3 Choose the correct words.

a A best friend **should / doesn't have to** always be honest and tell the truth.

b John **doesn't have to / must not** do any homework tonight. He did it all last night.

c I **have to / don't have to** call Jack. I talked to him at school today.

d You **have to / don't have to** keep Monica's secret. She thinks you're extremely honest.

Second Conditional

4 Write sentences using the second conditional.

you do / you saw your best friend stealing ?
What would you do if you saw your best friend stealing?

a you had an argument with your best friend / you apologize first ?

____

b Steve gave me a present / I / buy him lunch

____

c I / be very angry / my best friend weren't honest with me

____

d I were famous / I / still spend time with my friends

____

Grammar Buildup 4

1 2 3 4 5 6 7 8

5 Choose the correct answers.

Penny Hey, Mom says I can have a party.
Sian Great! You **a** ______ invite me. Please!
Penny Of course! Who else should I invite?
Sian You **b** ______ invite Glyn. I really like him.
Penny But you **c** ______ Bob too.
Sian No. Glyn's **d** ______ than Bob.
Penny OK. And I have to invite Clara because I went to her party.
Sian Oh yeah. I didn't go. I was **e** ______ sick.
Penny It was a great party. Really amazing!
Sian If it were my party, I **f** ______ Brian. He's really funny.
Penny I'd ask Brian if I **g** ______ him, but we've never met.
Sian When **h** ______ the party?
Penny In two weeks.

a	**1** don't have to	**2** should
b	**1** have to	**2** shouldn't
c	**1** like	**2** have liked
d	**1** funnier	**2** more funny
e	**1** enough	**2** too
f	**1** 'd invite	**2** 'll invite
g	**1** know	**2** knew
h	**1** will you have	**2** are you going to have

VOCABULARY IN PICTURES

Making Friends

arrive early

be late

be polite

be rude

bring a present

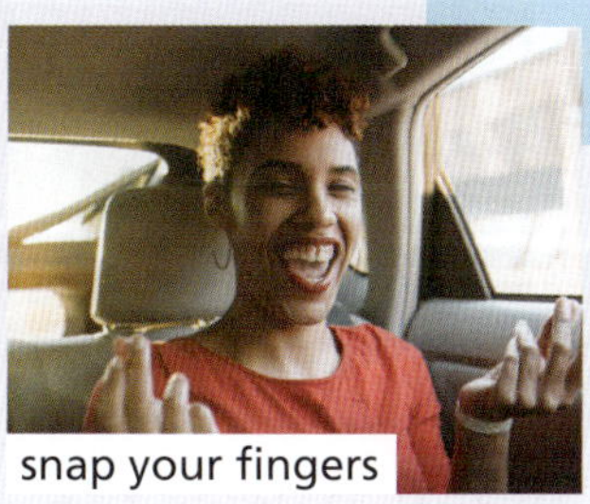
snap your fingers

interrupt a conversation

jump a line

point at someone

shake hands

take off your shoes

tell jokes

Verb and Noun Collocations

give advice / receive advice

give praise / receive praise

give presents / receive presents

have an argument

have fun

spend money

spend time

tell lies

tell the truth

REVIEW 2

VOCABULARY

Complete the sentences with the correct words. Find these words in the same page word search.

1 Some habits help us live in a more sustainable way, like mending ________________, for example.

6 A wise way to save the environment is traveling by ________________ transportation.

2 Fake news are created to ________________ people. Always double-check information on reliable sources.

H	V	H	A	Q	T	J	Z	T	W	Y	V	X	D	K
K	N	W	L	Y	M	L	Y	W	P	L	B	L	L	V
U	V	Q	K	F	P	U	B	L	I	C	O	J	K	B
U	P	S	P	P	R	K	W	H	D	Q	W	U	I	M
N	E	Y	O	L	D	C	L	O	T	H	E	S	E	T
D	G	F	B	V	T	I	B	M	N	O	C	C	J	T
E	A	E	J	D	U	M	V	Y	W	V	D	N	V	Q
R	Y	L	A	G	R	J	B	Q	Y	Z	A	M	Y	I
C	M	I	S	I	N	F	O	R	M	W	R	X	T	J
O	X	G	E	Z	O	O	V	E	R	E	A	T	E	N
O	W	P	W	A	F	J	I	W	M	X	L	W	R	B
K	I	S	Q	B	F	J	B	P	M	N	C	N	R	M
E	R	M	Y	G	E	E	I	O	U	L	W	R	K	Q
D	V	P	F	I	K	G	K	F	P	P	G	S	F	S
L	R	E	C	Y	C	L	E	C	F	O	H	S	P	C

3 He's ________________ and now he's feeling stuffed.

4 If you want to live in a sustainable world, you should ________________ your trash.

7 To save energy, we must ________________ the lights of a room when we're not there.

5 If Anthony rode his ________________ to the office more often, he would improve his health.

8 Some dishes at this restaurant have ________________ meat. Do you like it or do you prefer eating something different?

9

The little girl was singing out loud inside the plane, but she didn't mean to be ____________________ to the passengers.

10

Sandra had an ____________________ with Jane, but later they apologized to each other.

11

The student raised her hand and the teacher ____________________ at her.

12

You should always ____________________ hands with your interviewer. It's ____________________.

13

Nathalie prefers to ____________________ her allowance on books and games.

14

If you go to Japan, take off your ____________________ before entering someone's house.

E H P U I Q U M R X J M H L N
J O K E S I T N U G N P F U A
S J R R A A S N D I O O G Q S
P J W F P S G Y E J Y L F E T
O X K G D O T V L A D I Y L V
I R D V M T V D Z C L T G P M
N A K D D U Q W P R M E U I A
T J C C U Q W S X T F Q I C X
E I B S I W X I D I A Z T N Z
D V Y H T J Y M E M A R N Y Y
X I T A R G U M E N T I K Q T
U J S K X A R S P E N D O X R
K H Q E B R H T B U L O Y U J
N G H D Z I D X F D Q A Q X C
O Y N S H O E S O F U R X O Z

15

Robert told a ____________________ to his host father, and both of them laughed a lot.

REVIEW 2

GRAMMAR

Present Perfect + *for, since, how long*

1 Complete the chart with the time expressions in the box.

1995	the start of the month
a very long time	~~three days~~
~~May 20~~	we finished our exams
several days	weeks
six hours	yesterday

for	*since*
three days	May 20

2 Write sentences using the present perfect and *for* or *since*.

a Bob (not have) a day off / three months.

b I (know) my best friend / we were three years old.

c My soccer team (not win) a game / last year.

d Susan (not talk) to Melanie / two months.

3 Write questions with *How long* ...?

Paul / work / at this school ?
How long has Paul worked at this school?

a you / have / your jeans ?

b she / be / your English teacher ?

c they / live / in France ?

d he / play / the violin ?

4 Write answers to the questions in activity 3. Use *for* or *since* and the time expression in parentheses.

(six years)
He has worked at this school for six years.

a (last week)

b (about eight months)

c (three years)

d (six years old)

Present Perfect + *still, yet, already, just*

5 Rewrite the sentences using the words in parentheses.

I've done this exercise. (already)
I've already done this exercise.

a My friends haven't seen that new movie. (still)

b I've spoken to Liam. (just)

c Have you called your parents? (yet)

d I have bought you a birthday present. (already)

e It's one in the afternoon and you haven't gotten dressed. (still)

f We have praised her for the new job. (just)

Obligation, No Obligation, Prohibition, Advice

6 Read the sentences. Then write O for *obligation* or N for *no obligation*.

Class must start at 9 o'clock. [O]

a Do you have to wear a school uniform? [ ]

b Students don't have to have lunch in school. [ ]

c Sara doesn't have to walk to school. [ ]

d Ivy must wear glasses to drive. [ ]

7 Complete the sentences with *must not* or *shouldn't* and the verbs in the box.

feed	forget	play	~~point~~	touch

"Have you seen that tall man over there?" "Anna, you ___shouldn't point___ at him. It's rude!"

a It's Patrick's birthday next week. We ________________ to send him a card.

b Jack is only six so he ________________ that video game. The age rating is 14.

c You ________________ animals at the zoo.

d Soccer players ________________ the ball with their hands.

8 Complete the sentences with *should* or *shouldn't* and the verbs in the box.

~~arrive~~	eat	put	switch off	talk

You ___should arrive___ ten minutes before the movie starts. It's annoying when people are late.

a You ________________ your cell phone before the movie starts.

b You ________________ quietly.

c You ________________ loudly to your friends during the movie.

d You ________________ your feet on the seat in front of you.

Second Conditional

9 Underline the correct words.

If I **didn't** / **wouldn't** work hard, I **didn't** / **wouldn't** pass my exams.

a If he **played** / **'d play** a musical instrument, he **chose** / **'d choose** the saxophone.

b Where **did** / **would** you live if you **moved** / **'d move** to another country?

c My parents **were** / **would be** delighted if I **went** / **'d go** to college.

d If you **had** / **'d have** $10,000, what **did** / **would** you spend it on?

10 Complete the first half of the sentences with the simple past or *would* / *wouldn't* + infinitive. Then match the sentence halves.

a [4] I ___'d be___ (be) extremely rich

b [ ] What ________________ you ________________ (say)

c [ ] If we ________________ (have) an argument,

d [ ] If I ________________ (not know) where I was,

e [ ] My parents ________________ (complain)

1 if someone jumped the line you were in?

2 if they didn't like the food in a restaurant.

3 we wouldn't be happy.

4 if I won the lottery.

5 I'd ask for directions.

Cyberbullying

Online Cruelty

1 Read and listen. Then write *T* for true or *F* for false. Correct the false sentences.
42

a ☐ Grace dated a guy named Will a couple of times.

____

b ☐ Will wanted to break up with Grace and she got mad.

____

c ☐ Will created a fake profile in Grace's name as a tribute.

____

d ☐ Will uses Grace's fake profile to offend her schoolmates.

____

e ☐ Grace's schoolmates think it's Grace who's doing the attacks.

____

f ☐ Grace has already asked her parents for help.

____

g ☐ Lily convinces Grace to talk to her parents.

____

2 Discuss the following questions with a classmate. Then share your ideas with the class.

a Why does Grace feel guilty about the situation she is going through?

b In your opinion, why do many victims of cyberbullying feel guilty for the aggressions they suffer? What would you say to these victims?

c Why is it important to support a friend who is being cyberbullied, as Lily did for Grace?

3 According to Unicef, the UN agency that provides aid to children and teenagers, these are some examples of cyberbullying:

Examples of cyberbullying

1. Spreading lies about or sharing embarrassing photos of someone on social media.

2. Send hurtful or threatening messages via messaging platforms.

3. Impersonating someone and sending mean messages to others on their behalf or through fake accounts.

- Which of these three examples match what Will is doing with Grace?

____

4 Unicef asked teenagers around the world what they would like to know about cyberbullying. Read some of the questions asked by teens.

1 Am I being bullied online? How do you tell the difference between a joke and bullying?

2 Who should I talk to if someone is bullying me online? Why is reporting important?

3 I'm experiencing cyberbullying, but I'm afraid to talk to my parents about it. How can I approach them?

4 How can I help my friends report a case of cyberbullying especially if they don't want to do it?

5 How do we stop cyberbullying without giving up access to the internet?

CYBERBULLYING: What is it and how to stop it. *Unicef*. Available at: www.unicef.org/end-violence/how-to-stop-cyberbullying#1. Accessed on: July 13, 2022.

a Work in groups of 2-3. Choose a question from the list and discuss how you would answer it.

b Write your answer as completely as possible. If necessary, look for information on the internet.

c You will record a short advice video or podcast to help your classmates fight cyberbullying. One of you will read the Unicef question and the other will read the group's response.

d Rehearse a few times and then do the recording. Share it with your classmates and friends.

You've Got a Friend in Me!

- **In your opinion, what is friendship? What makes someone a good friend?**
- **Have you ever heard of the International Day of Friendship? What is it about?**
- **What does this celebration day have to do with respect for diversity?**

1 What does it mean to be a good friend? Write A for *always* and T for *try not to*. Share your ideas with your classmates.

a ☐ Share the conversation so that you are both a listener and a talker.

b ☐ Brag about what you have or what you have done.

c ☐ Be aware of others' feelings: think before you speak.

d ☐ Argue if your friend doesn't agree with you about something.

e ☐ Be prejudiced: make any negative comments about someone's religion, country, skin color, or physical appearance.

f ☐ Fight your friends' battles instead of helping them deal with their own problems.

g ☐ Talk about your friends without their permission.

h ☐ Try to understand people by thinking about things from their point of view.

I ☐ Use your manners: say "please" and "thank you."

j ☐ Praise your friends when they do something well.

k ☐ Do things for your friends without keeping score of who's done the most favors.

2 What do these images have in common? Discuss your ideas with your classmates. Then match them with the quotes below.

____

____

a

b

c

☐ "Love is the only force capable of transforming an enemy into a friend." – Martin Luther King, Jr.

☐ "Friendship is the hardest thing in the world to explain. It's not something you learn in school. But if you haven't learned the meaning of friendship, you really haven't learned anything." – Muhammad Ali

☐ "Diversity is not about how we differ. Diversity is about embracing one another's uniqueness." – Ola Joseph

3 Read the caption about the International Day of Friendship. Then match the sentences.

The International Day of Friendship is a day designed to promote friendship and bridge the gaps between races, colors, religions, and other factors which keep humans from enjoying each others' company.

- **a** The International Day of Friendship was proclaimed by the United Nations (UN) in 2011 …
- **b** The UN encourages governments, groups, and organizations to host …
- **c** The date suggested by the UN is July 30, but many countries celebrate it …
- **d** Studies point out that individuals …

- ☐ events that promote dialogue, acceptance, and understanding between people of different backgrounds.
- ☐ on the first Sunday of August.
- ☐ with the objective of building communities and helping move towards world peace.
- ☐ with stronger relationships live longer.

4 Friendship keeps the world going! Do you know how to say "friend" in other languages? Write the "friend" words in the box next to their respective languages.

ami dost Freund péngyou priyatel tomodachi vriend

- **a** Mandarin: ____________________
- **b** Dutch: ____________________
- **c** French: ____________________
- **d** German: ____________________
- **e** Hindi: ____________________
- **f** Japanese: ____________________
- **g** Russian: ____________________

Can you add more words to the list?

A Recipe for Friendship

How about preparing a "friendship recipe?" Follow the steps below.

DOING

1 Work in pairs. Think of a name for your recipe which includes the words *friend* or *friendship*.

2 Write how long it will take to prepare the "dish." (*Preparation time: ...*)

3 Mention the number of servings the recipe will provide. (*Serves ...*)

4 List the ingredients you will need and their respective quantities or proportions. (*You will need ...*)

- **Suggested ingredients to choose from:** happiness, kindness, sharing, helpfulness, empathy, tolerance, laughter, compassion, listening, patience, sensitivity, support, forgiveness, trust, honesty, conversation, understanding, affection, hugs, respect
- **Suggested quantities:** a cup of …, 1 tbsp (tablespoon) of …, 2 tsp (tea spoon) of …, a pinch of …, a sprinkle of …, a liter of …, 50g of …, a bag of …

5 Write how to prepare the dish. (*Method* or *Directions*)

- **Suggested verbs:** put, add, mix, stir, blend, pour, use, finish, serve, warm, bake

6 Include a photograph of the "finished dish."

PRESENTING

7 Tell your classmates what you took into consideration when you wrote your friendship recipe.

8 Hang the recipes in the school halls or post it on a student-friendly social media with the hashtag **#friendshipday**.

REFLECTING

9 Do you think your concept of friendship has changed? How?

10 After all this reflection on friendship, can you name the **three** most important qualities of a friend?

5

FOLLOWERS OF FASHION

1

2

3

4

5

VOCABULARY 1

Style Adjectives

1 Use your dictionary to look up the meaning of the adjectives in the box. Which can you use to describe the pictures?

The sneakers are very sporty.

casual	formal	sporty
colorful	glamorous	tight
comfortable	impractical	trendy
conventional	loose	
fashionable	old-fashioned	

1 ______________________

2 ______________________

3 ______________________

4 ______________________

5 ______________________

2 Listen and repeat.

43

3 Complete the sentences with words from the box.

a I don't like wearing boring black and brown clothes – I prefer ______________ designs.

b Those plain leather shoes are very ______________ – I prefer more unconventional designs.

c My dad isn't allowed to wear ______________ clothes at work. His office is very formal, so he wears a suit.

d My sister always follows the latest fashions. She never wears anything ______________!

e This skirt is too ______________ – I need a smaller size.

4 Choose the correct words.

My aunt loves shoes. She has so many pairs, it's unbelievable. She buys new shoes every week. She goes to the gym every day, so she has lots of sneakers, which are all **a sporty / old-fashioned**. They're also very **b trendy / conventional** because she always buys the latest designs by famous brands. Her favorite shoes are the high heels she wears on Saturday nights – they're really **c casual / glamorous** but so **d sporty / impractical**. I tried them on and I couldn't walk! Finally, she has her work shoes. She's a businesswoman, so she wears very **e formal / cool** shoes. She has to stand up a lot at work, so her shoes are **f comfortable / uncomfortable** – they can't be too **g conventional / tight**. What does she do? She owns a shoe store, of course!

READING 1

1 Read the lead and the topics in red to choose the best headline for the text.

a A short history of shoes

b FASHIONABLE FEET!

c High heels are bad for you

www.fashionworld.com

Look at the people around you. Now look at their feet. What type of shoes are they wearing? What do the shoes have in common? Color? Material? Design?

The basic design of shoes has not changed much since they were first invented. Most shoes have a sole on the bottom, a heel at the back, and an upper, the piece of material that covers the foot. However, fashion designers have found many creative ways to make shoes look different.

Let's start with heels. They can be low or incredibly high. In the 1950s, Italian designers created a glamorous new shoe: the stiletto, which has a very thin pointed heel. Shoemakers around the world loved the design and stilettos are still popular today. The ultimate pair must be the 40.5cm high stilettos produced by LadyBWear in the UK. Heels don't have to be thin to look different though: one American designer has created huge heels filled with water and toy goldfish! Of course, Lady Gaga is famous for wearing the "heelless shoes" made for her by Noritaka Tatehana of Tokyo. These shoes have a high sole but no heel, so they're very difficult to walk in.

Shoe designers have also had creative ideas for soles. Platform boots became trendy in the 1970s when lots of glam rock bands such as Kiss began to wear them. Recently, shoe designer Christian Louboutin famously decided to paint the soles of all his shoes bright red to make them instantly recognizable and extremely glamorous. Soles can also be made to look unusual. What about a pair of grass flip-flops? The grass is real and you have to water it!

Finally, designers can make the uppers fashionable. Sports brand Nike has produced shoes that look like human feet. Then there are sneakers that look like melting ice cream! But if you want something really original, some websites allow you to design your own shoes.

With all these creative fashion ideas for shoes, it's not surprising that people begin to collect them. Well-known shoe collectors include Madonna and Sarah Jessica Parker. But no one has a bigger shoe collection than the woman who owned around 3,000 pairs: Imelda Marcos, the wife of a former president of the Philippines. She had so many shoes that she even opened a shoe museum in Manila! Many of the shoes in the exhibitions have never even been worn – it would have taken her over seven years to wear all her shoes!

READING STRATEGY

Notice how texts are structured to identify their *genre*. This helps you access previous knowledge about similar texts to predict the content and make the reading process more meaningful.

2 How is the information organized in the text presented?

a It consists of a title, extensive data, and a deep analysis in formal language.

b It contains a headline, a lead, topics, and the language is relatively informal.

3 What text genre does it illustrate?

a a newspaper / magazine / blog article

b a scientific journal article

4 44 Read and listen to the text. Then write T for *true* or F for *false*. Correct the false sentences.

a ☐ Designers try to make shoes that are unusual.

____

b ☐ Stilettos have only recently become popular.

____

c ☐ Noritaka Tatehana makes shoes for Lady Gaga.

____

d ☐ Nike makes shoes that look like human hands.

____

5 Scan the text and answer the questions.

a What is an upper?

____

b How high are the world's highest stilettos?

____

c Why are Noritaka Tatehana's shoes difficult to walk in?

____

d Where can you design your own shoes?

____

e Why do people collect shoes?

____

6 INTERFACE Join a classmate. What do you think about collecting and accumulating clothing items? How do you believe this impacts the environment? Discuss.

GRAMMAR 1

Relative Pronouns

1 Read the sentences below. Write if the words in **bold** refer to people (P), things (T), locations (L) or time (TI). Then write the words they refer to.

[T] the stiletto In the 1950s, Italian designers created the stiletto, **which** has a very thin pointed heel.

a [ ] ______________ Sports brand Nike has produced shoes **that** look like human feet.

b [ ] ______________ No one has a bigger shoe collection than the woman **who** owned around 3,000 pairs.

c [ ] ______________ Italy is the country **where** fashion is a must.

d [ ] ______________ Trendsetters **that** wear heelless shoes find them difficult to walk in.

e [ ] ______________ Platform boots became trendy in the 1970s **when** rock bands began to wear them.

2 Based on the rules below, complete the chart.

a Relative pronouns are used to connect sentences. They refer to nouns (people, places, and things mentioned previously).
b When we talk about people we can use *who* or *that*.
c When we talk about things we can use *which* or *that*.
d When we talk about places / locations, we use *where*.
e When we talk about time, we use *when*.

people
The woman ____________ lives in that house owns a shoe store.
things
Chinese factories produce a lot of clothes ____________ are sold in Europe.
time
An engineer invented the bikini in 1946, ____________ Americans were testing atom bombs in the Bikini Atoll.
place
Milan is a city ____________ many glamorous shoes are made.

3 Choose the correct words.

a Noritaka Tatehana is the man **who / which** designs shoes for Lady Gaga.
b The 1950s is **that / when** stiletto shoes became fashionable.
c The jackets **which / when** my brother bought were really expensive.
d She's the girl **that / which** I met at the party.
e Where's the scarf **who / that** I lent you last night?
f San Francisco is **that / where** my cousins live.

4 Match the columns to make sentences.

a	That's the store	[ ] that cost you $100?
b	I'm the person	[ ] where I bought my suit.
c	New Year's was	[ ] which bit me.
d	Is that the dress	[ ] when I last saw him.
e	He's the man	[ ] who called you yesterday.
f	That's the dog	[ ] that emailed me last week.

5 Complete the sentences with *who, which, where*, or *when*.

H&M is a very popular clothes store in England. How much do you know about it? Read on to find out more.

Erling Persson is the man ___who___ started the company. Västerås in Sweden is **a** ____________ the first store opened. 1947 is **b** ____________ Persson opened his first store. There are now over 160,000 employees **c** ____________ work for the fast fashion company. H&M employs 100 designers **d** ____________ work on the clothes. 4,553 is the number of stores **e** ____________ the company owns. The things **f** ____________ the company sells include clothes, shoes, and cosmetics.

TIP

- In informal language, we can omit *which*, *who*, or *that* when the pronoun refers to the **object** of the sentence.
  ***The shoes they are wearing** have a basic design.* (Notice that "the shoes" are the **object** of the verb "wear"; in this case, we don't need to use *that* or *which*.)
- *Which*, *who*, or *that* can never be omitted when they refer to the **subject** of a sentence.
  *It was **Lady Gaga who / that first wore "heelless shoes."*** (In this case, Lady Gaga is the **subject** of the verb "wear," so *who / that* cannot be omitted.)
- *Whose* is used to indicate possession.
  *Boots **whose** platform soles became trendy in the 1970s can be seen in lots of different styles.*

6 Read the text about fashion for teens and underline the appropriate relative pronouns. X refers to omission of the pronoun.

If your teen doesn't like the clothes **a that / X** are perfect for them in your opinion, you are not alone. He or she is not the only adolescent **b which / who** thinks you don't have a clue about fashion. Don't worry! As teens grow, fashion is one of the ways **c X / where** they use to express their feelings and show how they see the world. Teens **d who / X** undergo "style-change" are just trying to express themselves.

7 **INTERFACE** Work in pairs. Ask and answer the questions using relative pronouns.

> What's a food that you really don't like?
> What's the name of a person who makes you laugh?

GRAMMAR GUIDE page 100

LISTENING

A Famous Designer

1 Look at the pictures. Who is the woman in the picture on the left? What is her job?

____

2 45 Listen to the first part of the interview. Check your answers.

3 46 Listen to the second part of the interview and answer the questions.

a Where did she grow up?
  1 in London
  2 near London

b What sort of school did she go to?
  1 an expensive private school
  2 the local state school

c When did she become interested in fashion?
  1 as a teenager **2** as a grown-up

d Where did she study fashion?
  1 in Paris **2** in London

e Who modelled at her first fashion show?
  1 Kate Moss **2** Claudia Schiffer

f When did she start working for Chloé?
  1 1997 **2** 2001

g Who did she design a wedding dress for in 2000?
  1 Kate Moss **2** Madonna

h Why doesn't she use leather or fur?
  1 because she is against animal cruelty
  2 because they are very expensive

SPEAKING

Prom Night

47 Nathalie and Jude are talking about what to wear to their high school prom. Listen and complete the dialogue.

Jude, what are you planning to wear to the prom?

Well, I haven't made up my mind yet … you know, it's an **a** ______________ I'll hopefully look back and always remember …

Yeah, it asks for a very special **b** ______________! After all, it's not an average **c** ______________ like birthdays or holiday seasons …

It's our special day, but I don't want to feel **d** ______________ or wishing I had chosen something different …

What about a lacy black slip **e** ______________?

Well, I personally don't like black … I think a floral dress is perfect for a summer or **f** ______________!

The dance will take place on the grass, so we must choose our **g** ______________ carefully … no stilettos!

Maybe a **h** ______________ …

Good idea!

In short, a lightweight dress, not too **i** ______________, and comfortable clothes! Perfect!

FUNCTIONAL LANGUAGE

Talking about Outfits

What are you planning to wear … ?
I haven't made up my mind yet …
It's a special occasion …
What about … ?
I personally don't like …
I think …
Maybe …

Speaking Task

Talk to a classmate about dressing for a special occasion.

Step 1

Choose a special occasion to talk about. Some ideas:

A wedding party

A rock concert

A friend's birthday party

Make notes about what to wear for the occasion / event.

Step 2

Write the information down to discuss it with your partner.

Step 3

Work with your partner. Take turns practicing your dialogue.

CULTURE

Fashion Revolution in South Africa

South Africa is a melting pot of cultures and traditions and therefore has become an inspiration for many designers all over the world. Rather than just copying overseas trends, local designers look into what it means to be fashionable in South Africa. Following their inspiration, they choose fabric, beads, and cultural aspects which can bring life to unique South African attire.

The ethnic look is a rule: *dashikis* – colorful garments worn by men and women in West Africa – come embellished in beads and are paired with pants. Many designers have also found ways to recycle by reusing clothes which allude to specific national and personal histories.

During Apartheid, *Loxion Kulca* – street slang for "Location Culture" – was a term used to refer to townships (underdeveloped segregated urban areas). Nowadays, it is the hottest brand worn on the streets and reflects the lifestyle of urban Africa through apparel, shoes, accessories, and handmade items.

African garments reveal something about heritage and perpetuation of local practices. Take *Seshoeshoe*, a printed dyed cotton fabric widely used for traditional African clothing. It is manufactured in different colors and patterns and, because it is quite popular, it is always in fashion.

That is South Africa: breaking waves in the industry and bringing the country's style to the world!

Dashikis multi-colored garments

Dashikis embroidery flower

Traditional African garments

1 Read and listen to the article and answer the questions below. 48

a Why has South Africa become an inspiration for designers all over the country?

____

b What are *dashikis*?

____

c During Apartheid, what did *Loxion Kulca* refer to?

____

d What is *Loxion Kulca* today?

____

e What is *Seshoeshoe* fabric?

____

2 What is the latest fashion in your country?

____

3 Do you know any fashion trends inspired by traditional or local cultures? Do you like them? Why or why not?

____

VOCABULARY 2

Phrasal Verbs: Clothes

1 Use your dictionary to look up the meaning of the phrasal verbs in the box. Then match them with the pictures below.

separable:	give away	pick out	pick up
	put away	put on	take off
	throw away	try on	wear out
inseparable:	get into	go with	look for

a

____

b

____

c

____

d

____

e

____

f

____

g

____

h

____

i

____

j

____

k

____

j

____

2 Listen and repeat.

49

3 Rewrite the words in **bold** using five of the phrasal verbs in activity 1.

This sweater's too small! I can't **fit into** it.
get into

a This T-shirt's really old – I'm going to **put it in the trash**. __________

b I like this sweater. I'm going to **find out if it fits**. __________

c I love sales. I always **find** good bargains in the stores. __________

d Does this black jacket **look good** with these black pants? __________

e I'm not going to wear this top often. I don't want it to **deteriorate**. __________

4 Complete the sentences with the other phrasal verbs from activity 1.

a I don't know what to wear. Can you __________ something __________ for me?

b When my room's messy, my mom tells me to __________ my clothes __________.

c It's so hot in here. I'm going to __________ my jacket __________.

d Do you want this belt? I want to __________ it __________.

e It's cold. __________ your coat __________.

f I can't find any sneakers I like! Can you help me to __________ some?

TIP

Some phrasal verbs have multiple meanings (e.g., *pick up*), so always read the context to decide on the appropriate meaning.

READING 2

1 Look at the messages on page 97. What is happening on Saturday evening?

____

Hi, Anna!

Hi, Lucy.

Are you going anywhere Saturday evening?

Yeah, it's Jenny's party. Aren't you going?

Wow, how could I have forgotten! Are you wearing anything special?

I don't know. I might wear my new blue skirt. How about you?

I'm going to wear my new green dress.

I want to wear my black boat neck top, but I've lent it to someone. Was it you, by any chance?

Er … don't think so. Let me check, it might be somewhere in my messy closet.

Thanks, it'll be great if you find it. Otherwise I'll have to go to the mall to buy something to go with that skirt.

Remember that this Saturday is a national holiday, nothing will open!

Right, I must get it tomorrow, then!

But hey, your top's here. I've just found it!

Yay!

And how are you getting there on Saturday? Is anyone driving you?

Nope, no one will be home on Saturday.

I'll ask my dad if he can take us there.

Thanks! Let's talk tomorrow to arrange it.

Yeap, bye!

TIP

In **text messages** we usually use informal language with slang and interjections. **Interjections** are words that are grammatically independent of the others around them and that communicate an emotion rather than an idea. Examples of interjections are *ouch* (pain), *eek* (fear), *phew* (relief).

2 Read and listen to the messages. Then write T for *true* and F for *false*.

50

- **a** ☐ Lucy is going to Jenny's party.
- **b** ☐ Anna was planning to go to the party when Lucy called.
- **c** ☐ Anna's wearing her black dress to the party.
- **d** ☐ Anna once lent her top to Lucy.
- **e** ☐ Lucy immediately remembers having Anna's top in her closet.
- **f** ☐ Anna's top was in Lucy's closet.
- **g** ☐ Anna's dad will drive the two girls to the party.

3 Complete the chart below with informal language from Anna and Lucy's messages.

Meaning	Informal language
Denial (*not*)	Nope
Affirmation (*yes*)	
Surprise	
Joy	
Hesitation	

4 INTERFACE Work in pairs. Do you often lend clothes or other personal items to your friends? Why? Why not? Share your ideas with your partner.

GRAMMAR 2

some, any, no Compounds

1 Look at the indefinite pronouns in **bold** in the sentences below. Write (P) for the ones which refer to *people*, (T) for those which refer to *things*, and (L) for the ones which refer to *locations*.

a ☐ I'll have to go to the mall to buy **something** to go with that skirt.

b ☐ Are you wearing **anything** special?

c ☐ I've lent my black top to **someone**.

d ☐ It might be **somewhere** in my messy closet.

e ☐ Is **anyone** driving you?

2 Look at the chart and complete the rules below with: *things / people / locations*.

I want to buy **something** really original.
I never go **anywhere** without my cell phone.
No one has a bigger shoe collection than Imelda Marcos.

a We use *someone*, *anyone*, and *no one* to talk about ____________________.

b We use *somewhere*, *anywhere*, and *nowhere* to talk about ____________________.

c We use *something*, *anything*, and *nothing* to talk about ____________________.

3 Underline the most appropriate indefinite pronouns in the sentences below.

a My uncle is participating in a fashion week event in New York. He's staying **somewhere / someone** near Central Park.

b **No one / Nothing** wears casual clothes at that school. It looks like they're all going to a party.

c I haven't bought **anything / anyone** for my mom's birthday. Do you think she'll enjoy a bright pink shirt?

d **Something / Someone** called you while you were in the shower.

e I've had **nothing / nowhere** to eat today. I must go grab something!

4 Complete the rules with the words in the box.

affirmative (2×)	negative	questions

a We use *some* compounds in ____________________ sentences.

b We use *any* compounds verbs in the ____________________ and in ____________________.

c We use *no compounds* in ____________________ sentences with negative meaning.

5 Complete the dialogue with the correct *some*, *any*, or *no* compounds.

Amy I'm going out tonight for my dad's birthday and I need to buy a new pair of shoes. Do you know **a** ________________ that sells cheap shoes?

Jo Well, there's **b** ________________ in town. All the shoe stores are really expensive.

Amy Oh no. I've got to get **c** ________________. My old shoes are torn.

Jo Well, maybe I can lend you **d** ________________. What do you need?

Amy Some formal black shoes. **e** ________________ very trendy or glamorous – I want a simple design.

Jo I don't have **f** ________________ like that but I know **g** ________________ who does.

Amy Who?

Jo Kerry. She has lots of shoes. She'll lend you **h** ________________.

Amy Great idea. Let's call her.

6 Complete the sentences so they are true for you.

a ________________ I know lives in ________________.

b I have never been anywhere ________________.

c ________________ in my family plays tennis.

d There's nowhere to buy ________________ in my town.

➜ GRAMMAR GUIDE page 100

CLIL

ART

Victoria and Albert Museum main entrance

Fashion designer Daniel Lismore poses his creations at the V&A's Fashion in Motion Series

The Victoria and Albert Museum

The Victoria and Albert Museum, commonly known as the V&A, is a museum of art and design in London. It was established in 1852 and is named after Queen Victoria and her husband, Prince Albert.

The museum's collections cover a wide variety of art forms from different historical periods and from all around the world. These include architecture, ceramics, painting, design, and fashion, among many others. Visitors can see everything from medieval sculpture to oriental carpets.

Many famous British designers have their work on display in the popular fashion collection. There are designs by Vivienne Westwood, miniskirts created by Mary Quant, and a selection of boots by Biba, the iconic London fashion boutique of the 1960s and 1970s. As well as contemporary clothes, there are fashion designs from previous centuries, including King James II's wedding suit from his 1637 marriage to Mary of Modena.

Special exhibitions are also held at the V&A. In 2007, there was an exhibition called *Kylie – The Exhibition*, a display of Kylie Minogue's extravagant costumes from her concert tours.

1 Read and listen. Answer the question.

51 Where can you find Vivienne Westwood's designs in the V&A?

____

2 Rearrange the letters to complete the crossword with collections you can see at the Victoria and Albert Museum.

Down

1 MICRECAS

3 STULCERUP

4 GISAPINTN

5 OHFSINA

Across

2 NISDEG

6 RETACRHICTUE

GRAMMAR GUIDE

Relative Pronouns

- we use relative pronouns to give extra information about people, places, time, and things. We join two sentences using a relative pronoun.

  That's the man. He lives on my street.
  That's the man **who** lives on my street.

- we use *who* for people, *which* for things, *when* for time, and *where* for places.

people	things	time	places
who	which	when	where
that	that	–	–

The man **who** lives in that house is from Athens.
Stella McCartney designs clothes **which** are fashionable.
I was living in Philadelphia **when** I met John.
That's the store **where** I bought my new shoes.

- we can use *that* instead of *who* or *which*.

  The man **that** lives in that house is from Athens.
  Stella McCartney designs clothes **that** are fashionable.

some, any, no Compounds

- we add *-one* to talk about people, *-thing* to talk about things, and *-where* to talk about places

people	places	things
someone	**some**where	**some**thing
anyone	**any**where	**any**thing
no one	**no**where	**no**thing

- *some* is used with countable and uncountable nouns in affirmative sentences

  I want to go **somewhere** hot on vacation this year!

- *any* can be used in both negative sentences and questions

  I haven't bought **anything** all week.
  Has **anyone** seen that new movie yet?

- *no* can only be used in negative sentences

  There's **nothing** interesting on television tonight.

- we can also replace *-one* with *-body*.

  Somebody has stolen my bike.
  There's **nobody** here!
  Did **anybody** watch the news last night?

Name: ___________
Class name / Period: ___________
Teacher: ___________
Date: ___________

PROGRESS CHECK

Style Adjectives

1 Complete the sentences with style adjectives.

a I love Marilyn Monroe. She was so g_______________.

b Heelless shoes look great but they're very i_______________.

c I hate going to weddings because I have to wear f_______________ clothes.

d My old sneakers are too t_______________. I'll have to buy a bigger pair.

e My dad's very c_______________. He even wears a suit on the weekend.

f My sister isn't very t_______________ like me. She isn't interested in fashion.

Phrasal Verbs: Clothes

2 Match the phrases to make sentences.

a Can I try

b I can't get

c Why don't you take

d I'm giving this T-shirt

e I've worn

f Pick

☐ out my jeans. I'll have to buy a new pair.

☐ away. Do you want it?

☐ up your clothes and put them in the wardrobe!

☐ on these shoes, please?

☐ into these shoes. They're too small.

☐ off your jacket? The weather is hot today.

Relative Pronouns

3 Use relative pronouns to join the two sentences.

I was born in a house. My father was born in the same house.

I was born in the house where my father was born.

a She's a designer. She designed my sister's wedding dress.

____

b This is a T-shirt. I wore it yesterday.

____

c We met in 1998. In 1998 we were 7 years old.

____

d I visited the museum. Your aunt works in this museum.

____

some, any, no Compounds

4 Complete the sentences with the correct compounds.

a Where are my sunglasses? I can't find them _______________.

b I want to go _______________ hot this summer. I need some sunshine.

c Did you get _______________ nice for your birthday?

d I didn't know you were sick. _______________ told me.

e The store is _______________ near here. We'll have to go on the bus.

f I need to find _______________ to wear to the job interview.

Grammar Buildup 5

1 2 3 4 5 6 7 8

5 Choose the correct answer.

Mila Hey, Karen.

Karen Hi, Mila. Hey, cool jeans. Where **a** **did you get** / **do you get** them?

Mila They were a present.

Karen Really! Who **b** **did give** / **gave** them to you?

Mila My grandma. Well, she gave me the money and I **c** **have bought** / **bought** them.

Karen Lucky you. Your grandma is really generous.

Mila Yeah, she **d** **gives** / **used to give** me presents for my birthday but now she gives me money. It's much better.

Karen When was your birthday?

Mila Last weekend.

Karen **e** **Did you have** / **Are you going to have** a party?

Mila No, I haven't had it **f** **already** / **yet**. Don't worry. I **g** **might** / **'m going** to invite you.

VOCABULARY IN PICTURES

Style Adjectives

casual

comfortable

colorful

conventional

fashionable

formal

glamorous

impractical

loose

old-fashioned

sporty

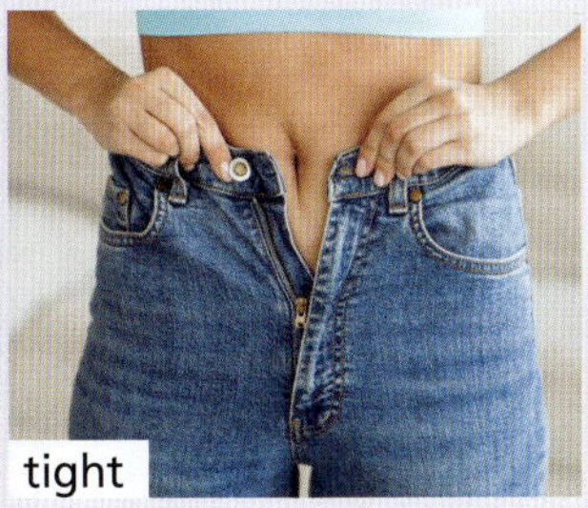
tight

trendy

Phrasal Verbs: Clothes

get into

give away

go with

look for

pick out

pick up

put away

put on

take off

throw away

try on

wear out

6

WORK AND MONEY

1

2

3

4

VOCABULARY 1

The World of Work

1 Look at the words in the box. Use your dictionary to look up the meaning of any unknown words. Then match pictures 1-4 with the words in the box.

allowance	☐	expenses	☐
application form	☐	job advertisement	☐
apprenticeship	☐	pay raise	☐
benefits	☐	pension	☐
bonus	☐	promotion	☐
conditions	☐	wage	☐
contract	☐	work experience	☐

52 **2** Listen and repeat.

3 Choose the correct words.

From: Diana
To: Greg
Subject: Good news! :-)

Hi, Greg!
Guess what? I have a part-time job! I'm a shop assistant at a bookstore in town. I'll only work there on Saturday afternoons, so I'll still have time for school and homework. I saw the **a pension / job advertisement** in the store window, so I went in and asked how to apply. I had to fill out **b a contract / an application form**, and then I had an interview this morning and they offered me the job. I'm going tomorrow to sign my **c contract / promotion**. The working **d expenses / conditions** are great (I get a free lunch!) and the **e wages / promotion** are quite good too. And if I sell a lot of books, I'll get a **f salary / bonus**! Isn't that great?
Talk soon,
Diana

4 Complete the sentences with words from activity 1.

My brother wants a job with a good ___pension___, so he'll have enough money when he retires.

a My mom travels a lot for business. Her company pays all her ______________ such as flights and hotels.

b My parents give my older sister a monthly ______________ to buy clothes and pay for her cell phone.

c My mom has been given a ______________ at work. She's going to be a senior manager now.

d My brother's doing an ______________. He's training to be an electrician.

e My uncle gets great ______________ at his new job, including medical insurance and a company car.

f My dad's boss was so pleased with his work that she's given him a ______________. He'll get $3,000 more a year!

g I want to be a nurse so I'm going to get some ______________ at a hospital this summer.

READING 1

1 Look at the pictures and the title of the magazine article. What do you think Ben's job is?

a lifeguard **b** caretaker **c** soccer player

2 Read and listen. Choose the correct answers.

53

a Queensland is in **the USA / Australia**.

b The caretaker had to **swim / write a blog**.

c Ben is from **the UK / the USA**.

d Ben made **47 / 60** video diaries.

The BEST Job in the World

What do you think is the "best job in the world?" Movie star? International soccer player? Politician? The problem is that you can't apply for these jobs. If you're a talented soccer player, you'll be successful. If you aren't, you won't. Music and acting are the same. If Shakira and Keira Knightley weren't good at what they do, they wouldn't be rich and famous.

However, in 2009 the Australian state of Queensland advertised what became known as "the best job in the world", and people from all over the world could apply. The only job requirement was that applicants had to be able to speak English.

So what was the job? Caretaker of Hamilton Island, a tropical paradise in the Great Barrier Reef. Duties included sunbathing, walking on the beach, and cleaning the swimming pool. But the most important tasks were to write a blog post once a week and keep a video diary. The aim of the job was to promote tourism in Queensland.

The contract was for six months, and in return the caretaker received a generous salary of over €73,000 and lived in a multi-million dollar beach house. It was certainly a job with excellent working conditions.

Over 30,000 people filled out application forms for the post, and 16 of them had an interview. Queensland offered the job to Ben Southall, a 34-year-old charity worker from the UK.

However, the world's best job was also quite a difficult job. Ben often worked 19 hours a day, seven days a week. He visited 90 exotic locations, made 47 video diaries, and gave more than 250 media interviews – including one with famous TV presenter Oprah Winfrey. He spoke with local politicians, gave speeches, held meetings with travel industry representatives, and shook hands with thousands of tourists. He wrote more than 75,000 words in 60 separate blog posts, uploaded more than 2,000 pictures, and wrote more than 730 tweets. After he finished, Ben was so tired he needed a vacation!

Now Ben has a new job as Queensland's international tourism ambassador. He's still earning a great salary, and now he's traveling the world to promote the state. He's very busy again, but if he has time he'll write a book about his experience on the island. It should be an interesting story!

3 Read the text again. Then write T for *true* or F for *false*.

a ☐ Keira Knightley applied for a job as a movie star.

b ☐ The job applicants had to be English.

c ☐ The job was six months long.

d ☐ Only 16 people applied for the job.

e ☐ Ben doesn't earn a lot of money now.

4 Answer the questions. Write full sentences.

a Who advertised "the best job in the world?"

____

____

b Why was the job created?

____

____

c Why was it called "the best job in the world?"

____

____

d What was difficult about the job?

____

____

e What does Ben do now?

____

____

READING STRATEGY

Make connections between texts and your prior knowledge. This will enhance your text comprehension and make reading a more meaningful experience.

5 INTERFACE Work in pairs. Ask and answer the question.

What do you think is the best job in the world?

I think it's chocolate consultant! Can you imagine spending your day trying chocolate?

GRAMMAR 1

First and Second Conditionals

1 Read the sentences below. Underline the sentences which express conditions.

a If Ben has time, he'll write about his experience on Hamilton Island.

b If Shakira and Keira Knightley weren't good at what they do, they wouldn't be rich and famous.

2 Look at the chart and underline to complete the rules.

first conditional	
condition	**consequence**
If Ben **has** time,	**he'll write** about his experience.

second conditional	
condition	**consequence**
If they **weren't** good at what they do,	they **wouldn't be** rich and famous.

a We use the first conditional when we talk about **real and possible / unrealistic or not probable** situations in the future.

b We use the second conditional when we talk about **real and possible / unrealistic or not probable** situations in the future.

c The structure of the first conditional is *if* + verb in the **simple present / simple past** (condition) and **would / will** + base form of the verb (consequence).

d The structure of the second conditional is *if* + verb in the **simple present / simple past** (condition) and **would / will** + base form of the verb (consequence).

3 Read the sentences. Write P if the sentence is possible and NP if it doesn't reflect a current possibility.

a ☐ If my brother saves money, he'll buy a car.

b ☐ If I had a better job, I'd earn more money.

c ☐ I'd pass my exams if I worked harder.

d ☐ If my dad works hard, he'll get a promotion.

4 Complete the first conditional sentences with the correct form of the verbs in parentheses.

a If my Dad ___________ (work) hard, he'll get promoted.

b She ___________ (not get) paid if she's late for work.

c If she ___________ (not lend) you the money, I will.

5 Complete the second conditional sentences with the correct form of the verbs in parentheses.

a If she ___________ (like) her job, she'd work better.

b She ___________ (get) a promotion if she worked better.

c I'd have more money if I ___________ (buy) fewer clothes.

PRONUNCIATION

Sentence Stress and Contractions

54 Listen and repeat the sentences. Which syllables have the main stress?

a If she's late for work, she'll lose her job.

b If I tell you the truth, you won't believe me.

c If he liked the car, he'd buy it.

6 Choose the correct answers.

I've always wanted to be a vet. It's my dream job. I know exactly what I have to do to become one. If I pass my exams when I'm older, I **a 'll / 'd** study science for the next two years. If I had time, I **b 'd / 'll** study English too, but I don't think it's possible. If I **c want / wanted** to go to college, I **d 'll / 'd** need to get good marks, so I need to work hard. There won't be time for English. But that's OK. I **e 'll / 'd** read lots of novels this summer if I have any free time. If I **f have / had** enough money, I'd go to Africa this summer, but it's too expensive. I'd love to see wild lions. If I **g save / saved** my allowance, I'd be able to afford it. But I can't – I spend all my money on books!

7 Look at the charts. How do we form conditional questions? Check (✓) the correct information.

question	condition
What **will** you watch	if you **go** to the movies later?

question	condition
Where **would** you go	if you **went** to South America?

- **a** ☐ In questions, *will* and *would* come before the subject.
- **b** ☐ In questions, use *do* and *did* in conditions.

8 Choose the correct word.

- **a** What **will / would** you study if you go to college?
- **b** What **will / would** you say if you met the president of the USA?
- **c** Where will you go if you **go / went** on vacation this summer?
- **d** What would you do if you **meet / met** David Beckham?
- **e** If you **find / found** $50 in the street, what would you do?

9 Order the words to make questions.

- **a** didn't / would / your town / you / live / Where / if / you / live / in ?
  ____
- **b** will / you / go out / see / this weekend / if / you / Who ?
  ____
- **c** Who / you / if / you / would / could / meet / meet / someone / famous ?
  ____
- **d** choose / What / job / would / you / if / you / tomorrow / started / work ?
  ____
- **e** What / million / you / if / would / you / had / do / one / dollars ?
  ____

10 INTERFACE Work in pairs. Ask and answer the questions in activity 9.

GRAMMAR GUIDE page 116

LISTENING

Part-time Jobs

1 
2 
3 

1 Look at the pictures above and the phrases in the box. What tasks do you think the people in the pictures do at work?

> do the washing up ☐
> give customers advice ☐
> make a playlist ☐ make coffee ☐
> play music at a party ☐
> sell clothes ☐ serve customers ☐

2 55 Listen to the radio show and match the speakers to the jobs.

- **a** ☐ Jimmy (Speaker 1) — **1** store assistant
- **b** ☐ Charlotte (Speaker 2) — **2** DJ
- **c** ☐ Rob (Speaker 3) — **3** waitress

3 55 Listen again and choose the correct answers.

- **a** Jimmy plays music **in a disco / at parties**.
- **b** Jimmy earns **$15 / $100** for each event.
- **c** Charlotte works for eight hours every **Saturday / Sunday**.
- **d** Charlotte **likes / doesn't like** getting an allowance from her parents.
- **e** Rob enjoys selling **CDs / guitars**.

4 55 Listen again. Then write T for *true* or F for *false*.

- **a** ☐ Jimmy makes sure people want to dance.
- **b** ☐ Charlotte doesn't do the washing up.
- **c** ☐ The customers at Charlotte's café are unfriendly.
- **d** ☐ Rob's shop sells magazines.
- **e** ☐ Rob earns a wage.

SPEAKING

A Job Interview

1 Bert has his first job interview today. Read, listen, and answer the questions.

56

a What kind of job is Bert looking for?

____

b What kind of store is the job vacancy in?

____

c What does Bert plan to study in college?

____

Hiring manager Good morning, Bert. Please take a seat.

Bert Good morning, Mrs. Pham. Nice to meet you.

Hiring manager I read your application form so I know you are in high school. Could you tell me about your goals for the future?

Bert Yes, I want to attend a fashion course at college.

Hiring manager Interesting! I also see that you are looking for a part-time job as a store assistant. Why should we hire you, Bert?

Bert Well, I'm a hard-working person with good communication skills. I'm also good at dealing with the public.

Hiring manager You haven't had any work experience yet, have you?

Bert Not a proper work experience … But since January I have volunteered as a salesperson at a church bazaar.

Hiring manager Excellent! And why do you want to work specifically for this clothing store?

Bert I've known about your company for a long time and really admire it. Furthermore, I identify with the style of clothing that you offer. They are comfortable and trendy at the same time!

Hiring manager It was a pleasure talking to you, Bert. Thank you for coming to the interview. We will contact you later this week to give you an answer.

Bert Thank you, Mrs. Pham. Have a good day!

2 CLASS VOTE Do you think Bert should be hired? Why (not)?

FUNCTIONAL LANGUAGE

Asking / Answering Questions in a Job Interview

Questions

Could you tell me about your work experience?
Why should we hire you?
Why do you want to work for this company?

Answers

I'm a hard-working / pro-active person.
I'm good / skilled at dealing with the public / working under pressure.

Speaking Task

Role-play a job interview.

Step 1

Work in pairs. One of you will play the hiring manager while the other will be the candidate for a job vacancy. Then switch roles.

Choose one of the part-time jobs on page 109 or use your own ideas.

Step 2

Think about the questions you will ask to find out if the candidate really matches the position offered. In addition to the questions proposed in the Functional Language box, consider other possibilities.

Could you tell me about extracurricular courses / volunteer work you have done?
What are your strengths and weaknesses?

Also think about the answers you will give to your partner's questions. Take notes under three headlines:

- *your plans for the future*
- *your skills*
- *your life experience (studies, extra courses, volunteer work).*

Step 3

Interview each other. Your teacher will invite some pairs to repeat the job interview in front of the class.

CULTURE

Working Teenagers in the US

Many American teenagers look for part-time jobs in the US – to help support their families, to save for college or simply to earn some extra money for personal expenses. However, there are some facts which employers must consider when hiring a teen.

There are some rules the American Department of Labor sets for working teenagers, and these rules vary according to the age of the minor and the job involved. As a general rule, the Fair Labor Standards Act (FLSA) establishes an age limit (14 years of age) as the minimum age for employment, and also prohibits a minor from working in hazardous job positions such as work involving driving, operation of power-driven equipment, and agricultural work.

It is also important to check working hours: 14 and 15-year-olds can only work 3 hours a day, 18 hours in a school week, 8 hours on a non-school day, and 40 hours during a non-school week. Teens in that age-group are allowed to work from 7am to 7pm, and no later. However, students ages 16 and 17 can work unlimited hours. When they turn 18, they can work unlimited hours and hazardous jobs are not a problem.

Although the American law does not forbid teens from working, parents must monitor their children to make sure they are not spending too much time at work and leaving their studies behind.

1 Read and listen to the information. Then write T for *true*, F for *false*, or NM for *not mentioned*.
57

- **a** ☐ American teenagers look for a part-time job for no specific reasons.
- **b** ☐ The American Department of Labor sets rules for working teens starting at age 14.
- **c** ☐ Parents must sign a legal document giving permission for their teen to work.
- **d** ☐ 14 and 15-year-olds can only work 3 hours a day, 18 hours in a school week, 8 hours on a non-school day, and 40 hours during a non-school week.
- **e** ☐ The American law forbids teens from working.
- **f** ☐ All part-time working students have good grades at school.

2 Can teens work in your country? What does the law say about it?

____

3 Do you think it is a good idea to have a part-time job while in high school? Why (not)?

____

VOCABULARY 2

Work Verbs

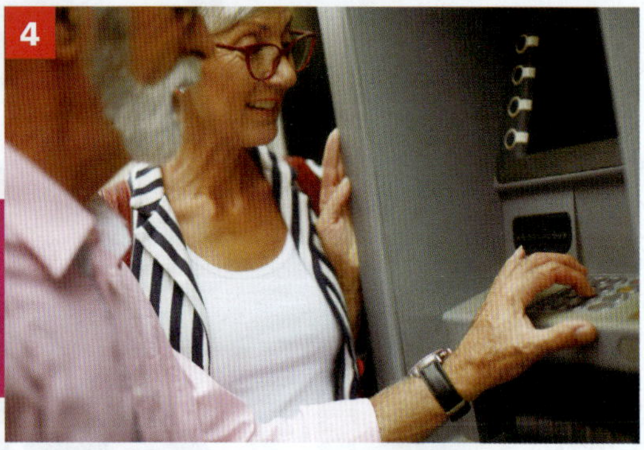

1 Match pictures 1-5 with expressions in the box. Use your dictionary if necessary.

apply for a job	☐	get a pension	☐
be unemployed	☐	have a full-time job	☐
claim expenses	☐	have an interview	☐
earn a salary	☐	lose a job	☐
fill in an application form	☐	sign a contract	☐
get a job	☐	work part-time	☐

2 Listen and repeat.

58

3 Match a-f with 1-6 to make sentences.

a ☐ My mom loves her job. She can claim
b ☐ Can you help me fill out
c ☐ My brother is
d ☐ My sister lost
e ☐ Tom has finished college. Now he can get
f ☐ Lauren earns

1 unemployed, but he has an interview today.
2 a modest salary, but even so she likes her job.
3 her job when the company closed down.
4 expenses for all her meals and travel.
5 a full-time job.
6 this application form for a weekend job?

4 Complete the sentences with the verbs in the box.

applied	earn	get
got	has	have

a My uncle always wears a suit when he ____________ a job interview.

b After working for 35 years, my grandpa finally ____________ a pension.

c Do you want to ____________ a high salary?

d Have you ever ____________ for a job?

e Is it difficult to ____________ a job where you live?

f It is often good for teens to ____________ a part-time job during high school.

READING 2

1 Read the leaflet and listen. What is an apprenticeship?

59

a a way to learn about a job and get experience

b a way to earn a lot of money

Finding a job can be difficult when you have no experience in the world of work. So before applying for a job, why don't you get some work experience while you're still at school?

Summer apprenticeships might involve some training, as well as practical experience of working in a job you think you might enjoy. Your boss will supervise your work and help you learn new skills.
There are lots of different job opportunities to choose from. Think about the skills you have and what types of jobs you might enjoy. Do you enjoy working with animals? You could apply to do an apprenticeship at the local zoo. Or if you love playing soccer and tennis, you might want to work as a sports coach for children at a summer camp.
Apprenticeships usually last for one month, and there are apprenticeship schemes all over the US for students aged 16-18.

What are you waiting for?
Apply for an apprenticeship now!

2 Read the leaflet again and answer the questions.

a What does an apprenticeship involve?

____

____

b Which jobs does the leaflet mention?

____

____

c Who can do an apprenticeship?

____

d How long does an apprenticeship typically last?

____

____

3 Leaflets usually encourage the reader to take action. Underline the sentence that **does not** try to convince us to sign up for an apprenticeship.

a "Try an Apprenticeship!"

b "[...] why don't you get some work experience while you're still at school?"

c "What are you waiting for?"

d "Apprenticeships usually last for one month [...]."

e "Apply for an apprenticeship now!"

4 In small groups, look for information about apprenticeship schemes in your country.

Apprenticeship in	______________
Minimum / maximum age	
Working time limit	
Average length of apprenticeship	

5 INTERFACE Choose an apprenticeship opportunity that interests you, seek information about it, and present your findings to your groupmates.

I'm interested in an apprenticeship at a water park.

Cool! What can you learn from it?

Ensuring safety in public spaces, providing first aid ...

Is it related to what you want to do in the future?

Yes, because I wanna be a health worker.

GRAMMAR 2

Gerunds and Infinitives

1 Read the sentences. Circle the verbs in the infinitive form and underline those in the gerund form.

a Finding a job can be difficult when you have no experience in the world of work.

b Do you enjoy working with animals?

c You could apply to do an apprenticeship at the local zoo.

d You might want to work as a sports coach.

e Summer apprenticeships might involve practical experience of working in a job.

2 Look at the examples in the charts and then match them with the sentences below.

gerunds as the subject of a sentence
a **Finding** a job can be difficult.

gerunds after verbs
b Do you enjoy **working** with animals?

gerunds after prepositions
c Before **applying** for jobs, get some work experience.

infinitives after verbs
d Did you learn **to speak** Italian at school?

infinitives after adjectives
e He's happy **to meet** you at ten o'clock.

☐ No, I learned French instead.

☐ That's perfect! I'll be here on time.

☐ I sure do, especially dogs and cats.

☐ I know. It took me two years to find a new job after my long stay in Europe.

☐ Thank you for the suggestion. I'll start sending out my résumé.

3 Use gerund or infinitive forms of the verbs in the box to complete the sentences below.

be	live	see	travel	work

a __________ rich doesn't make you happy.

b I want __________ that movie.

c __________ long hours makes me feel tired.

d __________ in a house in New York is very expensive.

e He'd like __________ to Asia.

4 Complete the sentences with the correct form of the verbs in parentheses.

a My dad really enjoys __________ (play) golf.

b I wanted __________ (watch) the movie but it was too frightening.

c I would really like __________ (go) out tonight.

d I can't afford __________ (buy) a new pair of shoes.

e I'm really looking forward to __________ (see) Marvel's new movie.

5 Underline the correct verbs to complete the dialogue.

Sara Mom, can you help me? I don't know what to wear for my job interview. What about **a to wear / wearing** my new jeans?

Mom I'm not sure **b going / to go** in jeans will impress the interviewers. I think you need **c to wear / wearing** something more formal.

Sara Yes, I suppose you're right. **d To look / Looking** smart is all part of making a good impression, I guess. I'll wear my red dress.

Mom Yes and **e to be / being** on time for the interview is also important.

Sara Oh dear! I'm a bit late.

Mom Is that the time? It is difficult **f seeing / to see** how you will get there on time …

Sara Oh Mom! Would you like **g giving / to give** me a ride? I can't afford **h to take / taking** a taxi.

Mom Come on, of course I'll take you!

➜ GRAMMAR GUIDE page 116

WRITING

A Letter of Application

1 EXPLORING THE CONTEXT

1 Read and listen. Why is Louise writing to Universal Computers?

60))

____

1 Dear Sir/Madam,

2 I am writing to apply for a work experience position at Universal Computers.

3 I am 14 years old and currently in 9th Grade at Highfields School. I am taking my exams in May and plan to continue studying at school for the next four years. In the future, I would like to study Business in college.

4 I have been interested in computers since I was eight years old. I can use Word, PowerPoint, and Excel, and I am also learning to write computer programs. My favorite subjects at school are ICT and art, especially graphic design.

5 I am a hard-working and responsible person and I am sure that I would learn a lot from working with your company for two weeks.

6 I would be very grateful if you could send me more information about your company and the work experience position.

7 I am enclosing my résumé and a reference from my ICT teacher. I am available to attend an interview.

8 I look forward to hearing from you.

9 Sincerely,

10 Louise Greene

2 Read the letter again and match descriptions a-j with paragraphs 1-10.

- **a** ☐ specific requests
- **b** ☐ final statement
- **c** ☐ age and future plans
- **d** ☐ signature
- **e** ☐ purpose of the letter
- **f** ☐ greeting
- **g** ☐ personal qualities
- **h** ☐ closing
- **i** ☐ interests and skills
- **j** ☐ notes on enclosures

2 PLANNING

1 Write a letter applying for a work experience position (150-170 words).

2 Decide what company you want to write to. What relevant skills do you have? Plan to give and ask for information.

LANGUAGE FOCUS

Job Application Letters

Dear Sir/Madam,
I am writing to apply for ...
I would be very grateful if ...
I am enclosing ...
I look forward to hearing from you.
Yours faithfully,

Order the words to make sentences.

a look / I / hearing / to / you / forward / from

____

b for / I / am / to / your café / apply / a job / writing / at

____

c some information / I / very grateful / if / would be / you could / send me

____

d I / my / am / résumé / enclosing

____

e available / am / I / attend / an interview / to

____

3 WRITING

1 Write a first draft.

2 Include information about your experience and personal qualities.

4 CHECKING & EDITING

1 Work in small groups. Ask your partners:

- **a** Did I use formal language and appropriate greetings?
- **b** If you were the hiring manager, would you call me for an interview? Why or why not?

2 Listen to their opinion and improve your letter.

5 SHARING

Each group chooses their favorite letter and a representative reads it aloud to the class.

GRAMMAR GUIDE

The First Conditional

condition	consequence
If you're a great singer,	you'll get a record contract.

consequence	condition
You'll get a record contract	if you're a great singer.

- we use the first conditional to talk about possible situations and their consequences
- we form the first conditional with *if* + subject + simple present (for the situation), and then subject + *will* / *won't* + infinitive without *to* (for the consequence)
  If we go to Madrid, **we'll stay** in a hotel.
  If he arrives late, **he won't get** a seat.
- we can put either the situation or the consequence first; if the situation comes first, we use a comma
  If you go out in the rain, **you'll get** wet.
- if the consequence comes first, we don't need a comma
  You'll get wet **if you go** out in the rain.

The Second Conditional

condition	consequence
If I had more money,	I would buy that dress.

consequence	condition
I would buy that dress	If I had more money.

- we use the second conditional to talk about imaginary or unlikely future situations and their consequences
- we form the second conditional with *if* + subject + simple past (for the situation), and then subject + *would* / *wouldn't* + infinitive without *to* (for the consequence)
  If I sold my car, **I'd buy** a motorbike.
  If they did more exercise, **they wouldn't** be so unfit.
- we can put either the situation or the consequence first; if the situation comes first, we use a comma
- if the consequence comes first, we don't need a comma

Gerunds and Infinitives

gerunds as the subject of a sentence
Making cakes is easy if you have a good recipe.

gerunds after verbs
I like singing in the shower.

gerunds after prepositions
After watching the movie, they had ice cream.

infinitives after verbs
Do you know how to play the piano?

infinitives after adjectives
She wasn't pleased to see the dog in the garden.

Gerunds as the Subject of a Sentence

- gerunds (the *-ing* form of the verb) can be the subject of a sentence
  Finding a job can be difficult.

Gerunds after Verbs

- some verbs are followed by a gerund
  I **enjoy playing** the trumpet.
  I **don't mind working** until 7pm.
  Have you **finished eating**?

Gerunds after Prepositions

- the gerund is generally used after prepositions
  I'm dreaming **about going** on vacation.
  She's good **at playing** the violin.
  I'm interested **in working** for you.

Infinitives after Verbs

- some verbs are followed by the infinitive
  I don't **want to talk** to you.
  We **expect to arrive** at ten o'clock.
  Did they **help to pay** for the car?
- be careful: some verbs can be followed by either a gerund or an infinitive but with slightly different meanings

Infinitives after Adjectives

- the infinitive is generally used after adjectives
  I am **pleased to see** you.
  We were not **happy to be** there.
  I was **surprised to hear** that.

6

PROGRESS CHECK

Name: ____________________

Class name / Period: ____________________

Teacher: ____________________

Date: ____________________

The World of Work

1 Choose the correct word.

a Jo's **wage / apprenticeship** is $25,000 a year.

b My parents give me **a bonus / an allowance** if I help with the housework.

c My grandparents get their **pension / pay raise** every two weeks.

d My brother is looking for a job with good **conditions / expenses**.

e My dad doesn't get any **benefits / promotion** at work. He doesn't even get a pension.

Work Verbs

2 Complete the sentences with the words in the box.

claimed filled has lost signed worked

a My mother ____________ a full-time job and looks after five children.

b Li has ____________ a contract to play soccer in Europe.

c I ____________ my job because I was late for work so often.

d My grandfather ____________ part-time in the library after he retired.

e My dad ____________ in an application form yesterday – I hope he gets an interview!

First and Second Conditionals

3 Complete the sentences using the correct form of the verbs in parentheses.

a If I ____________ (become) a doctor, I'll earn a lot of money.

b If he saved his money, he ____________ (be) able to go on vacation.

c If you ____________ (not apologize), she won't talk to you.

d What ____________ (do) if you had $1 million?

e I ____________ (lend) you some money if you promise to pay me back.

Gerunds and Infinitives

4 Complete the sentences with the verbs in gerund or infinitive.

a I enjoy ____________ (play) golf with my dad. It's great fun.

b He spends so much time ____________ (talk) on the phone.

c I've arranged ____________ (meet) Monica at 8:30pm.

d I don't want ____________ (see) that movie. It looks boring.

e She's decided not ____________ (leave) school next year.

Grammar Buildup 6

1 2 3 4 5 6 7 8

5 Underline the correct answer.

Ben Hi, Jan. You look great. Where **a are you going / do you go**?

Jan My grandma's having a party. She **b retires / 's retiring** today.

Ben Really?

Jan Yes, she's a cook. She **c 's worked / worked** in the same restaurant for 33 years. Today's her last day.

Ben Wow. So is she sad about retiring?

Jan No, she's really excited. She has lots of plans. She **d will / 's going to** travel and learn Italian.

Ben So where's the party?

Jan In the restaurant where she **e was working / works**.

Ben Who **f does organize / has organized** the party?

Jan Her boss. He's giving her a present too.

Ben What is he going to give her?

Jan I don't know. But I hope it's not a cook book. If he **g will give / gives** her a cook book, she'll be really angry!

Ben Why?

Jan Because she **h 's going to / might to** write a cook book now that she's retired. It's one of her plans.

VOCABULARY IN PICTURES

The World of Work

allowance

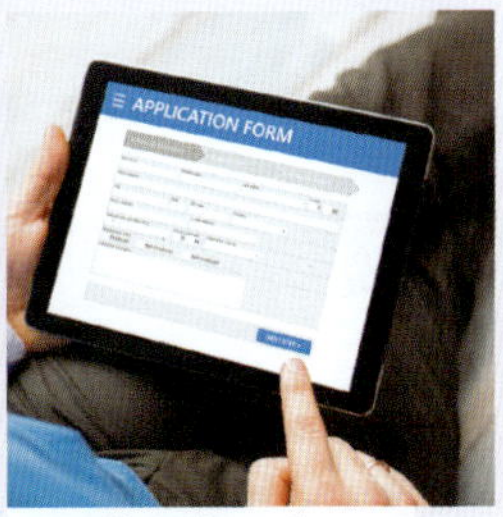

application form

apprenticeship

benefits

bonus

conditions

contract

expenses

job advertisement

pay raise

pension

promotion

wage

work experience

Work Verbs

apply for a job

be unemployed

claim expenses

earn a salary

fill in an application form

get a job

get a pension

have a full-time job

have an interview

lose a job

sign a contract

work part-time

REVIEW 3

VOCABULARY

Start

1 Maureen has finished college and now she's doing an _ _ _ _ _ _ _ _ _ _ _ _ _ _.

2 I love wearing very _ _ _ _ _ _ _ _ _ _ _ clothes when I'm relaxing at home!

7 I can't believe Seán has just _ _ _ _ his _ _ _ . He's an amazing professional!

8 Lisa's just gotten her month's _ _ _ _ _ _ _ _ _ and she'll buy a new pair of jeans.

9 I don't know if I should _ _ _ _ _ _ _ the jeans or the cotton dress today.

10 Look at Ann's wardrobe, most of her clothes are _ _ _ _ _ _ because she goes to the gym every day!

15 They had to _ _ _ _ a contract in order to move to the new house.

Finish

3

When I visit a customer, I must wear _ _ _ _ _ _ clothes.

4

After working hard for a long time, my cousin finally got a _ _ _ _ _ _ _ _ _ _ _.

5

Grandpa has lived on his _ _ _ _ _ _ _ since he retired ten years ago.

6

These clothes in the ad look like they're from the 90s. They're so _ _ _ - _ _ _ _ _ _ _ _ _!

11

My mom always _ _ _ _ _ _ _ _ her high heels as soon as she gets home.

12

Will _ _ _ _ _ _ a good salary at his new job.

13

Jimmi has just had a job _ _ _ _ _ _ _ _ _ _ today. He's confident he'll get hired!

14

We'd better _ _ _ _ _ these boots to make sure they're the right size.

REVIEW 3

GRAMMAR

Relative Pronouns

1 Complete the sentences with *who, which, when*, or *where*.

Alice Walker is a writer ___who___ writes about social problems.

a The first day of primary school was ________ I met my best friend.

b That's the trash can ________ we recycle our garbage.

c That's my brother's friend ________ got into trouble with the police.

d A myth is a story ________ includes gods, heroes, and magic.

2 Use a relative pronoun to join the two sentences.

I'm visiting my grandparents. They live in Texas.
I'm visiting my grandparents who live in Texas.

a We went to a beautiful beach. It had white sand and blue water.

____

____

b I met a famous actor. He's been in several movies.

____

____

c We went to a new gym. You could try all kinds of martial arts.

____

____

d It was New Year's. My dad fell in love with my mom.

____

____

3 Write complete sentences using the correct relative pronoun.

meet / was in *America's Got Talent* / I'll / the girl
I'll meet the girl who was in *America's Got Talent*.

a is the place / French / study / this / I

____

b is / got married / that / my parents / the year

____

c don't have / the shoes / these / shoelaces / are

____

d created / was / Chanel / the jersey suit / the designer

____

some, any, no Compounds

4 Complete the sentences with the words in the box.

~~anything~~	anywhere	no one
nowhere	someone	something

I'm hungry. Do you have ___anything___ to eat?

a I can't find my keys ________.

b Nathan was upset because ________ tried his cake.

c We're looking for ________ to wear for the wedding.

d While I was sleeping, ________ called.

e There's ________ better than home.

5 Underline the correct options.

My sister doesn't have **anything / nothing** to match her red pants.

a We wouldn't be here if we had **nowhere / anywhere** better to go!

b I have a bad headache. I need **something / nothing** to relieve it.

c There is **someone / anyone** at Kristen's house she wants to introduce to us.

d In the future, **someone / no one** will need oil. All fuel will come from renewable sources.

The First Conditional

6 Write complete sentences in the first conditional.

If / I / go / abroad / I / make / new friends.
If I go abroad, I'll make new friends.

a If / he / take off / his sweater / he / be / cold.

____

b We / save / energy / if / we / switch off / the lights.

____

c If / you / not listen / you / not understand.

____

The Second Conditional

7 Turn the sentences in the first conditional into second conditional sentences.

We'll save a lot of water if we don't take a shower every day.
We'd save a lot of water if we didn't take a shower every day.

a If I'm rich and famous, I'll buy a helicopter.

____

____

b Lucy will work in a store if the conditions get better.

____

____

c If my sister finds a good job advertisement, she'll apply for it.

____

____

The First and Second Conditionals

8 Complete the sentences with the correct form of the verbs in parentheses. Use the first conditional or the second conditional.

__I'll go__ (go) to the movies if it rains tomorrow.

a If my family won a lot of money, we__________ (move) to a new house.

b If I __________ (get) a good grade on the test, my parents will buy me a new bike.

c If I found a dog in the street, I __________ (keep) it.

9 Match the items to make sentences.

a I'll go by bike
b I'd get a part-time job
c If I wasn't happy at college,
d If you wear out those sneakers,

☐ I'd drop out.
☐ mom'll get angry.
☐ if I needed money.
[a] if the weather is good.

Gerunds and Infinitives

10 Underline the correct words.

a He hopes **to arrive / arriving** before 9pm.
b I love **to play / playing** the piano.
c My mom avoids **to eat / eating** cheese.
d Tim was happy **to hear / hearing** the good news.

11 Complete the sentences with the correct form of the verbs in parentheses.

a I don't enjoy ______________ (make) cakes.
b It's easy ______________ (learn) French.
c My brother's good at ______________ (play) baseball.
d Do you mind ______________ (help) me clean the house?

Phishing

Hooked Like a Fish

1 Read and listen. Then answer the questions.

61

a Daniel was about to fall victim to an internet scam. What kind of scam was it?

____

b What did the scammers offer to convince Daniel to click on the link?

____

____

c Daniel believed it was a promotion from his mobile operator. Why did he think so?

____

____

d What detail of the website made Lily realize it was a scam?

____

____

2 Find the words in the comics for definitions a–d.

a ____________: Any type of application whose purpose is to cause harm to the user. This term comes from the merger of "malicious" with "software."

b ____________: Crime of tricking people into sharing confidential information such as passwords and credit card numbers. The name was given for a sound similarity with "fishing," as criminals try to "fish" a victim's data.

c ____________: Software that, once installed on a mobile phone or computer, encrypts files and prevents user access to them. The criminal then demands that the victim pay an amount of money (a ransom) to recover his or her data.

d ____________: A spy software that is installed on a cell phone or computer without the user's consent. Once installed, the program monitors the user's online activities, which makes it capable of stealing passwords and banking information.

3 Discuss the following questions with a partner. Then share your ideas with your classmates.

a Did you know the criminal practices cited in the comics? Have you ever fallen victim or know someone who has fallen victim to a phishing scam? How was it?

b What can be the consequences if you fall victim to a phishing attack?

c In addition to offering promotions or freebies, phishing scammers sometimes issue alarming messages to their victims. For example, "your computer is infected with a virus!," "your electricity bill is overdue!," "your miles are about to expire!," etc. How would you describe the psychological strategy used by these criminals?

4 How to avoid phishing attacks? Complete the following tips with the verbs from the box.

avoid be (2×) check follow keep move review ~~use~~ watch

a ___Use___ antivirus software and ________ it up to date.

b ________ wary of alarming messages or offers that are too good.

c ________ plugging unknown devices into your computer's USB ports.

d When receiving a message supposedly from a company or government agency, ________ for grammatical or spelling errors. Another sign of fraud is poorly made logos.

e ________ out for messages that use generic greetings like "Dear Customer" rather than actual names.

f If the sender claims to be a company, ________ suspicious if the email address is private (e.g., @gmail).

g ________ the URL before clicking. It may look like the real URL, but it's actually a little different.

h Even if the link description points to the legitimate address of the company's website, ________ your mouse cursor over it. Sometimes the fraudulent link is disguised, but if you hover over it you will be able to see it.

i ________ security procedures even if the message was sent by people you know. Your friend may have been tricked, or his or her device may be sending messages without him or her knowing.

7

CRIME DOESN'T PAY

POLICE

1

2

3

4

VOCABULARY 1

Crime Verbs

1 Use your dictionary to look up the meaning of the verbs in the box. Then write C if the actions are done by *criminals* and P for actions done by the *police*.

arrest a suspect	☐	go to prison	☐
be guilty	☐	investigate a crime	☐
be innocent	☐	look for clues	☐
catch a thief	☐	pay a fine	☐
commit a crime	☐	question a suspect	☐
do community service	☐	solve a crime	☐
go on trial	☐	suspect someone	☐

2 Listen and repeat. Which expressions can you use to describe pictures 1-4?

62

1 ______________________________

2 ______________________________

3 ______________________________

4 ______________________________

3 Underline the correct words.

One of the most mysterious crimes in history were the Jack the Ripper murders. Five women were killed in East London, UK, during three months in 1888. The police never **a committed / solved** the crimes. They **b looked for / caught** and found many clues and **c suspected / questioned** suspects but nothing helped them.
The detective who **d committed / investigated** the murders, Inspector Frederick Abberline, never **e suspected / caught** the murderer – he never even **f solved / arrested** anyone. No one ever **g paid a fine / went to prison** for the murders. Even today we have no idea who was **h innocent / guilty** of the terrible crimes.

READING 1

1 Look at the poster. What kind of animals do people smuggle?

____

Watch Out for ANIMAL SMUGGLERS!

Imagine this situation. You're at the airport waiting to collect your suitcase. A man is standing next to you. He picks up a large leather suitcase from the baggage carousel. His bag moves.
What do you think?
a There must be something alive inside his bag.
b It's none of my business.

You look closely at the suitcase. It moves again.
What could it be?
a It can't be a person. It might be an animal.
b I don't know and I don't care.

He picks up the bag and looks around him. He looks nervous.
Who is he?
a He might be an animal smuggler.
b Sorry, I have no idea.

The bag moves again.
What do you do?
a Call a customs officer.
b Nothing.

THE CORRECT ANSWER TO ALL THESE QUESTIONS IS A.

Animal smuggling is cruel. Many of the animals that people smuggle are endangered species that should not be removed from their natural habitat. A large number of them die during the journey because they travel in boxes, suitcases, or even inside people's clothes.

Animal smuggling is a crime. Buying and collecting smuggled animals is illegal. Punishments can include heavy fines and imprisonment.

Animal smuggling is increasing. It's the second most portable illegal activity in the world. Only drug smuggling makes more money.

Help us stop animal smuggling! If you see something suspicious, REPORT IT!

Sleeping Snakes in a Suitcase

Customs officers in Jakarta arrested two men suspected of having animals in their suitcases. The men were trying to fly from Indonesia to Dubai. When airport officials looked in the men's bags, they found 40 pythons. The snakes had been given drugs to make them sleep. The suspects were questioned by airport authorities and the pythons were taken to the animal quarantine center at the airport.

Tiger Smuggling in Thailand

Police caught a 31-year-old woman trying to smuggle a baby tiger into Thailand. The tiger cub was inside a suitcase with a toy tiger. Although the woman had drugged the animal to keep it quiet, airport officials noticed that one of the two tigers was moving when they scanned her suitcase. The smuggler went to prison for six years.

2 Read and listen. Check your answer to activity 1.
63

3 Write T for *true* or F for *false*. Try to correct the false sentences.

a ☐ Many smuggled animals are very rare.
____

b ☐ The journey kills many animals.
____

c ☐ Animal smuggling is more profitable than drug smuggling.
____

d ☐ Criminals smuggle dangerous animals.
____

e ☐ Customs officials arrested the snake smugglers in Dubai.
____

f ☐ The woman was smuggling two tigers into Thailand.
____

GRAMMAR 1

Modals of Deduction and Possibility

1 Read the sentences below. Do they express *deduction* (D), *possibility* (P) or *impossibility* (I)?

a ☐ There must be something alive inside his bag.

b ☐ It can't be a person.

c ☐ It might be an animal.

d ☐ He may be an animal smuggler.

e ☐ It could be a dangerous snake.

2 Look at the sentences in activity 1 again. Complete the rules with the words in the box.

can't	isn't true	it is possible
might	must	believe

a We use the modal verbs *may*, __________ and *could* + base form of a verb when we think __________ that something is true.

b __________ + base form of a verb is used when we __________ something is true.

c __________ + base form of a verb is used when we are sure something __________.

3 Match the deductions to their meanings.

a He must be a smuggler.

b He might be a smuggler.

c He can't be a smuggler.

☐ I'm certain he's not a smuggler.

☐ I think it's possible he's a smuggler.

☐ I'm certain he's a smuggler.

4 Read sentences a-f and match them with the deductions.

a She speaks French and has a French passport.

b She used to live in Paris.

c Joanne hates dogs! A dog bit her when she was a child.

d I think Sheila likes dogs, but I'm not sure.

e I think I saw him on television yesterday.

f He's in that new movie we saw last week!

☐ That can't be Joanne's dog.

☐ He must be a famous actor.

☐ She may be French.

☐ He might be an actor.

☐ She must be French.

☐ That could be Sheila's dog.

5 Choose the correct words.

a He **must / can't** be guilty. He's never committed a crime in his life!

b There **could / must** be a dog in that bag. It's moving.

c You **must / can't** be hungry. It's four o'clock and you haven't had lunch.

d He **might / can't** be American. He speaks English.

e Ask John. He **can't / might** know the answer.

f This movie's terrible. You **might / can't** like it.

6 Look at the pictures of stolen items. Then complete the sentences with the most appropriate modal verb.

a The speaker __________ be Jane's. She never listens to music.

b The sunglasses __________ be Pete's. Jane never wears them.

c The money __________ be Jane's, but it __________ be Pete's too.

d The camera __________ be Pete's. He doesn't have one.

e The e-book reader __________ be Pete's or Jane's. They both love reading.

f The earrings __________ be Jane's. She bought a pair like those last year.

7 Listen to the sounds. Then write T for *true* or F for *false*.
64

a **1** ☐ It might be New Year's Eve.
2 ☐ It can't be a celebration.
3 ☐ It could be fireworks for the Fourth of July.

b **1** ☐ He can't be happy.
2 ☐ He must be happy.
3 ☐ He may have heard some good news.

c **1** ☐ It can't be a cat.
2 ☐ A thief might be trying to steal something from the house!
3 ☐ It must be a cat.

d **1** ☐ It might be a restaurant.
2 ☐ It must be a library.
3 ☐ Someone may be cooking dinner.

8 Choose the correct words.

Jack Hey, look! That's Andy Samberg, the actor.
Cath Who?
Jack Andy Samberg. He's in *Brooklyn Nine-Nine* on TV.
Cath No, it **a can't / must** be him!
Jack Why not? He **b might / can't** live near here.
Cath No way! Andy Samberg lives in California.
Jack Well, he **c must / could** be here making a movie.
Cath He **d can't / may** be Andy! He's wearing glasses.
Jack He **e must / might** wear glasses in real life. Hey, look! He's coming this way.
Andy Excuse me. I don't know this area. I **f must / can't** be lost. Can you help me?
Jack Of course. Are you Andy Samberg, the actor?
Andy Yes, I am. Do you watch *Brooklyn Nine-Nine*? You **g must / can't** miss it!

9 **INTERFACE** Think of a friend. What is he or she doing now? Write sentences giving evidence and using modal verbs. Then discuss your sentences with a partner.

What is Carlos doing now?

He must be on vacation in Key West, because he went there on Sunday. He might be at the beach.

GRAMMAR GUIDE page 138

LISTENING

Crime News

1 Listen to the three news stories. Put the robberies in the order you hear them.
65

a ☐ art theft
b ☐ jewelry theft
c ☐ a bank robbery

2 Listen again and answer the questions.
65

a Where was the bank robbery?
___
b What happened to the bank robbers?
___
c How long was the painting missing for?
___
d Who did the painting belong to?
___
e What did Horatio Mandeville steal?
___
f How many times has he been found guilty before?
___

3 Listen again and complete the sentences.
65

a Police investigated the bank robbery for ___ days.
b Mrs. Johnson was found ___ by the court.
c The painting was stolen from Paul Chambers' ___.
d Security guards found the painting after ___ minutes.
e The diamonds were worth more than ___ euros.
f Mandeville got out of prison ___ weeks ago.

SPEAKING

Witnessing a Crime

66 David is telling James how his bike has been stolen. Listen and complete the dialogue.

I'm so upset today...

Why? What **a** ____________________?

My bike was stolen last night.

How come? **b** ____________________ did it happen?

I **c** ______________ home to go to the gym. I left it in front of the gate for a few minutes to get my gym clothes in my bedroom.

d ____________________

e ____________________! I heard a noise and looked out of my window. A man was riding away on my bike!

Wow! That's absolutely incredible. I **f** ____________________ someone would do that. It **g** ____________________ be someone from another neighborhood.

h ____________________. Anyway, I called the police and went to the station to talk to them.

Good for you – it's really important to report crimes. I hope the police find your bike.

FUNCTIONAL LANGUAGE

Describing a Crime	Reacting
What happened?	*That's incredible!*
Where … ?	*It can't be true.*
I …	*It might / may / could …*
… the police.	*It must …*

Speaking Task

Talking about a crime with a classmate.

Step 1

Choose a fact file or use your own ideas to describe a crime you have witnessed.

CRIME: robbery at a supermarket
CRIMINALS: three thieves
EQUIPMENT: masks
ACTIVITY: stealing cash
ACTION: told the security guards

CRIME: mugging outside a restaurant
CRIMINALS: one man
EQUIPMENT: none
ACTIVITY: stealing a woman's handbag
ACTION: called the police and an ambulance

CRIME: animal smuggling
CRIMINALS: two smugglers
EQUIPMENT: a suitcase
ACTIVITY: smuggling a snake onto a plane
ACTION: told customs officials

Step 2

Describe what you saw.

I saw a robbery last night at …
The thief stole …
I called …

Think about what your classmate says.

You're joking! Tell me more.
What happened next?
I can't believe it.

Step 3

Practice your dialogue. Change roles asking and answering questions.

CULTURE

Cybercrime in India

Life has become much easier since technology started playing a role in our lives. The use of the internet has brought lots of advantages: paying bills, buying tickets for shows, booking hotels, among others. However, anyone can fall prey to online fraud and lose their confidential information, money and even reputation due to revenge, for instance.
India, being the home to IT innovation, has a strong internet and programming culture. However, this can also have a downside, because just as you have a huge army of amazing IT specialists, you also have a lot of cyber criminals with sufficient skills to break many security barriers. Malicious internet activities are called *cybercrimes*, which in India means "unlawful acts where the computer is used either as a tool or a target or both." Due to the rapid spread of this kind of criminal activity, there is a separate law for crimes committed on the internet.
Here are some examples of cybercrimes:

Against the Person

In this category, offenses include: *cyber stalking*, that is, threating people using computer technology such as emails, webcams, etc.; *hacking*, that is, accessing a computer system without permission; *defamation*, that is, using the net to damage a person's good reputation; *child pornography*, that is, using the net to spread, create or access materials which exploit minors.

Against the Government

Cyber terrorism, which refers to the use of information technology to cause disruption and fear among the population.
The list increases every day and the punishment also varies depending on the offense, from a fine to imprisonment. Therefore, certain precautions should be taken by netizens when using the web to avoid this terrible threat called cybercrime.

1 Read and listen to the information about cybercrime in India and answer the questions. 67

a What advantages has the use of internet brought?

b What does *cybercrime* mean in Indian law?

c What crime mentioned in the text relates to entering someone's computer or personal accounts?

d What example of crime against the government is given? Explain.

e Is there a punishment for cybercrime in India? Which?

2 Is there a law for cybercrime in your country? For which offenses? What is the punishment?

3 How do you think a cybercrime law can prevent offenses against people without threatening our freedom of expression?

VOCABULARY 2

Crimes and Criminals

1 Use your dictionary to look up the meaning of the words in the box.

burglar	murderer	theft
burglary	pickpocket	thief
kidnapper	pickpocketing	vandal
kidnapping	robber	vandalism
murder	robbery	

2 Listen and repeat.

68

3 Copy and complete the chart using the words in activity 1.

crime
burglary

criminal
burglar

4 Complete the sentences with words from the chart.

a A ______________ stole my bike from outside school.

TIP

Thieves rob places and steal things.
The thief robbed a bank and stole $200,000.

b I think ______________ is the most serious crime. Killing someone is unacceptable!

c A ______________ stole my cell phone from my pocket while I was waiting for the train.

d The police caught the ______________ after he released the victim. No one knew where she was for days!

e I saw three ______________ running away from the bank yesterday. They stole $100,000!

f There has been an increase in ______________ recently. Someone broke all the windows at the city hall.

g Be careful with your wallet on the street. ______________ is a real problem here.

READING 2

1 Look at the title and the pictures. What do you think the text is about? Read, listen, and check your answer.
69

____

www.ourdailynews.com/burglary-scene

Updated 2:29 p.m. ET September 19, 2022

Preserving a Burglary Scene

Detectives investigating crimes look for clues like fingerprints which can identify the criminals. Why? Because police officers know that all criminals sometimes make mistakes.
Check out what you must and must not do in case of a burglary.

1 **Call the police immediately.**
Besides making sure you get immediate help and some advice on how to preserve the crime scene, you must report the crime under your name in order to testify for the state if it prosecutes the burglar.

2 **Don't move things around!**
If you ever get home and realize your house's been broken into, although you might feel like immediately looking for your precious belongings, be careful! You must not touch some key items like internal door handles, faucets, and windows if you want the police to ever catch the criminals.

3 **Look for the suspect's movements.**
One of the most important things to help police locate the criminals is to have clues of how they entered and left the place. In order to help with that, you have to notice if there are any signs of open doors and windows or footsteps, and you must not close any doors or windows before the police arrive.

4 **Keep unauthorized people out.**
In order to preserve all evidence that you have taken care of in the previous items, avoid letting strangers into the house.

2 Read the text again and answer the questions.

a What text genre is it?
  1 A how-to list.
  2 A news report.

b Who did the author probably get information from to write the text?
  1 People who have had their home robbed.
  2 Police detectives.

c What must you do with entry and exit points?
  1 Leave them as they are.
  2 Close them all for safety.

d What should you do in case someone offers help?
  1 Let them help tidy your house.
  2 Don't let them in and accept help in other ways.

3 Now imagine that you received the following message from a friend.

Jess

Hi! I have bad news... ☹ Just now, when my parents and I got home from the cinema, we discovered that our house had been broken into. 12:01

As soon as we entered we realized that something was wrong. The living room was freezing! The windows were wide open and the wind was blowing hard. We closed the windows immediately. 12:02

Then my dad called the police. Meanwhile, my mom and I went through the rooms to see if they had taken anything. When we got to the backyard, we saw that my bike had been stolen! 12:04

When they took the bike, the thieves knocked over a vase of flowers and made a big mess. We had to wash everything away with the hose. Now we're waiting for the police to arrive. I'm so nervous! Call me when you can. 12:06

- Based on the information in the text "Preserving a Burglary Scene", answer: What did Jessica and her parents do wrong after getting home? And what did they get right?

____

____

GRAMMAR 2

Review: *must* / *must not*

1 Read the sentences below. Circle the ones showing *prohibition* and underline those which express *obligation* or *duty*.

- **a** When witnessing a crime, you must report it to the police.
- **b** Criminal offenses must be punished.
- **c** The police must not search your home without a search warrant.
- **d** If the police want to search your home, they must do it in your presence.
- **e** As a witness, you must not hide any details from the police.

2 Look at the chart below. Check (✓) the correct information as to the rules of *must* and *must not*.

obligation / duty	deduction	prohibition
You must report the crime.	The suspect must be from another neighborhood.	You must not carry a gun without permission.
The police must investigate that murder.		

- **a** ☐ *Must* can only be used to express obligation.
- **b** ☐ *Must not* is used to express prohibition.

3 Read the sentences below. Write (O) if *must* expresses *obligation* and (D) if it expresses *deduction*.

- **a** ☐ A crime scene reconstructionist must keep his or her report confidential.
- **b** ☐ Jonathan Blair must be the robber. He has already gone to trial for bank robberies.
- **c** ☐ All staff must wear safety equipment to access the area.
- **d** ☐ The robbers must have hidden the money … But where?

4 Underline the correct words in the paragraph beside.

www.legaltips.com

LEGAL TIPS

HOW TO SUE FOR DEFAMATION

Libel is the act of publicly offending someone, in written form, and lying about facts of this person's life. If you ever feel that you have been *libeled* or *defamed*, you can take the case to court. But in order to do that, you **a must / must not** only prove that what was written about you is a lie, but you **b must / must not** also prove that the person who wrote it actually knew that it was false. The text **c must / must not** also be a statement of fact that can be proven, and not just a personal opinion. Besides that, the text **d must / must not** cause damage to your reputation to be considered libel. It **e must / must not** be something that only hurts your feelings or makes you feel bad.

5 INTERFACE Talk to a classmate about crimes and punishment. Use *must* and *must not*.

> I think a person must be responsible for his or her acts.

> In my opinion, the person who accuses must provide evidence.

GRAMMAR GUIDE page 138

CLIL

ART

Graffiti – Inside or Outside the Law?

Graffiti is an Art

If art is a painting or a drawing that is created to be beautiful or to express ideas, then graffiti is art.

Major art museums, collectors and celebrities pay thousands of dollars for works by famous graffiti artists such as the English artist Banksy. When Banksy painted a mural of two Hollywood actors near a London underground station, art critics said that it could be worth $400,000. But the transportation authorities disagreed: it was their property and Banksy didn't have their permission, so they painted over the mural.

Graffiti is a Crime

In 2006, New York City tried to forbid any person under 21 from possessing spray paint or permanent markers. However, art students took the issue to court and won, legitimizing graffiti art in the city.

The Chicago Transit Authority now sues graffiti writers to recover the clean-up costs, and in some cases, the authors have to clean up the graffiti as well. The agency loses about $1 million in "vandalism" costs each year.

The Miami Design District in Florida, the USA.

A wall with graffiti in São Paulo, Brazil

A political message and art in a graffiti in Berlin, Germany

1 Read and listen. Is graffiti considered an art form or is it a crime?

70

____

____

2 Complete the sentences with the words in the box.

critic	graffiti	mural	Museum	works

a The art ______________ said that the painting was worth $400,000.

b A ______________ is a painting that is painted on a wall.

c The Los Angeles County ______________ of Art has a beautiful collection of paintings.

d Leonardo da Vinci's *Mona Lisa* is one of the most famous ______________ of art in the world.

e Many people think that ______________ isn't art – it's vandalism.

3 Do you think graffiti is a form of art and expression or a form of crime? Why?

GRAMMAR GUIDE

Modals of Deduction

modals of deduction
You **must** be tired after your journey.
He **can't** be guilty – he's the most honest person I know.

- we use *must* and *can't* for deduction
- *must* and *can't* take the same form for all subject pronouns
- we use *must* when we are certain about something because there is a logical explanation for it

  John has walked 20 miles today. He **must** be tired.
- we use *can't* when we are certain that something is impossible

  You **can't** be hungry now – you had a pizza and cake for dinner!

Modals of Possibility

modals of possibility
He **might** be Jessica's brother.
It **may** be sunny tomorrow.
She **could** be at the gym.

- we use *might*, *may* and *could* when something is possible or probable but not certain

  Joanne didn't answer the phone. She **might** have turned it off.

  My wallet isn't in my bag – I **may** have left it at the restaurant.

  The door is open. They **could** be in the house.
- *might*, *may* and *could* take the same form for all subject pronouns

Review: *must / must not*

obligation
To press charges, you **must** go to the police station.
He **must** appear in front of a jury.
They **must** stay in court until the end of the trial!

- we use *must* for obligation

prohibition
You **must not** interfere with crime evidence.
He **must not** touch what the burglars touched.
They **must not** cross the line.

- *must not* is used for prohibition
- to talk about something that is not an obligation nor a prohibition, we use *don't / doesn't have to*

  You **don't have to** call the police if it was just theft. You can report it over the internet.

Name: ______________________
Class name / Period: ______________________
Teacher: ______________________
Date: ______________________

PROGRESS CHECK

Crime Verbs

1 Match the phrases to make sentences.

a The man who stole the painting is going
b The vandals have to do
c He had to pay
d The police are suspecting
e Interpol has arrested
f A security guard caught
g The school security officers suspect

☐ five men for drug smuggling.
☐ the ambassador was kidnapped.
☐ a woman stealing books.
☐ a freshman graffitied the bathroom stalls.
☐ community service for six months.
☐ to prison for ten years.
☐ a $100 fine because he parked his car illegally.

Crimes and Criminals

2 Which criminals do these crimes?

a theft ______________________
b vandalism ______________________
c kidnapping ______________________
d murder ______________________
e pickpocketing ______________________
f robbery ______________________
g burglary ______________________

Modals of Deduction and Possibility

3 Choose the correct modal verb.

a He **must / can't** be Australian. He doesn't speak English.
b She **might / can't** be Ann's sister. They look quite similar.
c It **could / must** be his book. It has his name in it.
d He **can't / may** like football. I can't remember.
e He **can't / might** be the robber. He's too tall.
f You **must / can't** be thirsty. It's very hot outside.

Review: *must / must not*

4 Write O if the sentence refers to an *obligation*, P if it's a *prohibition* and D if it's a *deduction*.

a ☐ You must not take plants to a foreign country.
b ☐ We must carry an ID card at all times.
c ☐ He must have bought those flip-flops in Brazil.
d ☐ You walked past the store so you must have seen the robbers.
e ☐ They must get a vaccine for yellow fever to go to Costa Rica.
f ☐ She must not go out in the sun without sunscreen. Her skin is too sensitive.

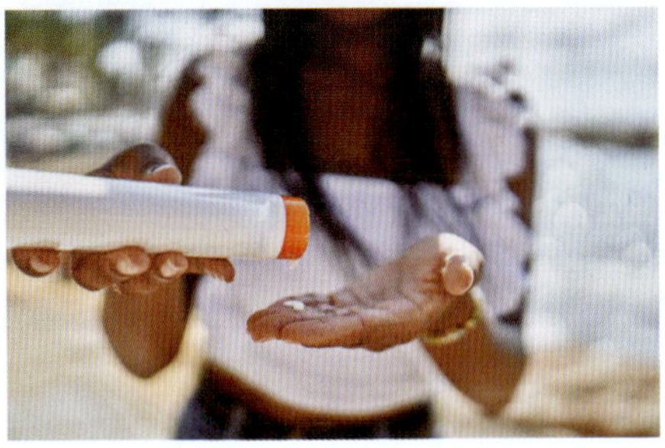

Grammar Buildup 7

1 2 3 4 5 6 7 8

5 Underline the correct answer.

The police **a are / have** investigating a recent increase in pickpocketing on buses in Chicago. In February, 157 people had their wallets **b stealing / stolen** on buses, and 70 more **c reported / report** their cell phone stolen.

Last week, Edna Thomas witnessed a pickpocket in action. "One man **d got / has got** on the bus at the same time as me. He looked ordinary – he **e has worn / was wearing** a pair of jeans and a blue jacket. The bus was full so he **f stand / stood** up. Suddenly, I saw him move his hand slightly. When he got off at the next stop, the man next to him **g was noticing / noticed** that his wallet was missing." "He **h must / can't** have stolen it," he said.

VOCABULARY IN PICTURES

Crime Verbs

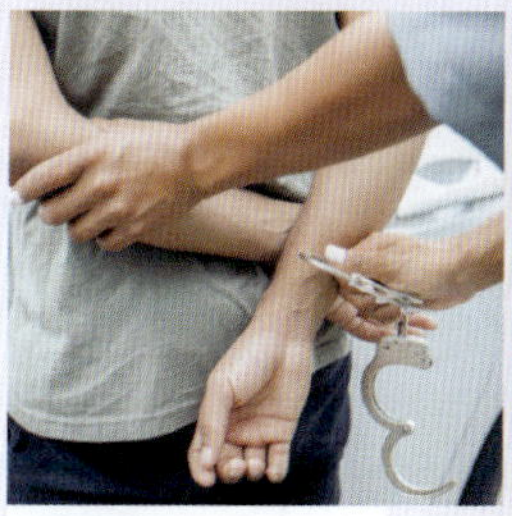
arrest a suspect

be guilty

be innocent

catch a thief

commit a crime

do community service

go on trial

go to prison

investigate a crime

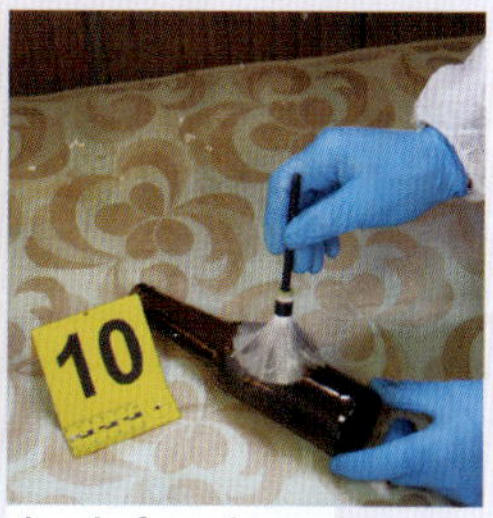

look for clues

pay a fine

question a suspect

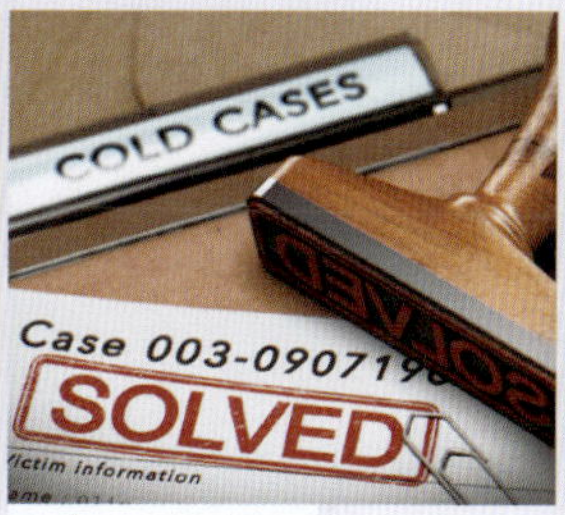

solve a crime

suspect someone

Crimes and Criminals

burglar

burglary

kidnapper

kidnapping

murder

murderer

pickpocket

pickpocketing

robber

robbery

theft

thief

vandal

vandalism

8

COMMUNICATE

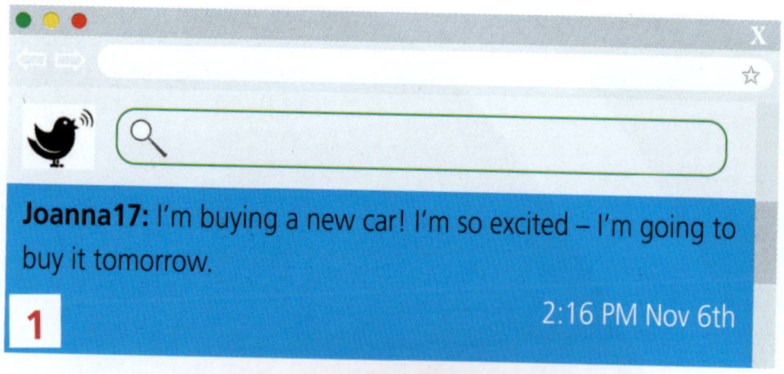
Joanna17: I'm buying a new car! I'm so excited – I'm going to buy it tomorrow.

2:16 PM Nov 6th

1

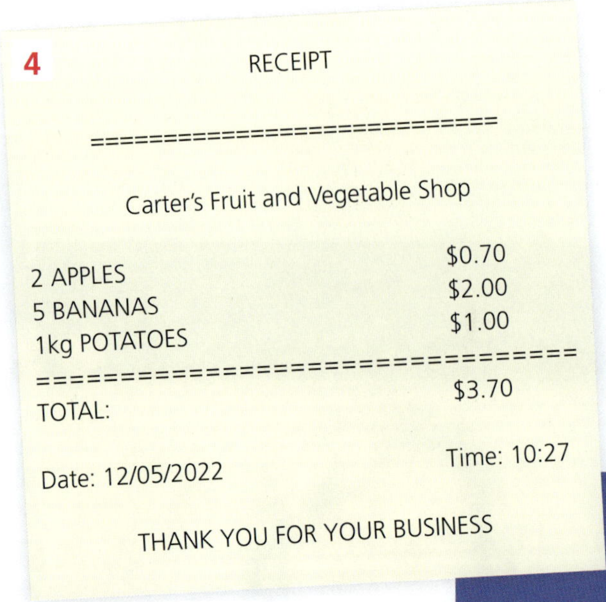
4

RECEIPT

============================

Carter's Fruit and Vegetable Shop

2 APPLES	$0.70
5 BANANAS	$2.00
1kg POTATOES	$1.00
TOTAL:	$3.70

Date: 12/05/2022 Time: 10:27

THANK YOU FOR YOUR BUSINESS

Smoked salmon pâté

450g smoked salmon, chopped in small pieces
1 tsp chopped fresh thyme
Juice of 1 small lemon
2 tbsp butter
85g soft cream cheese

1 Mix the smoked salmon, thyme, and lemon juice in a food processor.
2 Add the butter and cheese. Season with paprika.
3 Process again until the mixture is smooth.
4 Chill in the fridge overnight. Serve with fresh bread.

5

VOCABULARY 1

The Written Word

1 Match text genres 1-8 with one of the options in the box. Use your dictionary to check the meaning of the ones you didn't choose.

advertisement	☐	quote	☐
article	☐	receipt	☐
blog	☐	recipe	☐
cartoon	☐	review	☐
dictionary entry	☐	travel guide	☐
instruction manual	☐	tweet	☐
label	☐		

2 Listen and repeat.

71

3 Choose the correct options. Then answer the questions in pairs.

a Do you know any **quotes / advertisements** by William Shakespeare?

b Do you usually follow **recipes / receipts** when you cook or do you invent your own?

c Do you usually read **blogs / articles** in a newspaper or do you only look at the **cartoons / labels**?

d Do you usually read the **dictionary entry / instruction manual** when you buy a new gadget or do you try to work it out on your own?

e Do you usually read the **reviews / labels** before you see a movie?

f If you take a gap year, will you write a **blog / tweet**?

6

Andrew Garfield Wins a Golden Globe!

After the huge success of his musical *Tick, Tick... Boom!* it was no surprise that Andrew Garfield won the Golden Globe for best actor for his starring role as Jonathan Larson. Since the movie was released in 2021, it has made over $115 million dollars at the box office. Garfield is currently working on new projects.

R

ride1 /raɪd/ (past tense **rode** /rəʊd/; past participle **ridden** /ˈrɪd(ə)n/) verb
1 to sit on an animal, especially a horse, and control its movements as it moves along: *John used to ride his horse every weekend, but he doesn't have time now.*
2 to travel in a car, train, plane, etc. especially as a passenger: *They were riding on the subway when the train broke down.*
3 to take part in a race on a horse, bicycle, motorcycle, etc.: *Peter is going to ride in the race tomorrow. I hope he wins!*

7

BARGAIN BREAKS WITH TAYLOR'S TRAVEL

Need a vacation but can't afford an expensive trip abroad? **Think again ...** you can with Taylor's!

With a week's vacation in Europe starting at just $200 per person, including flights and accommodation. Your dream destination could be cheaper than you ever thought possible.

Call 0345 761987 TODAY to find out more!

8

READING 1

1 Look at the texts again. Which one do you think looks the most interesting? Why?

____
____
____

READING STRATEGY

Identify the genre of a text in order to know what to expect from it.

2 Read and listen to the texts. Write T for *true* or F for *false*. Then give reasons for your answers.
72

a ☐ Text 1: Joanna has bought a new car.
____

b ☐ Text 6: The movie *Tick, Tick... Boom!* hasn't been a success.
____

c ☐ Text 8: Taylor's Travel sells expensive vacations.
____

d ☐ Text 7: The dictionary entry only gives information about the meaning of the word.
____
____

e ☐ Text 4: Someone spent $3.70 on fruit and vegetables.
____

f ☐ Text 2: George Bernard Shaw thinks that communication is easy.
____
____
____

g ☐ Text 5: You have to make the salmon pâté one day before you want to eat it.
____

3 Find the words or phrases in the texts for definitions a-e.

a a false or wrong belief or idea (text 2)
____

b cut into tiny pieces (text 5) ______________

c metro (text 7) ______________

d a place to stay (text 8) ______________

e the main part in a play, movie or TV series (text 6) ______________

4 **CLASS VOTE** Do you agree with the quote in text 2? Why? Why not?

GRAMMAR 1

Tense and Form Review

1 **Read these sentences. Match the verbs in bold with their respective uses.**

- **a** John **used to** ride his horse every weekend, but he doesn't have time now.
- **b** You **thought** I might not want your flowers.
- **c** The flowers you bought **have lasted** all this time.
- **d** The biggest problem in communication is the illusion that it **has taken place**.
- **e** I**'m buying** a new car!
- **f** Garfield **is** currently **working** on his new movie.
- **g** Some men never **think** of buying flowers.
- **h** They **were riding** on the subway when the train broke down.
- **i** I**'m going to buy** a new car tomorrow.
- **j** We**'ll** definitely **watch** the movie!

☐ simple present for habits
☐ present progressive for an action happening now
☐ simple past for an action in the past
☐ past progressive for an action in progress in the past
☐ present perfect for an action that started in the past and continues until now
☐ present perfect for an action at an indefinite time in the past
☐ *used to* to talk about a past habit
☐ *be going to* to talk about a future plan
☐ present progressive to talk about a future arrangement
☐ simple future to talk about a future prediction

The Present

2 **Underline the most appropriate verb form to complete the paragraph.**

Nowadays, the internet **a is / is being** one of the most popular forms of communication. Over six billion people in the world regularly **b use / are using** smartphones every day. Nobody **c knows / is knowing** exactly how many people have internet access, but experts **d believe / are believing** it is around 63% of the world's population. Social networking sites and apps **e become / are becoming** more and more popular among all age groups. At the moment, IT specialists **f try / are trying** to improve internet connections to make our experience better.

3 **INTERFACE** **Complete the sentences about yourself. Then ask and answer questions about them in pairs.**

- **a** I often ...
- **b** I ... every day.
- **c** I don't usually ...
- **d** At the moment I'm ...
- **e** These days I'm ...
- **f** I'm not ... now.

What do you do every day?

The Past

4 **Complete the text with the correct form of the verbs in parentheses. Use the simple past, past progressive, or present perfect.**

The inventor Guglielmo Marconi ___sent___ (send) and **a** ________ (receive) the first radio signal in Italy in 1895. Marconi **b** ________ (work) in Italy when he **c** ________ (invent) the first radio transmitter, but he couldn't get money there to develop it, so he **d** ________ (go) to Britain.
Radio technology **e** ________ (grow) considerably since its early development. The first radio station **f** ________ (start) broadcasting in 1902. Nowadays there are millions of stations. For the past years it **g** ________ (be) possible to listen to the radio online.

The Future

5 Choose the most appropriate verb forms.

Frank I've had an argument with my friend. I **a 'll meet / 'm meeting** her later, but I'm a bit nervous.
Jessie Where are you going to meet?
Frank I'm not sure. We **b will probably meet / are probably meeting** at school.
Jessie I think you should meet somewhere quiet, then you can talk.
Frank Good idea, I **c will text / am texting** her soon and arrange to meet at a café.
Jessie Do you know what you want to say to her?
Frank Yes, I've thought about it, I know what I **d am saying / am going to say**. I think I **e will apologize / am apologizing** for forgetting her birthday.
Jessie Good idea.
Frank And I've bought some flowers. I **f am giving / am going to give** them to her.
Jessie Good luck! Don't forget to take her the flowers.
Frank Don't worry. I **g won't forget / am not forgetting**. Thanks.

6 Complete the sentences with the correct form of the verbs in parentheses. Use *will*, *be going to*, or the present progressive.

a Scientists predict that in the future communication ____________ (be) even faster. They say people ____________ (not have to) speak face to face if they don't want to.

b I ____________ (meet) Bill later, I've just arranged it. We ____________ (write) our article for the school newspaper together.

c I ____________ (not do) anything at all next weekend, I haven't made any arrangements at all. I ____________ (relax)!

d Experts say that the internet ____________ (grow) even bigger over the next few years, and soon everyone ____________ (be able) to control all the gadgets in their house with it.

TIP

The simple present is also used to talk about timetables in the future.
The train to London leaves at 18:50.
The movie finishes in 15 minutes.

GRAMMAR GUIDE page 154

LISTENING

Communication Quiz

1 Look at the words in the box. What do they all have in common?

alphabet · hieroglyphics · homing pigeons · microphone · newspapers · postal service · printing press · telegraph · telephone · typewriter

____

2 73 Listen to the quiz and choose the correct answers.

a The … developed the first alphabet.
1 Egyptians **2** Phoenicians

b The first use of homing pigeons was in …
1 England **2** Greece

c The … established the first postal service.
1 Romans **2** Chinese

d The printing press was invented in Europe in …
1 1450 **2** 1650

e Henry Mill patented the … in 1714.
1 telephone **2** typewriter

f Emile Berliner invented a box that could reproduce … in 1876.
1 sound **2** images

3 73 Listen again. Then write T for *true* or F for *false*.

a ☐ The Greeks started using homing pigeons around 1775 BC.

b ☐ The first message sent by a pigeon was about an invasion.

c ☐ The first daily newspaper appeared in 1650 in Germany.

d ☐ Emile Berliner invented the microphone.

SPEAKING

Good News

74 Josh is talking to his dad about a prize he won at the school art competition. Listen and complete the dialogue.

Dad, guess what?

What???

My group **a** ____________ the *Recycle and Create* art competition at school!

CONGRATS! I'm sure you deserved it! You **b** ____________ a great student! How many students took part?

Around 100, I guess! We were all evaluated based on creativity, percentage of use of recyclable and environmentally friendly materials.

I **c** ____________ how hard you and your friends **d** ____________ to collect all those bottles and cans and create a wonderful piece.

Yeah, and now we know how important **e** ____________ to reintroduce all that "trash" in the cycle of life ...

f ____________ so proud of you, son! **g** ____________ an exhibition of the projects, isn't there?

Yeah, **h** ____________ open till the end of next month.

Great! So, your mom and I can visit it next Friday. What **i** ____________?

FUNCTIONAL LANGUAGE

Talking about News and Sympathizing

What happened?
How was it?
You did a great job!
Congrats!
You deserved it!

Speaking Task

Plan a new dialogue between you and a classmate.

Step 1

Choose a situation or use your own ideas.

"I've failed my exams."

"I have a ticket for the music festival!"

Step 2

Think about what you say.

I've had some bad news. I ...
There's some good news too. I ...

Think about how your classmate responds.

Oh, no! How terrible.
Congratulations, that's wonderful news!

Step 3

Take turns practicing your dialogue.

CULTURE

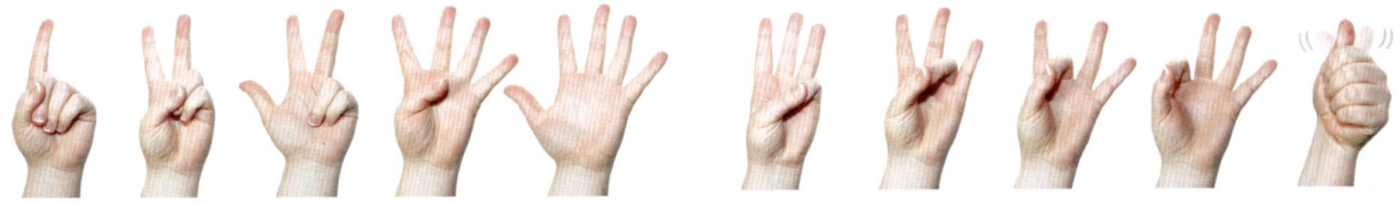

1 2 3 4 5 6 7 8 9 10

American Sign Language

American Sign Language (ASL) has been one of the primary means of communication for the hearing impaired since the 1800s. At that time, Thomas Hopkins Gallaudet, an American deaf educator, helped develop a language and co-founded the first institution for the education of the deaf in the USA, which is now known as the American School for the Deaf.

Millions of Americans use sign language as their native language. The deaf community is very large and the chance to interact in their own language is very important for them, especially if you understand that the language you speak represents your country's identity. Those who use sign language also love to see their language used before their eyes.

Besides, sign language can help bridge the gap between those who can hear and those who are hearing impaired.

Nowadays, the practice of teaching hearing children sign language is becoming popular all over the country. Studies have shown that learning ASL brings many educational benefits such as having the opportunity to gain cultural heritage of the deaf community, which includes various forms of cultural expressions, such as visual poetry, theater, and folklore. Another key factor is learning about values, beliefs, social, and educational aspects of the deaf community, which will certainly help understand other cultures as well.

1 Read and listen to the text. Then write T for *true* or F for *false*.

75

a ☐ ASL has been the only means of communication of the hearing impaired for a long time.

b ☐ Thomas Hopkins Gallaudet, whose son was deaf, helped develop a language for the deaf community.

c ☐ Sign language can help bridge the gap between those who can hear and those who are hearing impaired.

d ☐ Nowadays, the practice of teaching hearing children sign language is not popular in the USA.

e ☐ ASL provides no educational benefits.

2 What do you know about sign language in your country? Find as much information as you can about it. Record your findings.

____
____
____
____
____
____
____

3 Would you like to learn your country's sign language? Why? Why not?

____
____
____

VOCABULARY 2

Adjectives with *-able* and *-ible*

1 Complete the definitions with the adjectives in the box.

acceptable bearable flexible reasonable reliable responsible ~~visible~~

A person or thing that you can see: visible

a A person who can deal with a lot of responsibility: ______

b A person you can rely on: ______

c A person who shows reason: ______

d A person who adapts quickly to new situations: ______

e A situation that you can bear: ______

f A situation or thing that you can accept: ______

2 Match the adjectives from activity 1 with their opposites in the box.

inflexible invisible irresponsible ~~unacceptable~~ unbearable unreasonable unreliable

acceptable – unacceptable

______

______

______

______

______

______

3 Listen, check, and repeat.

76

4 Complete the sentences with words from activity 2.

Lucy never does anything she says she will do. She's very unreliable.

a We complained because their behavior was ______ and ______ – they completely destroyed the house.

b The magician made the rabbit ______ – you couldn't see it at all!

c This situation is awful. It's really ______ – I just can't tolerate it anymore.

d John is very ______. He doesn't like changes.

e My mom said I couldn't go to the party – she's so ______.

READING 2

1 Look at the cartoonist self-portrait on page 151. What three questions would you ask him?

______

______

______

2 Read and listen. Did you have similar questions?

77

3 Read the text again. Then write T for *true* or F for *false*. Correct the false sentences.

a ☐ Doug Savage created a webcomic.

______

b ☐ Doug had a creative job when he started working.

______

c ☐ When Doug was a child, his favorite comic strip was *Peanuts*.

______

d ☐ Doug draws his cartoons on the computer.

______

e ☐ He has drawn 1,000 cartoons.

______

The Man Behind the Chickens

Cartoonists are some of the most adaptable and creative people when it comes to communicating a complex idea in a small space. Doug Savage is best-known for his Savage Chickens webcomic – each cartoon is drawn on one single sticky note! Here he tells us all about himself.

Why do you draw chickens?

I drew cartoons a lot when I was younger, but when I started working in an office, I slowly lost the ability to draw. When I started drawing cartoons again, chickens were the only thing that I remembered how to draw!

When did you start drawing chickens?

I started drawing the chickens in autumn 2004 and I began posting them online in January 2005.

Why did you decide to start a webcomic?

I wasn't enjoying my office job because it wasn't very creative, so I was looking for some sort of artistic activity. A lot of people were starting blogs at the time. I thought it would be fun to create one too, so I started putting my comics on the web.

Did you read comics when you were younger?

Yes, I did. As a child, I read all of the comic strips I could find at the local library – especially *Peanuts*. I've always enjoyed authors who combine art and storytelling, such as Richard Scarry, Dr. Seuss, and Raymond Briggs.

What do you draw on?

I draw on actual yellow sticky notes, just like the ones you can find in an office. Then I scan them and edit the images on the computer.

What inspires you?

Everything, but mostly human behavior. People are so funny, and the world can be a very silly place.

What has been your biggest achievement so far?

A collection of my cartoons has been published in a book, which is incredible. But I'm also very proud of all the work that I've created over the past few years. I'm amazed that I've drawn over 1,600 cartoons!

What are your plans for the future?

I hope to publish more books and do more animation. And I'm always experimenting with new techniques, so I'd like to try more painting and maybe even write a graphic novel. I want to keep trying new things!

4 Complete the definitions with words and phrases from the text.

a A ______________________ is a type of comic book that tells a story via illustrations.

b A ______________________ is a sequence of drawings arranged in panels (usually three) that tell an amusing story.

c A ______________________ is a series of comic strips published online.

d ______________________ is the art of telling or writing stories or narratives.

5 Read again: "I hope to publish more books and do more animation. [...] I'd like to try more painting and maybe **even** write a graphic novel." Choose the correct option.

By the use of *even*, we understand that the cartoonist considers that writing a graphic novel would be a **less** / **more** surprising, unusual activity than the others he performs.

READING STRATEGY

Focusing adverbs are used to draw attention to a particular part of a sentence. *Even*, *at least*, *only*, and *just* are examples of focusing adverbs. Look:

Tom was relaxed at the party. He ate, talked to people, and ***even*** *danced.*
This car doesn't look good. I hope it ***at least*** *runs well.*
When I eat fruit, I eat ***only*** *fruit. No syrups or cream.*

In the sentences above, what words or phrases are being emphasized by the focusing adverbs?

____

GRAMMAR 2

Tense and Form Review: Questions

1 Read the sentences below. Underline the auxiliaries when provided.

- **a** Why do you draw chickens?
- **b** When did you start drawing chickens?
- **c** Who inspires you?
- **d** What has been your biggest achievement so far?

2 Complete the chart below with the questions from activity 1.

question forms	
Use the auxiliary when the subject is present in the question	Don't use the auxiliary when the subject is the question word

3 Order the words to make questions.

- **a** you / write / will / a blog post / later today ?
  ____
- **b** what / you / were / reading / when / arrived / your teacher ?
  ____
- **c** you / what / do / did / before / you / came to school ?
  ____
- **d** send / you / yesterday / did / any emails ?
  ____

4 Complete with the correct form of the verbs and the words in parentheses.

- **a** What ____________________ (your friends / do) when you arrived at school?
- **b** ____________________ (you / ever / make) a podcast?
- **c** ____________________ (your friends / arrive) at school yet?
- **d** Have you made any arrangements for this weekend? What ____________________ (you / do)?
- **e** ____________________ (you / buy) a new bike later this year?

GRAMMAR GUIDE page 154

WRITING

A Comment on a Blog Post

1 EXPLORING THE CONTEXT

1 Doug Savage started his blog in the early 2000s. Over time, vlogs (video blogs) became more popular, but people still write blogs of various types. Look at Chase's blog and answer: What type of blog is this?

- **a** a fashion blog
- **b** a travel blog
- **c** an opinion blog
- **d** a literature blog

2 Read, listen, and check your answer.

78

www.worldofchase.blogger.com

THE WORLD OF CHASE — movies | books | school life | everything!

I'm Chase Malich and I want to share my thoughts with you.
Here you can find my opinions on movies, books, school life, and the world in general.

LEARN MORE

What is the Best Way to Communicate?

by Chase, April 19, 2023

I've been thinking about the ways we communicate. On my post today, I'm discussing the best method of communication. In the past, people only used to communicate in person or by letter. However, nowadays there are many different ways to communicate, such as email, phone, and messaging apps.
As I see it, different forms of communication are appropriate at different times.
For example, it's better to spend time with friends in person because you can enjoy their company. What's more, the best way to solve problems is face to face. However, when you are out and you need to share information, then the quickest and easiest option is to send a text message. Finally, email and social networking sites are good ways of keeping in touch with a lot of people.
To conclude, in my opinion you should choose the best way to communicate depending on the circumstances. What do you think?

3 Read the post again and answer the questions.

- **a** What is Chase's post about today?
  ____
  ____

b In which of the blog sections was this post likely to be published?

____

____

c Chase asks, "What do you think?" How can readers respond?

____

____

4 Match descriptions a-e with passages 1-5.

a The author introduces the topic.

b The author provides general information on the topic.

c The author states his point of view.

d The author presents examples and arguments.

e The author reinforces his point of view.

1 ☐ "For example, it's better to spend time with friends in person [...]. However, when you are out [...], then the quickest and easiest option is to send a text message."

2 ☐ "To conclude, in my opinion you should choose the best way to communicate depending on the circumstances."

3 ☐ "In the past, people only used to communicate in person or by letter."

4 ☐ "As I see it, different forms of communication are appropriate at different times."

5 ☐ "On my blog today, I'm discussing the best method of communication."

2 PLANNING

1 Read this other post from *The World of Chase*.

> Hey guys! Many young people are addicted to social networking. What's your opinion about it? Write a comment (150-170 words) on my blog!

2 Accept Chase's invitation and write a post on the best method to communicate.

3 WRITING

Write your first draft. Plan at least three paragraphs.

LANGUAGE FOCUS

Linkers and Opinion Expressions

Use linkers to connect ideas and expressions to state your opinion.

However, *nowadays there are many different ways to communicate.*

As I see it, *different forms of communication are appropriate [...].*

What's more, *the best way to solve problems is face to face.*

To conclude, in my opinion *you should choose the best way to communicate [...].*

Rewrite the sentences using the words in the box.

as a result finally firstly from my point of view ~~furthermore~~ on the other hand secondly whereas

Sending texts is easy. It is cheap. (linker of addition)
Sending texts is easy. Furthermore, it is cheap.

a A disadvantage of social networks is that some teenagers stay up late. (opinion expression)

____

____

b Texts are easy to send. Some people send far too many. (linker of result)

____

____

c Making phone calls can be expensive. Sending texts is cheap. (linker of contrast)

____

____

d There are advantages to sending texts. They are cheap. You can send them from anywhere. It's quick. (3 linkers of sequencing)

____

____

____

e On the one hand, texts are easy to send. They can become addictive. (linker of contrast)

____

____

4 CHECKING & EDITING

1 Check your post for the appropriate use of:

a grammar, word order, spelling, and punctuation

b linkers and opinion expressions

2 Correct and write your final copy.

5 SHARING

1 Publish the posts on the class blog.

2 What are the most common opinions in the class?

GRAMMAR GUIDE

Tense and Form Review

simple present	
+	I **play** basketball.
–	He **doesn't like** rock music.
?	**Do** they **eat** dinner at 7pm? Yes, they **do**. / No, they **don't**.

simple past	
+	I **lived** in France for two years.
–	She **didn't watch** the tennis match.
?	**Did** he **read** the book? Yes, he **did**. / No, he **didn't**.

present progressive	
+	I'**m waiting** for the bus.
–	He **isn't talking** to Louise.
?	**Are** they **thinking** about the exam? Yes, they **are**. / No, they **aren't**.

past progressive	
+	I **was listening** to rock music.
–	She **wasn't reading** a book.
?	**Were** they **playing** soccer? Yes, they **were**. / No, they **weren't**.

present perfect	
+	I **have spoken** to Jenny.
–	She **hasn't bought** a new car.
?	**Have** you **seen** Brad Pitt's new movie? Yes, I **have**. / No, I **haven't**.

be going to	
+	I'**m going to** watch a movie.
–	He **isn't going to** sell his car.
?	**Are** you **going to** speak to John? Yes, I **am**. / No, I'**m not**.

will	
+	I **will** go to college in London.
–	She **won't** be late.
?	**Will** they **move** to a new house next year? Yes, they **will**. / No, they **won't**.

question forms
What is your name? How long have you been interested in music? What sports did you play when you were younger? What are you doing now? What are you going to do next? Will you go on vacation next year?

PROGRESS CHECK

Name: ____________________
Class name / Period: ____________________
Teacher: ____________________
Date: ____________________

The Written Word

1 Complete the sentences with the words in the box.

advertisements articles headlines instruction manual recipe

a When I read a newspaper, I look at the ____________ first to get an idea of what all the ____________ are about.

b I never watch the ____________ on TV because most of them are boring.

c This soup tastes horrible – I should have used a better ____________.

d I don't understand how to operate my smartphone. Have you seen the ____________?

Adjectives with *-able* and *-ible*

2 Choose the correct adjectives to complete the sentences.

a She's late again! That's completely **acceptable / unacceptable**.

b He wouldn't share his pizza with me – he's so **reasonable / unreasonable**.

c He didn't see me on the street yesterday – maybe I'm **invisible / visible**!

d My sister is absolutely **bearable / unbearable** – she's so noisy, and she always steals my clothes.

Tense and Form Review

3 Choose the correct answers.

a Yesterday I **read / have read** the newspaper.

b I think I **will send / are sending** an email tomorrow if we **don't / didn't** hear from Pete.

c I usually **listen / am listening** to music every morning before school.

d They know this cartoonist. They' **re / ve** read her cartoons before.

4 Complete the text with the correct form of the verbs in parentheses.

If you **a** ____________ (love) computer games, you **b** ____________ (be) happy to hear that an exciting new game console **c** ____________ (release) next month. Designed by Fusion, the console **d** ____________ (have) lots of innovative new features. Fusion **e** ____________ (design) other consoles in the past, including the BS-20 which **f** ____________ (sell) in Europe between 2014 and 2018.

5 Write questions for these answers.

a ____________________

Yes, I have written lots of articles.

b ____________________

No, I won't use that recipe.

c ____________________

No, I wasn't reading that travel guide when you arrived.

6 Write questions.

a what / you / do / yesterday ?

____

b what / you / do / next weekend ?

____

c how long / you / have / your cell phone ?

____

d what / you / do / now ?

____

Grammar Buildup 8

1 2 3 4 5 6 7 8

7 Choose the correct answers.

How much **a do you know / are you knowing** about text messages? Also known as SMS, the first one **b was sent / is sent** in December 1992 by engineer Neil Papworth. Since then, text messaging **c is becoming / has become** popular all over the world.
Text messages **d are / have been** an easy way to communicate, especially among people who don't like to make phone calls. Sending text messages can be dangerous, though: some people **e admitted / are admitting** to sending text messages while driving!
Text messages **f are still developing / will still develop**. You can send photos and videos by text message. Who knows what **g is happening / will happen** in the future?

VOCABULARY IN PICTURES

The Written Word

advertisement

article

blog

cartoon

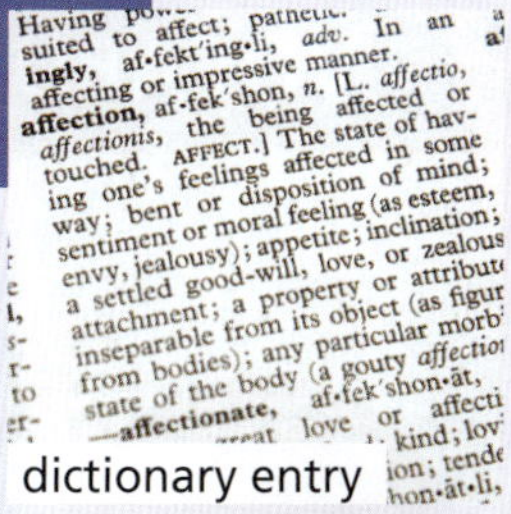
dictionary entry

instruction manual

label

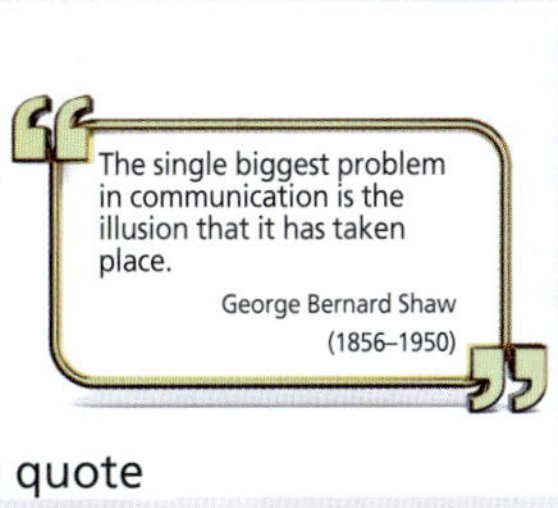

quote

receipt

recipe

review

travel guide

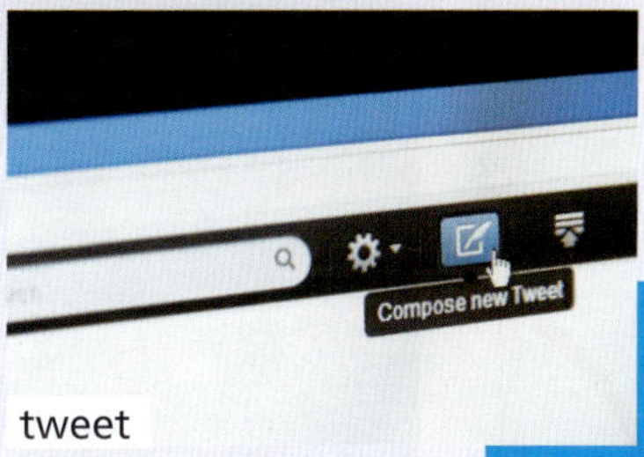

tweet

Adjectives with *-able* and *-ible*

acceptable

unacceptable

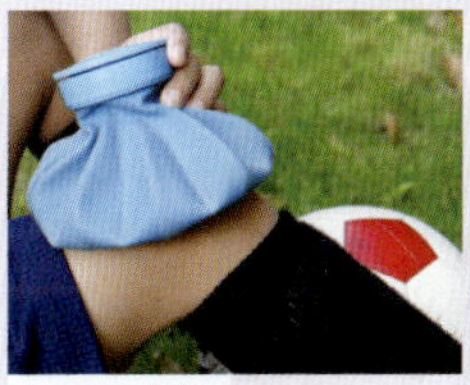
bearable

unbearable

flexible

inflexible

reasonable

unreasonable

reliable

unreliable

responsible

irresponsible

visible

invisible

REVIEW 4

VOCABULARY

START

1

In order to assemble the shelves, you must read the **instruction manual** / **label**.

2

He was arrested for **robbery** / **theft** after stealing that woman's cell phone.

8

The detective is **searching for** / **investigating** a crime.

7

I can barely see the glass in this picture. It's almost **visible** / **invisible**.

9

This definition is so precise, it looks like a dictionary **entry** / **description**.

10

To find out how to wash it, read the **recipe** / **label**.

15

Destroying the bus stop was pure **vandalism** / **theft**.

FINISH

3

Ethan is **irresponsible** / **reliable**.
He doesn't take care of any of his belongings.

4

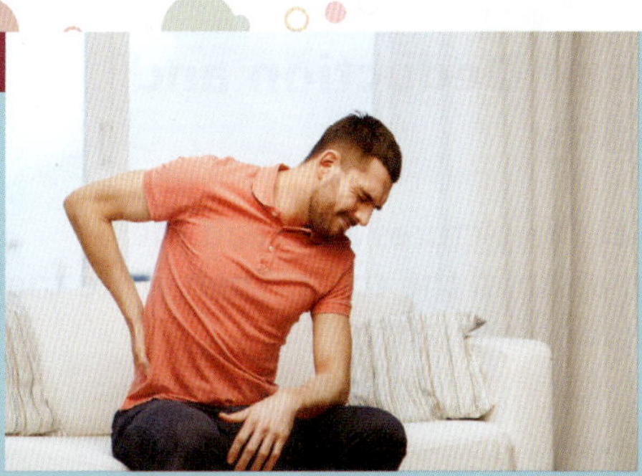

This back pain is just **unbearable** / **bearable**!
I need a painkiller to continue working.

5

The police officers are **interviewing** / **questioning** the suspect now.

6

The manager had to go on **trial** / **vacation** for not paying the staff's wages.

11

She's an experienced climber.
She's totally **reliable** / **unreliable**!

12

The forensic scientist is looking for **clues** / **tips**.

13

Always carry your bag in front of you to avoid **robbery** / **pickpocketing**.

14

You can find out how much tax is being charged if you read the **recipe** / **receipt**.

REVIEW 4

GRAMMAR

Modals of Deduction and Possibility

1 Look at the pictures and read the information in the chart. Then write the corresponding names.

a

____

b

____

c

____

	Larry	Rick	Steve
height	1.95m	1.85m	1.70m
weight	90 kilos	75 kilos	60 kilos
hair	hairless	gray	brown

2 Read the chart in activity 1 again and complete the sentences with *must*, *might*, or *can't*.

The short man __can't__ be Larry because he's tall.

a The short man _______________ be Rick either because he's 1.85m tall.

b The man has brown hair. It _______________ be Steve.

c The tall man _______________ be Larry.

d The man weighs less than 70 kilos. It _______________ be Larry or Rick.

3 Underline the correct words.

Ruth isn't at school. She **can** / **may** be on vacation.

a What's that noise? I'm not sure, but it **might** / **must** be the dog.

b It **can't** / **must not** be 11pm. It's light outside.

c Eva is making a snack. She **must** / **could** be hungry.

d My friends aren't here. They **could** / **can** be late.

4 Rewrite the sentences using *must*, *might*, or *can't*.

Where's Elisa? Perhaps she's at home.
Elisa might be at home.

a Ali's lived in England. I'm sure he speaks English.

____

b Luke was with me all day. I'm sure he isn't guilty.

____

c They're not answering the phone. Maybe they're asleep.

____

must / *must not*

5 Match the parts to make rules.

a To win at *Monopoly*,

b If you want the police to catch the thief,

c In order to apply for scholarship,

d To board the plane,

[ ] you must not carry sharp items.

[a] you must buy a lot of properties.

[ ] you must have excellent marks.

[ ] you must not eliminate any clues left.

Tense and Form Review

6 Write the name of the correct verb form of the verbs in bold.

They often **train** before school.
simple present

a Last night I **dreamed** about a ghost.
______

b We**'re going to** have a party soon.
______

c He **was walking** home when he met an old friend.
______

d They**'ve lived** here since 2015.
______

e She **does** her homework every day.
______

f I**'m reading** a great short story.
______

g You**'ll become** rich and famous one day.
______

7 Now match the verb forms in activity 6 with their uses.

a [a] Used for an action or event in the past.

b [ ] Used for an action or event that started in the past and continues until now.

c [ ] Used for talking about a future plan.

d [ ] Used for an action or event which is true at the present time or which happens regularly as a habit.

e [ ] Used for talking about a future prediction.

f [ ] Used for an action or event which is happening now.

g [ ] Used for an action or event in progress in the past.

8 Complete the sentences using simple past, past progressive, or present perfect.

We ___were___ (be) late so we ___didn't eat___ (not eat) breakfast this morning.

a I ______ (send) you a text message when I ______ (drop) my phone.

b I ______ (visit) the Guggenheim Museum in New York but I ______ (see) the Guggenheim Museum in Bilbao.

c He ______ (not ride) his bike since he ______ (have) an accident.

9 Write complete sentences using the correct future form.

When / I / (be) / older / I / travel around the world
When I'm older, I'll travel around the world.

a We / (meet) / at the party / at 6pm
______

b That child / (cry) / soon
______

c He / probably / (be) / an engineer / after finishing college
______

10 Write complete questions. Then write short answers.

you / often / argue / with your friends? ✓
Do you often argue with your friends? Yes, I do.

a you / take a shower / yesterday / when / the phone ring? ✓
______
______

b your friends / study / at college next year? ✗
______
______

c you / know / your best friend / since primary school? ✓
______
______

Clickbait

A Misleading Headline

1 Read and listen. Complete the sentences with the characters' names.

79

Daniel	Daniel's dad (4×)
Daniel's mom (2×)	Daniel's parents

Daniel's mom has back pain.

a ______________ is browsing the website of a newspaper.

b ______________ reads a headline and believes it's an article about a new drug.

c When clicking on the link, ______________ realizes that the text doesn't match the headline.

d ______________ are disappointed with the article.

e ______________ explains to them that this is not an article, but an ad. Creators of this content follow a strategy called "clickbait."

f ______________ considers clickbait a deceptive tactic.

g ______________ argues that, while not illegal, clickbait is unethical.

2 Read the questions about clickbait. Match them to their answers.

What is clickbait?
Why do even respected news websites have clickbait ads?
For what purpose is clickbait used?
Is clickbait illegal?
Why is it easy to confuse clickbait ads with news articles?

Clickbait FAQ

a ______________

As the name implies, clickbait is a strategy that consists of throwing a "bait" to the readers so that they click on a link. The bait often involves appealing to strong emotions like fear or curiosity.

b ______________

In most cases, it's used for advertising. An advertiser may disguise its message in the form of a news article, as in the comic strip. Or a website that earns income from ads may want many people to visit it, and for that purpose it creates sensational headlines that attract readers.

c ______________

Because a website does not select the ads it will publish. There are companies that specialize in placing ads on websites — and they publish ads from advertisers who pay the most. The process is mostly carried by computers, with little human participation.

d ______________

Because clickbait ads mimic the style and look of news articles. On news sites, they appear mixed with real news. In general, there is only a tiny disclaimer stating that it is advertising content.

e ______________

In most countries no. But it's generally considered an unethical practice. Platforms like YouTube and Twitter have guidelines against clickbait, and some reputable newspapers and magazines have already banned them.

3 Work in pairs. The following arguments could be used in a debate about banning clickbait. Read them and write *A* for arguments **against** the ban and *F* for arguments **in favor of** the ban.

a ☐ Clickbait ads deceive consumers and spread misinformation.

b ☐ In fact, all media companies use clickbait to some extent because they all want to get audience attention.

c ☐ It's very difficult to draw a line between misleading content and eloquent advertising.

d ☐ Clickbait can be a gateway to phishing attacks: The readers can participate in a fake survey, for example, and have their personal data stolen.

4 Write another argument *against* and one more *in favor of* banning clickbait.

a Against the ban: ______________

____

____

b In favor of the ban: ______________

____

____

5 Let's discuss this issue in a digital forum! Each student will present his or her point of view on the question: **Should clickbait be illegal?** Use good arguments!

6 Reply to your classmates, especially those who have a different opinion than yours.

A Better Me Every Day

What do you enjoy?

What are you good at?

What skills would you like to improve?

1 Before choosing a career path, it is fundamental to find out about your interests, skills, and qualities. Read the chart below and check (✓) the items that apply to you. Add extra information, if necessary.

interests	skills	personal qualities
At school or in your free time, do you enjoy:	Are you good at:	Do you:
☐ art?	☐ ICT?	☐ work well in a group?
☐ sports?	☐ science?	☐ plan ahead?
☐ pets?	☐ math?	☐ help people around you?
☐ socializing?	☐ communication?	☐ have original ideas?
☐ surfing the net?	☐ creative work?	☐ meet deadlines?
Other: ____________	☐ sports?	☐ listen to people with different views?
	☐ crafts?	Other: ____________
	Other: ____________	

2 Interview a classmate. Ask him or her the questions from activity 1. Do you and your classmate share the same interests / skills and personal qualities?

Are you good at math?

I'm terrible at math, but I'm really good at crafts!

3 The theory below was developed by American psychologist John Holland. In his view, there are 6 types of vocational personalities which could make people predisposed to certain jobs / occupations. Match the types to the descriptions provided.

a realistic ("doers")
b investigative ("thinkers")
c artistic ("creators")
d social ("helpers")
e enterprising ("persuaders")
f conventional ("organizers")

☐ They like to work with people, helping them whenever needed. They are caring, warm, and look for close relationships with others.

☐ They enjoy people's company but want to be in charge of the situation. They are good "talkers" and are always trying to persuade people to do what they want. They are leaders who value money, status, and power.

☐ They like to work with things and are very competitive. The outdoor type, they like working with tools and machines. They are not very good at socializing.

☐ These people like to work with ideas and express their feelings. They are usually very creative as they use their imagination a lot. However, they dislike rules and regulations.

☐ They prefer to think and observe. Logic and concepts are important so science is the field they often enjoy.

☐ They like rules and regulations and emphasize self-control. They are usually well-organized but have little or no imagination.

4 Read the job titles and write the most suitable type of vocational personality for each group of professionals.

a artist, actor, dancer, designer, DJ: ____________

b nurse, librarian, physiotherapist: ____________

c chemist, mathematician, pharmacist: ____________

d lawyer, manager, journalist: ____________

e secretary, clerk, supervisor: ____________

f farmer, truck driver, builder, carpenter: ____________

5 Discuss with a classmate.

a What vocational type(s) do you fit the most?

b Do you already have an idea of the career you want to follow? Is it related to the vocational type you fit?

Mission: Self Improvement

As you read the descriptions of vocational types, you've probably noticed that each type has its strengths and weaknesses. Self-knowledge involves identifying not only your current skills, but also those that need to be developed. In small groups, you will outline a plan to fulfill a mission: to improve a skill or personal quality.

DOING

1 Look again at the answers you gave in activity 1. Pay attention to the skills and personal qualities that you *didn't* check. Are any of them important for the career you intend to follow? Would you feel more satisfied with yourself if you improved any of these skills?

2 Fill in the first column of the chart below with the skills or personal qualities you would like to improve. In the second column, write one or two actions you could take to do it. For example, if you struggle to meet deadlines, it may be helpful for you to rely on a daily planner. If you have poor communication skills, it may be useful to participate in group activities, such as drama or role-playing games.

Skill / Personal quality I'd like to improve	Action(s) I'll take to improve it	Results – Week 1	Results – Week 2

3 For the next two weeks, use the other columns to record your progress. If you find it interesting, continue doing these self-assessments in your notebook for a longer period of time.

PRESENTING

4 Share your experience with your partners. Was it easy or difficult trying to improve a skill? Did the chosen strategies work or would it be better to try others?

5 Write down the group's main findings and present them to the class.

REFLECTING

6 Do you believe that 21st century professionals need to develop multiple skills? Why (or why not)?

7 In your opinion, can pursuing self-development increase personal or professional satisfaction? Why (or why not)?

8 What have you learned about yourself by doing this project?

IRREGULAR VERBS

80))

Infinitive	Simple Past	Past Participle
be /bi/	was / were /wɑz/, /wɜr/	been /bin/, /bɪn/
begin /bɪˈgɪn/	began /bɪˈgæn/	begun /bɪˈgʌn/
break /breɪk/	broke /broʊk/	broken /ˈbroʊkən/
bring /brɪŋ/	brought /brɔt/	brought /brɔt/
build /bɪld/	built /bɪlt/	built /bɪlt/
buy /baɪ/	bought /bɔt/	bought /bɔt/
choose /tʃuz/	chose /tʃoʊz/	chosen /ˈtʃoʊz(ə)n/
come /kʌm/	came /keɪm/	come /kʌm/
do /du/	did /dɪd/	done /dʌn/
drink /drɪŋk/	drank /dræŋk/	drunk /drʌŋk/
drive /draɪv/	drove /droʊv/	driven /ˈdrɪv(ə)n/
eat /it/	ate /eɪt/	eaten /ˈit(ə)n/
fall /fɔl/	fell /fel/	fallen /ˈfɔlən/
find /faɪnd/	found /faʊnd/	found /faʊnd/
fly /flaɪ/	flew /flu/	flown /floʊn/
forget /fərˈget/	forgot /fərˈgɑt/	forgotten /fərˈgɑt(ə)n/
get /get/	got /gɑt/	got /gɑt/, gotten /ˈgɑt(ə)n/
give /gɪv/	gave /geɪv/	given /ˈgɪv(ə)n/
go /goʊ/	went /went/	gone /gɔn/
have /hæv/	had /həd/	had /həd/
hear /hɪr/	heard /hɜrd/	heard /hɜrd/
know /noʊ/	knew /nu/	known /noʊn/
learn /lɜrn/	learnt / learned /lɜrnt/, /ˈlɜrnəd/	learnt / learned /lɜrnt/, /ˈlɜrnəd/
leave /liv/	left /left/	left /left/
lose /luz/	lost /lɔst/	lost /lɔst/
make /meɪk/	made /meɪd/	made /meɪd/
meet /mit/	met /met/	met /met/
pay /peɪ/	paid /peɪd/	paid /peɪd/
put /pʊt/	put /pʊt/	put /pʊt/
read /rid/	read /red/	read /red/
run /rʌn/	ran /ræn/	run /rʌn/
say /seɪ/	said /sed/	said /sed/
see /si/	saw /sɔ/	seen /sin/
sell /sel/	sold /soʊld/	sold /soʊld/
sing /sɪŋ/	sang /sæŋ/	sung /sʌŋ/
sit /sɪt/	sat /sæt/	sat /sæt/
speak /spik/	spoke /spoʊk/	spoken /ˈspoʊkən/
take /teɪk/	took /tʊk/	taken /ˈteɪkən/
teach /titʃ/	taught /tɔt/	taught /tɔt/
tell /tel/	told /toʊld/	told /toʊld/
think /θɪŋk/	thought /θɔt/	thought /θɔt/
wear /wer/	wore /wɔr/	worn /wɔrn/
win /wɪn/	won /wʌn/	won /wʌn/
write /raɪt/	wrote /roʊt/	written /ˈrɪt(ə)n/

WORKBOOK

CONTENTS

Starter 168

Unit 1 – Changing Lives 170

Vocabulary 1 | Life-changing Events 170

Grammar 1 | Review: Simple Past / *used to* 171

Vocabulary 2 | Verb + Preposition 173

Grammar 2 | Subject and Object Questions 174

Grammar Check 175

Listening 175

Extension 176

Vocabulary Plus | College Degrees 177

Unit 2 – Incredible Journeys 178

Vocabulary 1 | Travel 178

Grammar 1 | Review: Present Perfect and Simple Past 179

Vocabulary 2 | Extreme Adjectives 181

Grammar 2 | Review: Quantity and Uncountable Nouns 182

Grammar Check 183

Listening 183

Extension 184

Vocabulary Plus | Health Problems and Cures 185

Unit 3 – The World Around Us 186

Vocabulary 1 | Saving Environmental Resources 186

Grammar 1 | Review: Present Perfect + *for, since, how long* 187

Vocabulary 2 | Prefixes 189

Grammar 2 | Review: Present Perfect + *still, yet, already, just* 190

Grammar Check 191

Listening 191

Extension 192

Vocabulary Plus | Trees and Plants 193

Unit 4 – Good Friends 194

Vocabulary 1 | Making Friends 194

Grammar 1 | Obligation, No Obligation, Prohibition, Advice 195

Vocabulary 2 | Verb and Noun Collocations 197

Grammar 2 | Second Conditional 198

Grammar Check 199

Listening 199

Extension 200

Vocabulary Plus | Friendship 201

Unit 5 – Followers of Fashion 202

Vocabulary 1 | Style Adjectives 202

Grammar 1 | Relative Pronouns 203

Vocabulary 2 | Phrasal Verbs: Clothes 205

Grammar 2 | *some, any, no* Compounds 206

Grammar Check 207

Listening 207

Extension 208

Vocabulary Plus | Clothes and Accessories 209

Unit 6 – Work and Money 210

Vocabulary 1 | The World of Work 210

Grammar 1 | First and Second Conditionals 211

Vocabulary 2 | Work Verbs 213

Grammar 2 | Gerunds and Infinitives 214

Grammar Check 215

Listening 215

Extension 216

Vocabulary Plus | In the Office 217

Unit 7 – Crime Doesn't Pay 218

Vocabulary 1 | Crime Verbs 218

Grammar 1 | Modals of Deduction and Possibility 219

Vocabulary 2 | Crimes and Criminals 221

Grammar 2 | Review: *must / must not* 222

Grammar Check 223

Listening 223

Extension 224

Vocabulary Plus | Breaking the Law 225

Unit 8 – Communicate 226

Vocabulary 1 | The Written Word 226

Grammar 1 | Tense and Form Review 227

Vocabulary 2 | Adjectives with *-able* and *-ible* 229

Grammar 2 | Tense and Form Review: Questions 230

Grammar Check 231

Listening 231

Extension 232

Vocabulary Plus | The Newspaper 233

STARTER

Jobs and Life Events

1 Find in the word spiral the name of 18 jobs.

2 Match the columns to find at least 8 life events. Items can have more than one match.

a be	a house
b get	school
c start	drive
d learn to	born
e leave	home
f buy	children
g have	a job
	married

3 Write down the life events found in activity 2.

____
____
____
____
____
____
____
____
____
____

Clothes and Accessories

4 Number the clothes and accessories in the pictures according to the words in the box.

1 boots	2 dress	3 jacket	4 pants
5 shirt	6 skirt	7 sneakers	8 T-shirt

5 Complete the names of the clothes and accessories with the missing letters.

a c ___ ___ ___

b ___ e a n ___

c s ___ ___ ___ ___ ___ r

d s ___ ___ ___ f

e s ___ ___ ___ ___ s

Prepositions

6 <u>Underline</u> the most appropriate preposition to complete the sentences.

a Is this bus heading **toward / over** town?

b This is a very interesting town: Let me show you **across / around**.

c She could see a figure **along / through** the fog.

d Keep your hands **into / away from** the hot stove!

e Please put the bowl **into / along** the sink.

f The ship sailed **under / along** the coast.

make and *do*

7 Complete the sentences with the words in the box.

a decision a mistake charity work homework money

a Many students find it difficult to do ___________ under pressure.

b Sometimes you'll have to make ___________ between something bad and something worse.

c Everyone makes ___________ every now and then.

d There is no easy way to make ___________.

e The high school students are raising funds to do ___________.

should / *shouldn't*

8 Underline the words to complete the sentences.

a You **should / shouldn't** research your family tree. It would be so interesting!

b You **should / shouldn't** definitely follow your dream. It's really worth doing it.

c You **should / shouldn't** conquer your fear. There is no reason to be afraid.

d You **should / shouldn't** pass by those who need your help. Be compassionate.

e You **should / shouldn't** find time for studying. You'd feel more confident at school.

f You **should / shouldn't** be afraid to say no. Only you know what's best for you.

will and *be going to*

9 Order the words to make sentences.

a new book / a / think / bestseller / her / I / will become

____

____

b reopen / summer / That store / definitely / before / will

____

____

c class / going to / We / afternoon / this / have / English / aren't

____

____

____

____

d a retreat / spend / the weekend / going to / at / They're

____

____

____

____

e because / acting classes / won't take / too shy / I'm / I / the

____

____

____

____

First Conditional

10 Match the columns to make sentences.

a	If you go to bed late	if the forecast is for bad weather.
b	We won't go	if we agree to some rules.
c	If you miss the flight	we'll have time to watch some TV.
d	Everybody will be more comfortable	you'll have to buy another ticket.
e	If you finish doing your homework soon	you'll feel tired in the morning.

11 Write down the sentences formed in activity 10. Use commas when necessary.

a ______________________________

____

b ______________________________

____

c ______________________________

____

d ______________________________

____

e ______________________________

____

1

CHANGING LIVES

VOCABULARY 1

Life-changing Events

1 Complete the words with the vowels.

g _e_ t _i_ n t _o_ t r _o_ _u_ b l _e_

a b ___ c ___ m ___ r ___ c h

b g ___ ___ b r ___ ___ d

c c h ___ n g e s c h ___ ___ l s

d m ___ v ___

e t ___ k ___ ___ g ___ p y ___ ___ r

f s t ___ r t y ___ ___ r ___ w n b ___ s ___ n ___ s s

g b ___ w ___ d ___ w ___ d

2 Match the phrases with what the people say.

a [3] win an award

b [ ] settle down

c [ ] drop out of college

d [ ] have an accident

e [ ] go for a job interview

f [ ] retire

g [ ] make new friends

1 We're getting married next month. We've already bought a house.

2 What can you offer this company?

I'm very hard-working and I speak several languages.

3 And the winner of *Teenager of the Year* is Damien Arrowsmith.

4 I've moved into the house next door.

Would you like to come round for a coffee?

5 I'm only 19, but I've stopped going. Now I want to get a job and save some money to travel.

6 I'm 62 now. I've stopped working. I spend all my time in my garden.

7 What's wrong with your leg?

It's broken. I fell off my motorcycle.

3 Complete the sentences with the words in the box.

become rich change schools ~~go abroad~~ move start my own business take a gap year

I don't want to go to college here. I want to _go abroad_ to study, perhaps to the UK.

a I don't want to work for anyone. I want to ______________.

b My parents want to ______________ and live downtown. Then it will be much quicker for them to get to work.

c Some teenagers dream they can ______________ as famous musicians or sports stars.

d Two of her friends left the school, so she decided to ______________ too.

e When I leave school, I'm going to ______________ before I go to college.

GRAMMAR 1

Review: Simple Past / *used to*

1 Complete the sentences with the simple past form of the verbs in parentheses.

A lot of people in my class ___took___ a gap year before college. (take)

a She's very shy so she __________ new friends during her trip. (not make)

b The science teacher often __________ about rockets when we were in 8th grade. (talk)

c __________ Maria __________ about becoming famous before it came true? (dream)

d My little brother __________ into some serious trouble at school. (get)

e I __________ much about the trade on my first job interview. (not know)

f At what age __________ your grandparents __________? (retire)

2 Complete the questions and answers using the simple past form of the verbs in parentheses.

Q: Why ___did she get___ (she / get) so upset?
A: Because Eddie ___didn't invite___ (not invite) her to his party.

a **Q:** How much money ______________ (you / win)?
A: I ______________ (win) $500.

b **Q:** Why ______________ (you / be) late for school this morning?
A: I ______________ (not be) late. I ______________ (arrive) at eight fifteen.

c **Q:** When ______________ (they / break up)?
A: They ______________ (break up) about a year ago.

d **Q:** Where ______________ (he / lose) his cell phone?
A: He ______________ (leave) it on the bus, I think.

e **Q:** Why ______________ (you / take) the last chocolate cookie?
A: I ______________ (not take) it. Martin ______________ (take) it.

3 Underline the correct words.

We always **used to** / **didn't use to** go on vacation to Guatemala, but this summer we went to Peru.

a Caroline **used to** / **didn't use to** have long hair, but she had it cut last week.

b I **used to** / **didn't use to** like sports very much because I wasn't very good at it.

c There **used to** / **didn't use to** be a swimming pool here, but they built one last year.

d My parents **used to** / **didn't use to** hate camping, but they love it now.

e One hundred years ago, most women **used to** / **didn't use to** go to college or work outside the home.

4 When his family moved from Los Angeles to a village near the sea, Chris' life changed a lot. Complete the sentences using *used to* and *didn't use to*.

Before Chris ...	Now Chris ...
lived in a small apartment on a busy street	lives in a big house with a garden
had a small room with a view of a parking lot	has a big room with a view of the sea
met his friends at the shopping mall	meets his friends at the beach
spent all his free time playing computer games	spends all his free time surfing

He ___used to live___ in a small apartment on a busy street.
He ___didn't use to live___ in a big house with a garden.

a He ______________ a small room with a view of a parking lot.
He ______________ a big room with a view of the sea.

b He ______________ his friends at the beach.
He ______________ his friends at the shopping mall.

c He spends all his free time surfing now, but he ______________ all his free time playing computer games.

5 Write questions using *used to* and the words in parentheses.

(you / get) into trouble a lot when you were young?
Did you use to get into trouble a lot when you were young?

a (people / spend) more time cooking 20 years ago?
______
______

b What (you / do) in your free time when you were a teenager, Grandma?
______
______

c (your / brother) annoy you when he was younger?
______
______

d Where (you / go) to school before you moved to this town?
______
______

e What (you / watch) on TV when you were six years old?
______
______

6 Complete the dialogue with *used to* + the verbs in parentheses.

Grandma I was born here 93 years ago. It ___used to be___ (be) much quieter here in those days. It was a village, not a town, and there weren't many cars. Do you know, even the police officer **a** ______ (ride) a bike.

Ellie What **b** ______ (you / do) in your free time? **c** ______ (you / watch TV)?

Grandma Oh no, dear. We didn't have a television. But we sometimes **d** ______ (go) to the movie theater in Salinas. They **e** ______ (show) lovely black and white movies. Nice and romantic!

Ellie What kind of music **f** ______ (you / listen to), Grandma?

Grandma Well, people didn't have those things you put in your ears.

Ellie You mean ear phones?

Grandma Yes, dear. We just **g** ______ (listen) to the radio. And I **h** ______ (spend) a lot of time talking to my friend May.

Ellie On the phone?

Grandma No, no, dear. People didn't use those horrible cell phone things. We **i** ______ (visit) each other's houses.

7 Complete the text with the correct form of the verbs in parentheses. Use the simple past or *used to* + verb.

Lily Thompson ___was___ (be) a millionaire in the first half of the 20th century. She **a** ______ (live) in a big apartment in the middle of New York. She **b** ______ (not drive) because her chauffeur **c** ______ (drive) her everywhere. She **d** ______ (go) to Italy and France on vacation and she **e** ______ (wear) designer clothes. She **f** ______ (not work) and she **g** ______ (not have) any money worries. But things **h** ______ (not be) always like this for Lily. Before being a millionaire, she **i** ______ (work) in a café as a waitress. She **j** ______ (buy) cheap clothes and she **k** ______ (not go) abroad for her vacations. So when **l** ______ (things / change) for Lily? One day in 1926, a customer in her café **m** ______ (not have) enough money to give Lily a tip so he **n** ______ (give) her a race ticket instead. That lucky ticket **o** ______ (win) Lily a million dollars and **p** ______ (change) her life forever.

VOCABULARY 2

Verb + Preposition

1 Underline the correct phrase.

Some people always **argue about** / **dream about** being rich and famous one day.

a We always **wait for** / **look forward to** our camping trip during summer vacation.

b I don't **argue with** / **agree with** you about this, but we can still be friends.

c I need to **listen to** / **talk to** you about something important.

d Don't **worry about** / **dream about** Karen's health. I am sure she will be better tomorrow.

e Do you want to **depend on** / **participate in** an exciting new project?

2 Complete the sentences with the prepositions in the box.

about on ~~to~~ to to with

My mother loves listening ___to___ music.

a I usually agree ________ my best friend about most things.

b She's a great person to have on the team. You can always depend ________ her.

c I'm looking forward ________ seeing you next weekend.

d My brother always worries ________ school tests.

e When I'm worried I sometimes talk ________ my aunt Alice.

3 Match the phrases with what the people say.

a [4] agree with someone

b [ ] argue about something

c [ ] depend on someone

d [ ] dream about something

e [ ] look forward to something

f [ ] participate in something

g [ ] wait for someone

h [ ] worry about someone

1 I'd love to sail around the world in my own boat one day.

2 I have tickets for the concert on Saturday. It's going to be great!

3 It was really interesting.
No, it wasn't. It was really boring!

4 That book was really terrible.
Yep, you're totally right.

5 There's an athletics meet tomorrow. I'm going to be in it because I'm on our school athletics team.

6 We need you on the team. We can't succeed without you.

7 Where is she? It's 4:20 and I got here at 4pm. She's late!

8 Why does he want to climb that mountain? It's very dangerous. He might fall.

4 Complete the sentences with the phrases in the box.

agree about argue with depend on ~~dream about~~ talk to wait for worry about

I often ___dream about___ learning to fly a plane.

a If I'm staying out late, I call my parents so they don't ______________ me.

b If you're late, I'll ______________ you – but only for 15 minutes.

c We have the same taste in music so we always ______________ which bands are the best.

d He always does what he says he will do. We can ______________ him.

e I don't want to ______________ the teacher about that test. I know I did very badly on it.

f When I ______________ my father about politics he always wins because he knows more facts.

GRAMMAR 2

Subject and Object Questions

1 Write if the underlined question words refer to the *subject* (S) or the *object* (O).

[O] Who did you see in the park?

a [ ] What did you buy at the store?

b [ ] What happened at the store?

c [ ] Who told you about the party?

d [ ] What do you usually have for breakfast?

e [ ] Who's making that noise?

f [ ] What makes you laugh?

g [ ] Who do you know in this picture?

2 Order the words to make questions. Write S if the question word is a *subject* and O if it is an *object*.

[O] about / did / talk / What / yesterday / you ?
What did you talk about yesterday?

a [ ] movie theater / outside / the / did / meet / Who / you ?

______

b [ ] bag / fell / just / now / out of / What / your ?

______

c [ ] does / family / in / the / usually / washing up / Who / your ?

______

d [ ] about / did / dream / last / night / What / you ?

______

e [ ] family / in / makes / most / noise / the / Who / your ?

______

f [ ] at the / movie / end / happened / of / that / What ?

______

g [ ] do / talk to / when / Who / worried / you / you're ?

______

3 Write *who* questions from these sentences.

You listened to someone.
Who did you listen to?

Someone spoke to you.
Who spoke to you?

a You looked at someone.

______

b Someone smiled at you.

______

c She waved at someone.

______

d He spoke to someone.

______

e Someone gave you that number.

______

f Someone stole the money.

______

4 Write *what* questions from these sentences.

He took something out of that bag.
What did he take out of that bag?

a Something happened on the way to school.

______

b She bought something from the store.

______

c He is hiding something from us.

______

d Something frightened them.

______

e They are stealing something.

______

f Something fell out of the sky.

______

5 Write subject or object questions using *who* or *what* for the underlined information.

Picasso painted *Guernica*.
Who painted *Guernica*?

Picasso painted *Guernica*.
What did Picasso paint?

a Shakespeare wrote *Hamlet*.

______

b Shakespeare wrote *Hamlet*.

______

c Walt Disney created Mickey Mouse.

______

d Walt Disney created Mickey Mouse.

______

e Mark Zuckerberg started Facebook.

______

f Mark Zuckerberg started Facebook.

______

GRAMMAR CHECK

1 Read the text and circle the correct answers.

Even when he was a young child, Ben Adams **a** ______ surfing and skateboarding. He was also very interested in fashion and **b** ______ designing his own surfing and skating clothes. When he was only 15, he **c** ______ a prize for his T-shirt designs, and during the summer, he **d** ______ to work for Fashion First in New York. At 16, he **e** ______ out of school and started his own clothes company, Skate and Surf. He is now 17 and a multimillionaire. We interviewed him at his home in Malibu, California.

What **f** ______ *when you dropped out of school?*
My mom was worried, but my dad wasn't.

What did your teachers say?
They **g** ______. I **h** ______ in all the classes except physical education.

Did you **i** ______ *to get into trouble?*
I'm afraid so, but the teachers all like me now!

What **j** ______ *when you left school?*
I missed being with my friends at first, but now I have a new bunch of friends.

	A	B	C
a	loves	loved	was loving
b	enjoyed	did enjoy	enjoys
c	wind	winning	won
d	used to go	was going	went
e	was dropping	used to drop	dropped
f	did you happen	happening	happened
g	didn't care	cared not	didn't use to care
h	dreamt	dream	used to dream
i	use	used	usually
j	did you miss	you missed	you do miss

2 Listen and check your answers.

1

LISTENING

1 Listen to a radio show. Check (✓) the things you hear about.

2

- [✓] problems at school
- [ ] moving
- [ ] arguments with parents
- [ ] surfing
- [ ] changing schools
- [ ] starting a business
- [ ] traveling
- [ ] New Year's Eve
- [ ] the internet
- [ ] writing newspaper articles
- [ ] working in a restaurant
- [ ] teaching children

2 Order these events in Eddie's life. Number them 1 to 10. Be careful! There are two extra events which did not happen.

2

a [ ] He applied to college.
b [1] He argued with his parents about school work.
c [ ] He dropped out of school.
d [ ] He flew to Australia.
e [ ] He got a job at a surf shop.
f [ ] He opened his own restaurant.
g [ ] He put an advertisement in a local newspaper.
h [ ] He started giving surf lessons in Carmel.
i [ ] He started to earn $200 a day.
j [ ] He worked in a restaurant.
k [ ] His parents stopped speaking to him.
l [ ] The bank agreed to lend him money.

EXTENSION

Underline the correct words to complete the text.

Bethany Hamilton was born in Hawaii in 1990 and **a grew up / was growing up** near the ocean. Young Bethany **b used to spend / was spending** all her time in the water and she **c used to learn / learned** to surf before she could walk.

At the age of eight, she **d starts / started** to compete seriously. By the time she was 12, she was the world's number two under-eighteen surfer. She **e was planning / is planning** to become a professional and her sponsors **f were helping / help** her with her plan.

Then at the age of 13, Bethany's life **g changed / was changing** forever. She **h surfed / was surfing** off the Hawaiian island of Kauai with her friend Alana Blanchard and Alana's brother and father. Bethany **i had / was having** a rest. She **j was lying / is lying** on her surfboard with her arms hanging in the water. Suddenly a shark **k attacked / was attacking** her and **l used to pull / pulled** her left arm off just under her shoulder. Her friends helped her get back to the shore, but Bethany **m lost / was losing** 60% of her blood. She **n was / is** lucky to be alive today.

But Bethany **o didn't give up / doesn't give up** surfing. She told reporters that she had to work on her fear of sharks and that she sometimes still **p gets / is getting** scared. But one year after the attack, she **q was starting / started** competing again. Today she **r surfed / surfs** in world championships and **s was winning / wins** prizes. She also **t helps / helped** other victims of shark attacks through her charity, Friends of Bethany. She **u wrote / writes** her story, *Soul Surfer*, in 2004. There's also a movie of the book, but Bethany **v doesn't star / wasn't starring** in it.

VOCABULARY PLUS

College Degrees

1 ____________

2 ____________

3 ____________

4 ____________

5 ____________

6 ____________

7 ____________

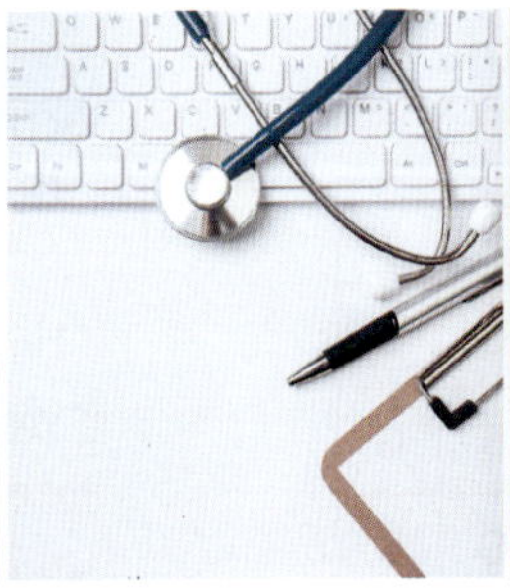
8 ____________

9 ____________

10 ____________

1 Label the pictures with the words in the box. Then listen and repeat.

3

architecture	law
business	media studies
computer science	medicine
engineering	nursing
fine art	teacher training

2 Underline the correct words.

She wanted to be a journalist so she studied **medicine** / **media studies**.

- **a** You learn how to design buildings when you get **a law** / **an architecture** degree.
- **b** If you enjoy looking after sick people, why don't you get a degree in **engineering** / **nursing**?
- **c** My dad loved designing machines so he studied **engineering** / **business**.
- **d** I'm terrible at drawing so I'd never get a **fine art** / **computer science** degree.
- **e** Jack loves reading about famous criminals and their cases. He should study **teacher training** / **law**.

3 What degree should they get? Write the correct words.

My brother wants to be a nurse.
nursing

- **a** My sister wants to be a doctor.
____
- **b** I'd like to start my own business.
____
- **c** My best friend would like to be a teacher.
____
- **d** My cousin is interested in working in TV.
____
- **e** My neighbor is always on his computer writing new programs.
____

4 Complete the sentences for you. Try to use words from activity 1.

- **a** I'd love to study
____
- **b** I wouldn't like to get a degree in
____
- **c** A lot of people in my school are going to study
____

2

INCREDIBLE JOURNEYS

VOCABULARY 1

Travel

1 Find ten words related to travel in the word search.

T	P	O	S	T	C	A	R	D	S	Y
R	A	C	Z	I	R	D	Z	H	Q	O
A	E	B	X	Q	F	V	U	R	S	G
I	Q	G	U	I	D	E	B	O	O	K
N	G	N	G	J	O	N	M	A	U	B
A	R	R	I	V	E	T	B	C	V	M
P	A	C	K	O	P	U	B	O	E	X
O	V	S	T	T	Z	R	W	B	N	E
K	I	U	S	L	T	E	P	U	I	S
S	U	I	T	C	A	S	E	S	R	X
J	O	U	R	N	E	Y	L	K	S	K

2 Match a-h with 1-8 to make travel phrases.

a send	**1** a journey
b buy	**2** a bus
c come back	**3** a suitcase
d get off	**4** a guidebook
e have	**5** home
f meet	**6** adventures
g pack	**7** people
h plan	**8** postcards

3 Complete the sentences with the words in the box.

adventures guidebook journey ~~people~~ postcards suitcase train

Have you ever met nice ___people___ while you were camping?

a I always send ________ to my friends when I go on vacation.

b My sister always packs her ________ a week before she leaves!

c I need to buy a ________ so I can plan my trip.

d We got on the ________ at nine this morning.

e You have to plan your ________ before you leave.

f We had a lot of ________ when we traveled around India.

4 Match the travel phrases in the box with the sentences.

arrive buy souvenirs have adventures ~~meet people~~ set off plan a journey

"Hi. Do you speak English?"
"Yes, I am Australian! Do you need help?"
meet people

a I have my passport, ticket, and money. Now I must go. Goodbye, everyone.

____

b Let's fly to Rome. Then we can get the train to Bari. From there we can get a boat to Patras, in Greece.

____

c Let's get a T-shirt that says I LOVE LONDON and a statue of Big Ben!

____

d On one Greek island there wasn't any room in the hostel, so we slept on the beach.

____

e That was a long journey, but we're here now. Fantastic!

____

GRAMMAR 1

Review: Present Perfect and Simple Past

1 Write SP for *simple past* or PP for *present perfect* next to each sentence.

[PP] Kim has gone to China.

a [ ] He went three weeks ago.
b [ ] Karen lived in Paris from 2001 to 2018.
c [ ] Karen didn't enjoy her time there.
d [ ] She's told me a lot about those years.
e [ ] Have you ever lived outside of Europe?
f [ ] I've traveled all around the world.
g [ ] I haven't been to South America.
h [ ] Where did you go for your last vacation?

2 Write pairs of sentences using the present perfect and the simple past form of the verbs in parentheses.

Luis ___has lost___ (lose) his glasses. (present perfect)

He ___left___ (leave) them on the bus yesterday. (simple past)

a **1** You ______________ (change)! (present perfect)

2 You ______________ (have) long hair the last time I saw you. (simple past)

b **1** Maria ______________ (break) her leg. (present perfect)

2 She ______________ (do) it on her skiing vacation last month. (simple past)

c **1** My parents ______________ (buy) a new car. (present perfect)

2 They ______________ (get) it yesterday. (simple past)

d **1** They ______________ (paint) the house. (present perfect)

2 Adam ______________ (choose) all the colors. (simple past)

e **1** We ______________ (write) a letter to Sylvia. (present perfect)

2 We ______________ (send) it this morning. (simple past)

f **1** I ______________ (spend) all my allowance. (present perfect)

2 I ______________ (buy) lots of new clothes during the weekend. (simple past)

3 Underline the correct words.

I've never **been** / **gone** to Switzerland. What's it like?

a Where's Tom **been** / **gone**?
b How many times have you **been** / **gone** to Segovia?
c Have you **been** / **gone** to the Guggenheim Museum in Bilbao?
d They're having a fantastic time in Australia. They've **been** / **gone** for six months.
e Vicki isn't here. She's **been** / **gone** to the movies with her friends.
f I'm at home on my own. Everyone's **been** / **gone** for a walk by the river.

4 Circle the correct answers.

I ______ to Italy last summer.

1 have been **2** (went) **3** have gone

a They ______ that dog for about three months.

1 had **2** hasn't had **3** have had

b "Did you get those jeans for your birthday?"

"Yes, I ______ ."

1 have **2** did **3** did get

c "Do you like duck?" "I don't know. I ______ it."

1 never ate **3** didn't eat
2 've never eaten

d "Has Jen learnt the vocabulary for her test yet?"

"No, she ______ ."

1 haven't **2** didn't **3** hasn't

e Sue can drive us to the airport. She ______ her test yesterday.

1 did pass **2** has passed **3** passed

5 **Write questions using the present perfect or the simple past.**

What time ___did you go___ (you / go) to bed yesterday?

___Has Mark already finished___ (Mark / already / finish) reading that long book?

a (they / meet) any nice people on their last vacation?

______

b What (Jen / say) to you last Tuesday?

______

c How many times (Lily / lose) her glasses this week?

______

d Where (you / buy) those amazing shoes?

______

e How long (you / know) your friend Carmen?

______

f (Josie / call) you at four o'clock?

______

g How much money (they / raise) since March?

______

h (Lucy / ever / go) to New York?

______

6 **Complete the dialogues with the present perfect or the simple past form of the verbs in parentheses.**

Beth ___Have you ever been___ (you ever be) to Italy?
John Yes, we **a** ______ (have) a vacation in Pisa three years ago.
Beth **b** ______ (you / fly) there?
John No, we **c** ______ (drive).

Liz Where's Ben? **d** ______ (you / see) him anywhere?
Pete Yes, he **e** ______ (go) to the gym five minutes ago.
Liz What about Luke?
Pete I don't know. I **f** ______ (not see) him since lunchtime.

Ann Do you know Penny's brother?
Jim I **g** ______ (see) him a few times at parties, but I **h** ______ (never speak) to him. **i** ______ (you / ever / talk) to him?
Ann Yes. I **j** ______ (meet) him after the game on Saturday. He's really nice.

7 **Write questions for the answers. Only use the present perfect or the simple past.**

___Have you ever been to Berlin?___

Yes, I have, once.

a ______

At four o'clock.

b ______

No, I haven't.

c ______

Yesterday.

d ______

Since Monday.

e ______

For three years.

f ______

No, never.

g ______

Two months ago.

h ______

No, he didn't.

VOCABULARY 2

Extreme Adjectives

1 Complete the extreme adjectives with the vowels. Then match them with the normal adjectives in the box.

bad big cold frightening ~~good~~ happy hot small tired

a m a z i n g — good

a ___ w f ___ l ______

b b ___ ___ l ___ n g ______

c d ___ l ___ g h t ___ d ______

d ___ n ___ r m ___ ___ s ______

e ___ x h ___ ___ s t ___ d ______

f f r ___ ___ z ___ n g ______

g t ___ r r ___ f y ___ n g ______

h t ___ n y ______

2 Circle the correct words.

Can we open the window? It's … in here!

1 (boiling) **3** tiny
2 freezing

a It's a movie about a man who kills people. It's … ! Don't go and see it.
1 enormous **3** terrifying
2 tiny

b Can you lend me a sweater and a hat, please? I'm …
1 enormous **3** tiny
2 freezing

c My parents gave my little sister a puppy for her birthday. She's … with it.
1 terrifying **3** awful
2 delighted

d My feet are much bigger than yours. I can't wear these … shoes of yours!
1 awful **3** freezing
2 tiny

e You look … Why don't you go to bed early tonight?
1 delighted **3** exhausted
2 amazing

f This book is … You'll love it.
1 amazing **3** delighted
2 awful

3 Complete the sentences with the correct extreme adjectives from activity 1.

It's ___boiling___ today. The temperature is about 40°C.

a She was ______ when she received two free tickets to the concert.

b I wrote the number on a ______ bit of paper and now I can't find it.

c We can't camp in Scotland in the middle of winter. It will be ______.

d Look at the size of that elephant. It's ______.

e Our vacation in Greece was ______. I loved it and I want to go back next year.

f We were swimming near the boat when we saw a shark. The shark was ______.

g The cake and the flowers are for me? Really? That's so lovely. Thank you so much. I'm ______.

h The average temperature in January in Novosibirsk, Siberia's largest city, is -24°C. It's ______.

i The average temperature in August in Jeddah, Saudi Arabia, is 40°C. It's ______.

j The Leshan statue of Buddha in China is 71 meters high. His shoulders are 28 meters wide. It's ______.

k While we were on the boat, there was a storm. The waves were eight meters high. People were crying. It was ______.

l The world's smallest monkey is the pygmy marmoset. Adults are only about 11cm long and weigh 120 grams. They are ______.

GRAMMAR 2

Review: Quantity and Uncountable Nouns

1 Write C for *countable* or U for *uncountable* next to the nouns.

[U] tea

a [ ] money
b [ ] water
c [ ] candy
d [ ] people
e [ ] information
f [ ] space
g [ ] socks
h [ ] noise
i [ ] fruit
j [ ] ideas

2 Complete the questions with *much* or *many*.

Health Quiz

How ___much___ *fruit do you eat a week?*
How **a** ________ *hours of sleep do you get a night?*
How **b** ________ *time do you spend in front of the TV?*
How **c** ________ *glasses of water do you drink a day?*
How **d** ________ *times a day do you clean your teeth?*
How **e** ________ *sport do you do a week?*
How **f** ________ *tea or coffee do you drink a day?*

3 Match the sentence beginnings with the endings.

a [5] I can't make this cake because there isn't
b [ ] We went to the beach, but there wasn't
c [ ] The doctor says I mustn't drink
d [ ] You can have a party, but please don't invite too
e [ ] There are a lot of boys in this class, but there are only
f [ ] There were a lot of potatoes, but there was only
g [ ] There aren't any potatoes, but there is

1 a lot of meat.
2 a little meat.
3 many people.
4 much sun.
5 any butter.
6 a few girls.
7 a lot of coffee.

4 Complete the sentences with *much*, *many*, *a little*, or *a few*.

Let's put ___a few___ olives on this pizza.

a I'm not very sporty, but I like to do ________ exercise every day.

b Let's buy ________ apples for the picnic. I usually eat one after lunch.

c Don't eat too ________ candy. It's bad for you.

d I can't get her an expensive present because I don't have ________ money.

5 Circle the correct answers.

There wasn't ______ space in the car for our bags.
1 many **2** some **3** (much)

a There are just ______ vegetables in the fridge.
1 a few **2** a little **3** any

b Do you have ______ good ideas about raising money?
1 a little **2** any **3** much

c We saw ______ beautiful birds near the coast.
1 a little **2** some **3** any

d Did you buy ______ fruit at the market?
1 a lot of **2** many **3** a few

e Jack didn't know ______ people at the party.
1 much **2** many **3** a little

f We need ______ information about train times.
1 much **2** a few **3** some

6 Write true sentences about you, your friends, your family, or your home.

___My sister___ doesn't eat any ___fish___.
___I___ have just bought some ___new computer games___.

a ________ doesn't eat any ________.

b ________ have just bought some ________.

c We only have a few ________.

d There is only a little ________.

e ________ don't have much ________.

f ________ doesn't have many ________.

GRAMMAR CHECK

1 Read the text and circle the correct answers.

I **a** ______ to South America three times in my life. Last year, we **b** ______ to Argentina. We **c** ______ to dance the tango in Buenos Aires and bought **d** ______ souvenirs at San Telmo. We **e** ______ La Recoleta cemetery and found the tombs of **f** ______ famous people. Then we **g** ______ the sunset at Palermo. Mar del Plata was amazing, but we didn't spend **h** ______ time there. We only saw **i** ______ seals there, but we'll stay longer next time. What **j** ______ when you went to Argentina?

	1	2	3
a	went	were	have been
b	went	were	have been
c	were learning	learned	have learned
d	a lot	lot of	a lot of
e	have visited	visited	were visiting
f	some	any	much
g	watched	were watching	have watched
h	a lot	some	much
i	a few	a little	not much
j	did you	did you do	have you done

2 Listen and check your answers.

4

LISTENING

1 Listen to Melissa talking about her trip and check (✓) the things she still needs to do.

5

- ☐ book her flight
- ☐ pay for her ticket
- ☐ collect her ticket
- ☐ arrange travel insurance
- ☐ get her vaccinations
- ☐ decide which clothes to take
- ☐ buy a sun hat
- ☐ buy a new backpack
- ☐ pack her backpack
- ☐ order *pesos* and US dollars
- ☐ collect her money from the bank
- ☐ buy a mosquito net

2 Listen again and answer the questions.

5

a What does Melissa have to get on Monday?

____

b What did she buy when she paid for her ticket?

____

c What did she do the day before yesterday?

____

d What does she need to buy before she starts packing?

____

e What has she ordered from the bank?

____

f What cities is she staying in, in Mexico?

____

g What isn't she going to buy for space reasons?

____

EXTENSION

Circle the correct words to complete the text.

Karl Bushby **a** **started / was starting** walking around the world on November 1, 1998, and he is still **b** **walk / walking**. He **c** **has already walked / already walked** through South, Central, and North America. He is the first person who has **d** **ever / never** crossed the Bering Strait from Alaska to Russia on foot. Around the Bering Strait, he **e** **has become / became** terrified of polar bears. They **f** **attack often / often attack** humans when they are hungry. Luckily, they didn't **g** **tried / try** to get into his tent at night when he was camping there.

However, according to Bushby, the Bering Strait wasn't **h** **more / as** terrifying as the Darien Gap, the tropical jungle between Colombia and Panama. He says the Darien Gap was **i** **more frightening / the most frightening** than any other place. While he was **j** **walked / walking** through the jungle there, he needed to hide from local guerrilla wars. At one point, he was **k** **more / too** frightened to walk, so he swam down a river full of alligators for **l** **a few / a little** days.

Bushby **m** **gets / has gotten** fitter since he started his walk. And he says walking has made him **n** **more ambitious / most ambitious** and more responsible. He loves **o** **spend / spending** time in the world's wildest places. But he has been lonely **p** **many / some** of the time. So walking has taught him **q** **a lot / some** things about his most important friendships and relationships.

Bushby **r** **isn't / doesn't** walking for a special reason. He doesn't **s** **want / wants** to get rich from it or make money for charity. Apparently, every day people in cars offer him lifts, and every day he **t** **says / is saying** "No, thank you."

VOCABULARY PLUS

Health Problems and Cures

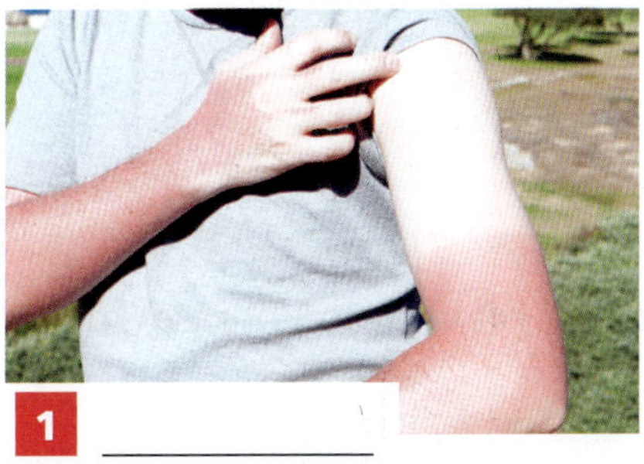
1 ___________

2 ___________

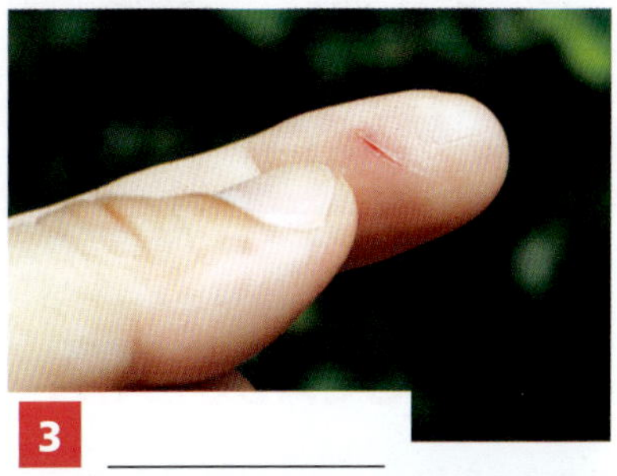
3 ___________

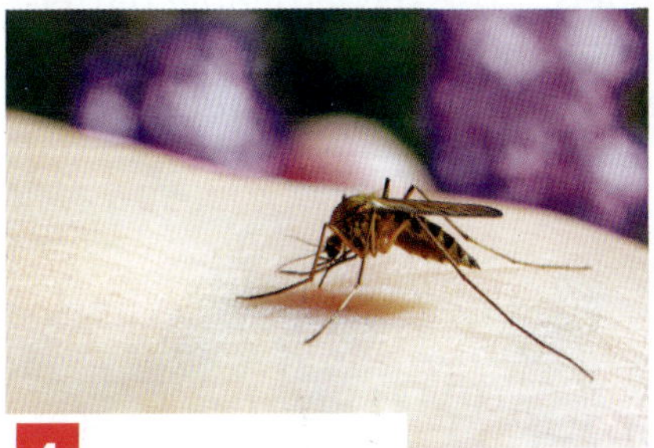
4 ___________

5 ___________

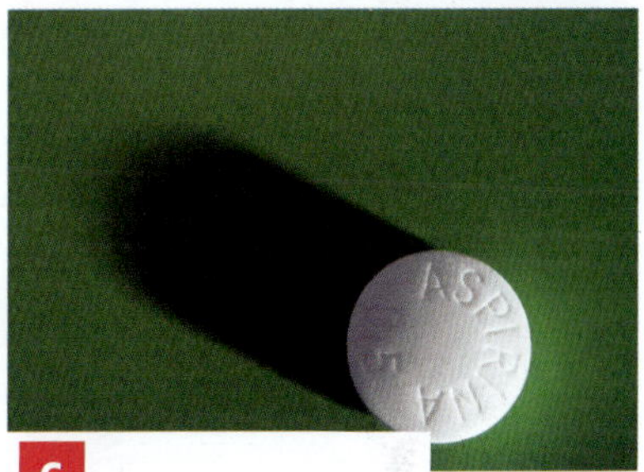
6 ___________

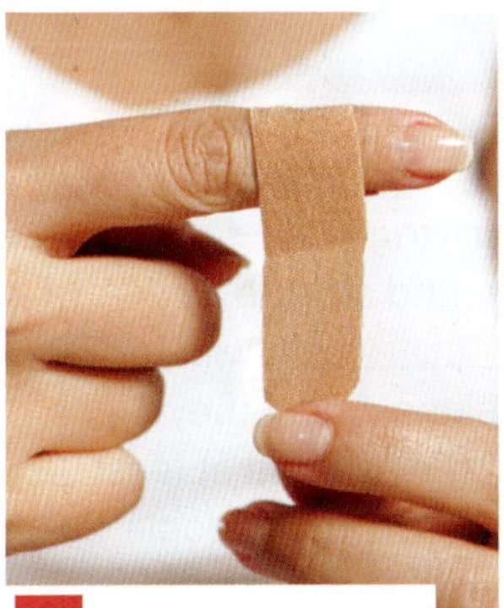
7 ___________

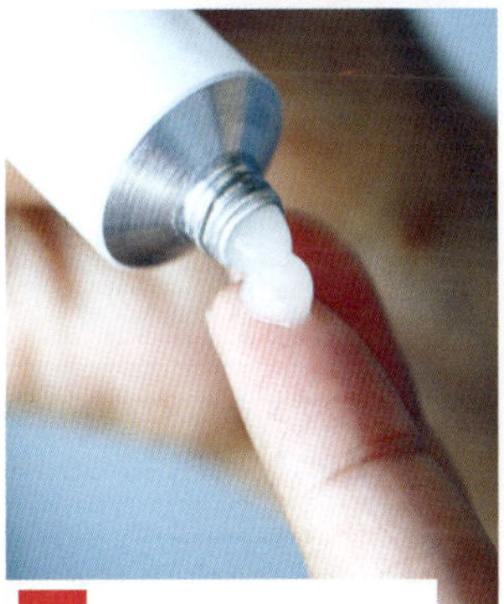
8 ___________

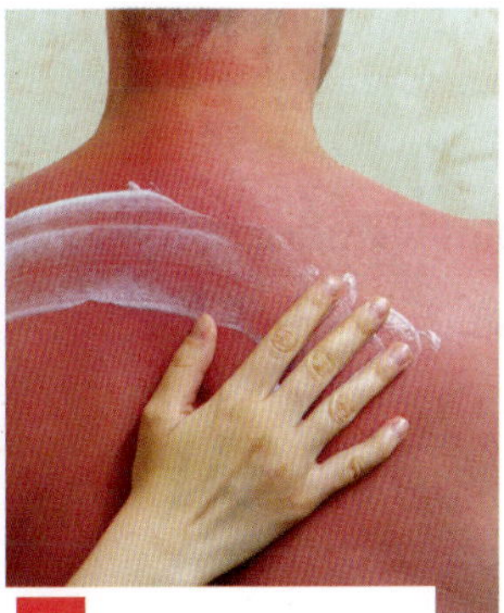
9 ___________

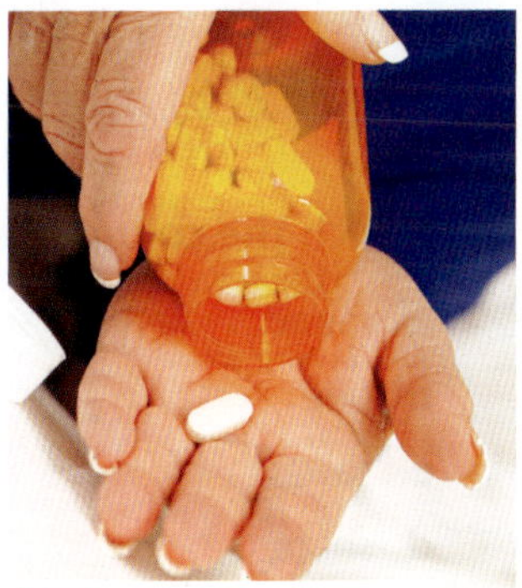
10 ___________

1 Listen to the words in the box. Then label the pictures with them.
6

a bandage	aspirin
a cut	an insect bite
a migraine	antiseptic cream
a motion sickness pill	sunburn
after sun lotion	motion sickness

2 Match the treatments a-d with the health problems in activity 1.

[4] antiseptic cream

a [ ] a motion sickness pill

b [ ] after sun lotion

c [ ] a bandage

d [ ] aspirin

3 Circle the correct words.

Turn the music down! I've got a terrible **insect bite** / **migraine**.

a If you spend a long time in the sun, you'll get a **cut** / **sunburn**.

b I take a **motion sickness pill** / **aspirin** because I always feel sick on planes.

c He woke up and he had four **insect bites** / **motion sickness** on his face.

d Take some **antiseptic cream** / **aspirin** and you'll feel better!

e Do you have any **after sun lotion** / **bandages**? I have a cut on my finger.

3

THE WORLD AROUND US

VOCABULARY 1

Saving Environmental Resources

1 Find five environment phrases in the word snake.

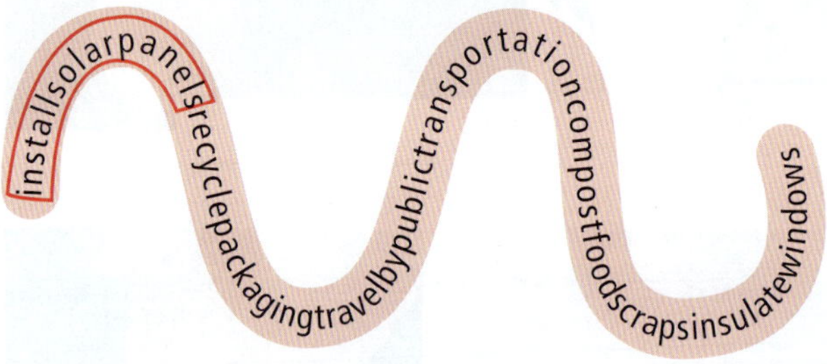

2 Match the columns to make phrases.

a	mend	a bike
b	ride	car journeys
c	save	old clothes
d	share	the lights
e	turn off	rechargeable batteries
f	use	water

3 Match the sentences a-f with the instructions 1-6.

a Don't throw them away.
b It's good for your health and for the planet.
c It's very good for the garden.
d We need to save electricity.
e Turn off the faucet.
f You'll save on central heating.

1 [d] Turn off the lights.
2 [ ] Compost your food scraps.
3 [ ] Mend your old clothes.
4 [ ] Insulate windows.
5 [ ] We need to save water.
6 [ ] Ride a bike.

4 Complete the text with the phrases in the box.

install solar panels   use rechargeable batteries   recycle packaging   share car journeys   ~~travel by public transportation~~

People should stop driving their own cars everywhere and start to _travel by public transportation_. It will reduce carbon emissions. And if they don't want to do that, they should at least **a** ____________ with people who work in the same area. We should all **b** ____________ in our cameras and phones. And in houses which get a lot of sun on the roof, it's a good idea to **c** ____________. Finally, we shouldn't throw away so much paper, plastic, and glass. The answer to that is to **d** ____________.

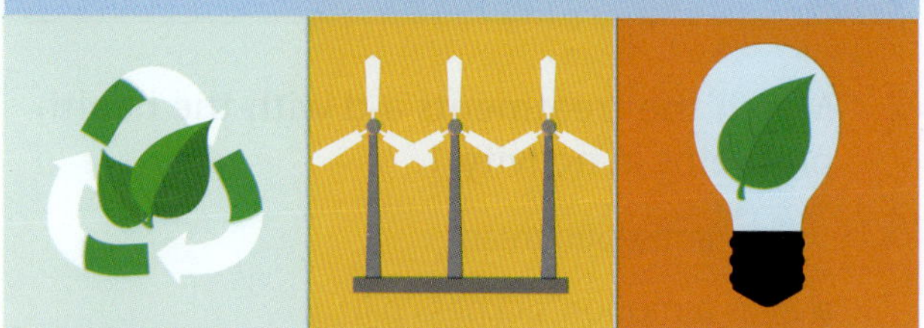

GRAMMAR 1

Review: Present Perfect + *for, since, how long*

1 Match the sentence beginnings with the endings. Then write sentences in the present perfect using *for* or *since*.

a [2] I (not see) a good movie
b [ ] We (know) each other
c [ ] The European Union (exist)
d [ ] Kate (have) a driver's license
e [ ] There (be) life on Earth
f [ ] You (be) sick with that cough
g [ ] Michael (work) in environmental projects

1 1993.
2 I saw *The Descendants 2*.
3 millions of years.
4 she was 17.
5 three days now.
6 two years.
7 we were in primary school.

a I haven't seen a good movie since I saw *The Descendants 2.*
b ______________________________
c ______________________________
d ______________________________
e ______________________________
f ______________________________
g ______________________________

2 Write questions with *how long* and answers with *for* or *since*.

Q: you / have / a compost bin?
A: six months
Q: How long have you had a compost bin?
A: I've had a compost bin for six months.

a
Q: she / know / how to make her own clothes?
A: 2014
Q: ______________________________
A: ______________________________

b
Q: you / be / interested in environmental issues
A: I was 11
Q: ______________________________
A: ______________________________

c
Q: he / work / at the recycling center?
A: the past few months
Q: ______________________________
A: ______________________________

d
Q: they / had / solar panels?
A: last month
Q: ______________________________
A: ______________________________

3 Complete the email using the present perfect form of the verbs in parentheses.

From: Amy
To: Rob
Subject: Life in the country

Dear Rob,
I'm sorry I haven't written (not write) for a few months. I **a** __________ (be) very busy since our move to the country. Since we arrived, we **b** __________ (install) solar panels on our roof ourselves, and we **c** __________ (insulate) all our windows. For the past few weeks, I **d** __________ (spend) a lot of time working in the garden. I **e** __________ (plant) a lot of vegetable seeds since the weather got warmer. We **f** __________ (have) a compost heap for a year now, which is really useful (that's me working on it in the picture!). But life on our little farm is very hard work. I **g** __________ (not see) a good movie for over six months and I **h** __________ (not be) on vacation for a year. **i** __________ (you / see) Peter since Thanksgiving? I **j** __________ (not hear) from him for a very long time. If you see him, say hi from me. Write soon!
Amy

4 Underline the correct words.

I **have made** / **made** pancakes for breakfast yesterday.

a **Have you found** / **Did you find** your glasses yet?

b **You've never met** / **You never met** my cousin from Canada.

c When **have you got** / **did you get** back from your vacation?

d We **have already bought** / **already bought** food for the picnic.

e Who **have you danced** / **did you dance** with at the party?

f Oh no! Somebody **has stolen** / **stole** my cell phone.

5 Write sentences using the present perfect and *for* or *since*.

a this school / be / at / three years / I
I've been at this school for three years.

b work / at / Gavin / the recycling center / 2017

c your grandparents / not / you / two months / see

d on vacation / go / Geraldine / ten days

e have / I / three years / my computer

f emails / not / I / two weeks / check

g live / 2015 / Ontario / Susie / in

h play / Alice / the electric bass / eight years

i the country / work / Ronan / 2010 / in

j eat / Fran / she was twelve / meat / not

6 Complete the texts using the present perfect or simple past form of the verbs in parentheses.

Joey lives in Sweden now. He has lived (live) there for a year. Before that he **a** ________ (live) in Norway. He **b** ________ (work) there for two years, but he **c** ________ (not / like) it very much. He **d** ________ (think) the weather was too cold.

Martin Do you know Carmen's sister?

Rob I **e** ________ (see) her at the gym a few times, but I **f** ________ (never / speak) to her. What about you? **g** ________ (you / ever / speak) to her?

Martin Yes. I **h** ________ (meet) her at a party two weeks ago. We **i** ________ (dance) together. It **j** ________ (be) fun.

Rob That's cool! I think Carmen **k** ________ (invite) me to this party, but I **l** ________ (not go) because it **m** ________ (be) my brother's birthday.

Emily **n** ________ (you / ever / be) to Rome?

Nick Yes, I **o** ________ (go) there on vacation last year.

Emily **p** ________ (you / have) fun?

Nick Yes, we **q** ________ (have) a great time. I **r** ________ (not be) to Florence, though. I'd like to go there this year.

VOCABULARY 2

Prefixes

1 Find seven verbs with prefixes in the word search beside.

M	I	S	P	L	A	C	E	T	R	M
Z	H	G	L	X	E	M	R	K	D	L
S	I	E	K	J	E	W	I	T	O	G
I	R	E	C	Y	C	L	E	W	V	P
B	B	Y	O	V	M	E	E	S	E	R
K	F	F	K	F	O	G	F	X	R	U
U	N	D	E	R	C	O	O	K	C	J
N	Z	W	G	X	J	C	T	N	R	D
U	N	D	E	R	P	A	Y	A	O	Z
O	V	E	R	E	A	T	E	A	W	K
R	E	P	L	A	C	E	P	G	D	B

2 Order the letters and write the words with prefixes.

mis + f r o m i n misinform

a over + l e t a p o u p ______

b re + y a l p ______

c under + e u s ______

d re + a g r i z o n e ______

e mis + d u n e r d a n t s ______

f under + a m i s e t t e ______

3 Complete the crossword using the clues and the words in the box.

misinform misplace ~~misunderstand~~ overcrowded overeat overpopulated recycle reorganize replace replay undercooked underestimate underpay underused

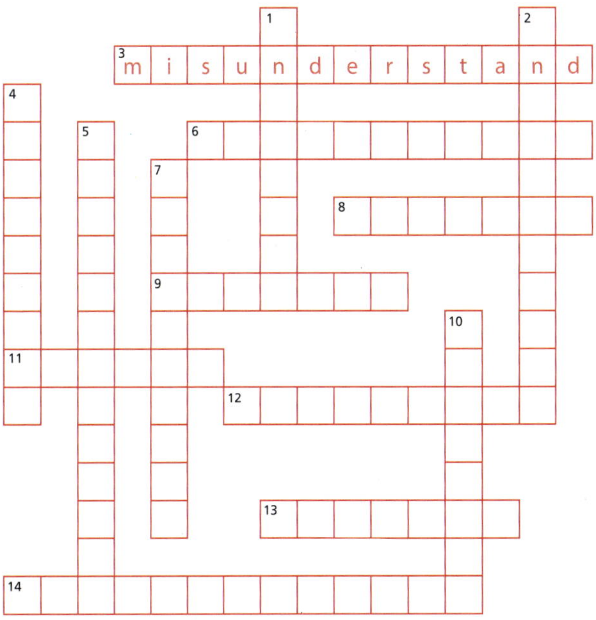

Across

3 I explained very clearly. Why did they misunderstand me?

6 Twelve of them live in a very small apartment. It's terribly ______.

8 I broke my mother's favorite vase. I want to ______ it with something similar.

9 Don't throw those bottles away. ______ them.

11 The game was a draw. They are going to ______ it next week.

12 They are going to shut down that gym. Nobody goes there. It is very ______.

13 Try not to ______. That is really harmful for your health.

14 Don't ______ him. He's very clever but he pretends to be stupid.

Down

1 The money is bad at that job. They always ______ their staff.

2 This meat is ______. Could you do it a little longer, please?

4 Check the facts on the internet. I don't want to ______ you.

5 There are too many people in this country. It's ______.

7 I need to ______ my cabinets. I can't find anything.

10 I don't often lose things so I hate it when I ______ something.

GRAMMAR 2

Review: Present Perfect + *still, yet, already, just*

1 Underline the correct words.

I haven't done the activity **yet** / **still**.

- **a** She has **just** / **still** put the leaves in the compost.
- **b** Have you recharged those batteries **still** / **yet**?
- **c** They haven't been to the recycling center **already** / **yet**.
- **d** You **still** / **already** haven't given me the tickets.
- **e** No more cake, thanks, I've **just** / **still** overeaten!
- **f** You've **still** / **already** told me that twice!

2 Write sentences in the present perfect using *still*, *yet*, *already*, and *just*.

already / Tim / leave?
Has Tim already left?

- **a** find / not / Peter / his keys / yet ______
- **b** already / they / meet / Luke ______
- **c** not / me / she / write / still / to ______
- **d** make / you / dinner / yet? ______
- **e** sort out / he / the garbage / just ______
- **f** the game / they / not / still / replay ______

3 The Jackson family want to be more environmentally friendly. Write sentences about their progress using *still* and *already*.

plant a vegetable garden (✓)
They've already planted a vegetable garden.

install solar panels (✗)
They still haven't installed solar panels.

- **a** insulate the windows (✓) ______
- **b** buy bikes (✓) ______
- **c** sell their car (✗) ______
- **d** read an organic gardening book (✓) ______
- **e** make a compost heap (✗) ______
- **f** get a container to catch rain water (✗) ______
- **g** start mending their old clothes (✓) ______
- **h** stop buying new clothes (✗) ______

4 Rewrite the *still* sentences in activity 3 using *yet*.

They still haven't installed solar panels.
They haven't installed solar panels yet.

- **a** ______
- **b** ______
- **c** ______
- **d** ______

5 You and a friend are planning a biking vacation. Write your questions using *yet* and your friend's answers using *still*, *yet*, *already*, and *just*.

Biking trip – things to do

buy the maps (already)
Have you bought the maps yet?
Yes, I've already bought them.

buy a tent (yet)
Have you bought a tent yet?
No, I haven't bought one yet.

- **a** plan the route (still) ______
- **b** choose the campsites (yet) ______
- **c** buy bike shorts (already) ______
- **d** check the bike lights (just) ______
- **e** practice changing a tire (still) ______

GRAMMAR CHECK

1 Read the text and circle the correct answers.

Two years ago my family **a** ______ to do something for the environment. First, we **b** ______ taking our own shopping bags to the supermarket so we **c** ______ to use the supermarket's plastic bags. Then we **d** ______ a compost heap in the garden for all our food waste. My parents **e** ______ their bikes to work for years. But to be even greener, they **f** ______ their car. We **g** ______ put solar panels on our roof, but we will soon. I haven't bought any new clothes **h** ______ a year but last week I **i** ______ half my clothes with a friend who's the same size as me. And since the beginning of the year my sister and I **j** ______ an environmental group raise money.

A	B	C
a decided	has decided	were deciding
b start	started	have started
c aren't needing	haven't needed	didn't need
d were building	built	have built
e were riding	have ridden	rode
f have just sold	were just selling	did just sell
g yet haven't	still haven't	just didn't
h since	for	yet
i was swapping	have swapped	swapped
j were helping	helped	have helped

2 Listen and check your answers.
7

LISTENING

1 Listen to four teenagers discussing environmental issues. Check (✓) the things you hear about.
8

- ☐ improving insulation
- ☐ nuclear accidents
- ☐ people wasting electricity
- ☐ rainfall
- ☐ rechargeable batteries
- ☐ reducing our garbage
- ☐ saving water
- ☐ solar energy
- ☐ the weather
- ☐ taking action
- ☐ the climate in the USA
- ☐ the need for better public transportation
- ☐ the need to recycle
- ☐ riding a bike

2 Listen again and complete the sentences with the correct names: Rawan, Jack, Anna, or Caleb.
8

a ________ isn't sure if using nuclear energy is a good idea.

b ________ says floods are caused by climate change.

c ________ says it's easy to cut our electricity use.

d ________ says nuclear power stations don't emit carbon.

e ________ thinks it's too late to do anything about climate change.

f ________ thinks nuclear energy is too dangerous to use.

g ________ thinks people should use their cars less.

h ________ thinks the government should invest in solar and wind energy.

EXTENSION

Underline the correct words to complete the text.

The United Nations Environment Programme **a has calculated / calculated** that there are 3,000 pieces of plastic waste per square kilometer of the world's oceans. And all this garbage **b was killing / is killing** birds and sea creatures. Plastic waste **c has caused / caused** the death of a million seabirds and 100,000 sea mammals last year. **d For / Since** the past ten years, scientists have found more and more cigarette lighters and toothbrushes inside the stomachs of dead seabirds. Seabirds **e had eaten / eat** these things because they think they are food and then they **f can't / couldn't** get rid of them.

Charles Moore, an American oceanographer, **g believes / is believing** there are now 100 million tonnes of plastic waste in the Pacific Ocean. Mr. Moore **h used to be / has been** a sailor and in 1997, while he **i sailed / was sailing** from Los Angeles to Hawaii in a yacht race, he found himself in a huge area of garbage. "I **j was moving / have moved** through garbage for a week," he said. **k Since / For** that time, he has become an environmental activist. The problem is that modern plastics **l are / were** not biodegradable. Plastic that got into the ocean 50 years ago **m still / yet** has not degraded.

The problem in the Mediterranean is very serious too. In a recent study of dead loggerhead turtles off the coast of Spain, 75% of them **n had swallowed / were swallowing** plastic bags. Why? Plastic bags **o are looking / look** like jellyfish, the favorite food of these endangered animals.

So what plastic things **p do people throw / throw people** away? Plastic bags, bottles, containers, golf balls, plates, knives, forks, toothbrushes, helmets, beach toys, syringes, and fishing lines is the short answer. And who **q does throw / throws** all this stuff away? We **r don't have / didn't have** any names. But please make sure it's not you.

VOCABULARY PLUS

Trees and Plants

1  ________

2  ________

3  ________

4  ________

5  ________

6  ________

7  ________

8  ________

9  ________

10  ________

1 Label the pictures with the words in the box. Then listen and repeat.

9 🔊

bark	branch	bud	leaf	petal
root	soil	stalk	trunk	twig

2 Underline the correct words.

In fall, the <u>**leaves**</u> / **stalks** fall off the trees.

- **a** The **trunks** / **buds** on a plant will grow into flowers.
- **b** Several **roots** / **branches** fell off the tree during the storm.
- **c** You'll need to keep the **soil** / **twigs** wet if you want the plant to grow.
- **d** This flower has bright pink **petals** / **bark**.
- **e** To make the fire, we need to collect some dry **buds** / **twigs**.

3 Read the definitions and write the correct words.

A small round thing on a plant that grows into a flower.
bud

- **a** The hard brown material that covers a tree. ________
- **b** A flat green thing that grows on a twig. ________
- **c** The part of a tree or plant that grows under the ground. ________
- **d** The main brown part of a tree. ________
- **e** The long green part of a flower. ________
- **f** A twig grows from this part of a tree. ________
- **g** Both trees and plants have roots that grow in this. ________
- **h** This is the part of a flower that is colorful to attract insects. ________

4

GOOD FRIENDS

VOCABULARY 1

Making Friends

1 Complete the phrases with the vowels.

interrupt a c_o_nv_e_rs_a_t_i_o_n

a jump a l__n__

b arrive ____rly

c be l__t__

d be r__d__

e be p__l__t__

2 Match the phrases with the pictures.

[f] bring a present

[ ] snap your fingers

[ ] point at someone

[ ] shake hands

[ ] take off your shoes

[ ] tell jokes

3 Complete the phrases with the words in the box.

jump ~~polite~~ rude shake snap take off

It's ___polite___ to write a thank-you letter after a meal at someone's house.

a It's ______________ to interrupt someone's conversation.

b Everybody is waiting their turn. Go to the back and don't try to ______________ the line.

c After a tennis match, we always ______________ hands to show we are still friends!

d Your house is very clean. Would you like us to ______________ our shoes in the hall?

e It's rude in Britain to ______________ your fingers to get the waiter's attention.

4 Match the phrases with the sentences.

arrive early be late bring a present ~~interrupt a conversation~~ point at someone tell jokes

Cam and I were talking and suddenly a guy came up and started talking about his phone.
interrupt a conversation

a Do you like chocolates? These are for you.

____

b Have you heard the one about two cats who had a swimming race?

____

c "Look at that man, Mommy. He's walking in a funny way." "Don't point, Emma. It's rude."

____

d "I've been waiting for an hour." "I'm really sorry. The traffic was terrible."

____

e My watch was wrong and we arrived at 11:10. The invitation was for 11:30. It was embarrassing.

____

GRAMMAR 1

Obligation, No Obligation, Prohibition, Advice

1 Write pairs of sentences with *must* and *must not*.

Be here by six. Don't be late.
You must be here by six. You must not be late.

a Go to bed early. Don't stay up late.
____

b Be polite. Don't be rude.
____

c Don't wear jeans. Wear nice clothes.
____

d Put your cell phone on silent. Don't disturb people on the train.
____

e Take off your shoes. Don't get the carpet dirty.
____

f Don't jump the line. Wait for your turn.
____

2 Complete the sentences with *has to* / *have to* or *doesn't have to* / *don't have to*.

a He ___has to___ be fit.
He ___doesn't have to___ wear a suit and tie.
1 He ____________ train a lot.
2 He ____________ use a computer in his job.

b **1** She ____________ be calm and reliable.
2 She ____________ wear a uniform.
3 She ____________ like children.
4 She ____________ travel for her job.

c **1** They ____________ stand a lot.
2 They ____________ have a driver's license.
3 They ____________ be creative and good with their hands.
4 They ____________ sit at a desk.

3 Write questions with *have to*. Then write answers for you.

In your country ...

How old / you / be / to drive a scooter?
How old do you have to be to drive a scooter?
You have to be 17 to drive a scooter.

a you / pay / to see a dentist?
____
____

b young people / do / military service?
____
____

c how old / you / be / to get a job?
____
____

At your school ...

d students / wear / a uniform?
____
____

e How much homework / you / do?
____
____

f students / go home / for lunch?
____
____

4 Complete the sentences with *must not* or *don't / doesn't have to*.

You ___must not___ tell anyone. It's our secret. OK?

a Great! I ____________ get up early. I can stay in bed until eleven!

b It's a pajama party, but you ____________ wear pajamas if you don't want to.

c The bus leaves at seven. He ____________ be late.

d My grandfather ____________ pay on the bus. He has a free pass.

e We have lots of time. We ____________ run to the bus stop.

f Your brother ____________ park there. The police will tow his car away.

5 What things do you have to do at home? What about your friend? Complete the sentences.

I have to ______make my bed______. ✓

I don't have to ______cook______. ✗

a I ____________________. ✓

b But I ____________________. ✗

c My friend ____________________. ✓

d He / She ____________________. ✗

6 Give advice for each situation. Use *should / shouldn't* and the verbs in the box.

do drink eat ~~go~~ have put on sit sleep smoke ~~start~~

GET HEALTHY NOW!

My top tips for teenagers by Dr. Suzanne Golden

You ______should start______ the day with a healthy breakfast.
You ______shouldn't go______ to school with an empty stomach.

a *You ____________ three meals a day.*

b *You ____________ plenty of water.*

c *You ____________ eight hours every night.*

d *You ____________ some exercise every day.*

e *You ____________ ever. It's the worst possible thing for your health.*

f *You ____________ in the sun in the middle of the day. It's bad for your skin.*

g *You ____________ sunscreen and a hat if you are out in the sun.*

h *You ____________ a lot of soft drinks, sweets, chocolate, or junk food.*

7 Write four tips for a happy life using *should* and *shouldn't*.

You ______should be friendly and helpful______.

You ______shouldn't worry too much______.

a You should ____________________.

b You shouldn't ____________________.

c You should ____________________.

d You shouldn't ____________________.

8 Underline the correct options.

Go back and take a shower, please. At this pool, you **must** / **should** have a shower before you go in it.

a I have a headache. Perhaps I **must** / **should** take an aspirin.

b The sign says NO SMOKING. That means you **must not** / **should not** smoke here.

c I don't have to do my homework today, but I think I **must** / **should**. Then I'll be free all weekend.

d People **must not** / **shouldn't** drive if it isn't necessary. It's bad for the environment.

e You **must not** / **shouldn't** touch things in the museum. If you do, you will get into trouble.

9 Complete the summer camp rules with *have to, has to, should, don't have to,* or *must not*.

Camp Rules

You can play music, but you ______must not______ make noise after eleven at night.

You **a** ____________ light fires. It's very dangerous here in the forest.

You can swim in the lake but you **b** ____________ dive. The water isn't deep enough.

Every child **c** ____________ pass a water safety test. If you can't swim, you **d** ____________ go out in the canoes.

You can do exercises before breakfast with Ms. Mortimer, if you like. You **e** ____________ do them but it's a great way to start the day.

Group activities start at ten every morning. You **f** ____________ be late. If you are late, we all **g** ____________ wait for you and it is a waste of everyone's time.

You **h** ____________ help with the cooking, but it's great if you do.

There are no cleaners so every camper **i** ____________ help with the cleaning. If you don't clean your room, you will be in serious trouble!

We do a concert at the end of your stay. You **j** ____________ be in it if you don't want to. But you **k** ____________ because it's a lot of fun!

VOCABULARY 2

Verb and Noun Collocations

1 Find these nouns in the word search.

advice argument fun lies money praise ~~presents~~ time truth

P	R	E	S	E	N	T	S	O	A
E	I	F	B	I	X	C	Y	J	G
A	R	G	U	M	E	N	T	O	Q
B	N	A	F	R	X	Y	N	Q	P
A	D	V	I	C	E	Y	T	P	A
Q	S	E	U	Z	R	O	I	S	T
P	R	A	I	S	E	I	M	Z	R
A	H	N	A	T	F	U	E	F	U
V	W	E	E	L	I	E	S	U	T
O	J	K	M	O	N	E	Y	N	H

2 Complete the phrases with the nouns from the word search in activity 1.

a give / receive ___presents___, ________, ________.

b spend ________, ________.

c have an ________.

d tell ________.

e tell the ________.

f have ________.

3 Match the sentence beginnings with the endings.

a [3] On weekends I usually spend

b [ ] Let's go now. You don't need to spend

c [ ] She wanted my honest opinion so I had to tell

d [ ] She had health problems but she didn't receive any

e [ ] There's a page in this magazine where they give

1 advice about teenagers' problems.

2 her the truth.

3 money on eating out or going to the movies.

4 time changing your clothes.

5 useful advice from her doctor.

4 Complete the sentences with the words in the box.

argument fun ~~lies~~ presents receive

I never believe her stories. She always tells ___lies___.

a I didn't want to have an ________, so I just agreed with her.

b We usually have ________ when we go to the beach.

c The best thing about birthdays is that you ________ presents from all your friends.

d How many people do you give ________ to at Christmas?

5 Answer the questions for you.

a What's the best thing you did for fun?

____

____

b Do you always tell the truth?

____

____

c What do you love spending money on?

____

____

d What's the best advice you have given to a friend?

____

____

GRAMMAR 2

Second Conditional

1 Match the sentence beginnings with the endings.

a [3] If I had enough money,
b [ ] If we had a cell phone with us,
c [ ] It would be fantastic
d [ ] I would tell you the answer
e [ ] If she didn't talk so much,
f [ ] I wouldn't ask her for advice

1 if I had wings and could fly!
2 she would be less annoying.
3 I'd buy an electric guitar.
4 if I were you.
5 we could call for help.
6 if I knew it.

2 Write sentences using the second conditional. Don't forget the comma where necessary.

If I (be) the prime minister / I (build) more hospitals
If I were the prime minister, I would build more hospitals.

a I (not ask) Bob for help / if I (be) you
______

b He (have) more money / if he (not spend) all his time dreaming
______

c If people (not drive) so much / this town (be) cleaner
______

d If you (wear) a coat / you (not feel) cold
______

e I (not have to) do the dishes / if we (have) a dishwasher
______

3 Complete the questions. Then choose your answers and write sentences with *I'd …*

Personality Quiz

Are you a lion or a mouse?
Find out with this quiz!

What would you do if you saw (see) a shark swimming towards you in the sea?
1 scream and prepare to die
2 stick your fingers in its eyes
3 swim away fast
I'd scream and prepare to die.

a What would you do if the principal ______ (ask) you to sing in front of the whole school?
1 pretend to be sick
2 agree to do it in a month
3 jump up and start singing
______

b What would you do if you ______ (break) your father's computer?
1 go and stay at a friend's house for a week
2 tell him and say sorry
3 start saving my allowance
______

c What would you do if you ______ (can) choose a vacation anywhere in the world?
1 choose a beach vacation in Europe
2 fly to New York and San Francisco
3 go walking in the Andes
______

d What would you do if you ______ (find) a snake in your tent when you were camping?
1 die of fright
2 get out of the tent fast
3 take a picture of it
______

e What would you do if you ______ (go) to a restaurant with a very unusual menu?
1 leave immediately
2 pretend to feel sick
3 order the snails and frogs' legs
______

GRAMMAR CHECK

1 Read the text and circle the correct answers.

WELCOME TO OAKWOOD SUMMER SCHOOL

We **a** _____ it if we didn't need to have rules! That's why we don't have very many. Please take the time to read them.

Rooms

Students **b** _____ pay a $20 deposit for their room key. If you lose your key, you will lose your deposit. For security reasons, you **c** _____ lock your room when you go out. It's OK to make hot drinks in your rooms, but you **d** _____ cook in them.

Classes

Every student **e** _____ sign the register before morning classes. No student **f** _____ ever sign in for another student. It is strictly forbidden. Classes start at 9:30 in the morning. You **g** _____ be late.

Excursions

Life wouldn't be much fun for our students if we **h** _____ offer a wide range of excursions. We really recommend them. Of course, you **i** _____ go on them, but we think you **j** _____ try them.

	1	2	3
a	would prefer (circled)	preferred	prefer
b	should	must	don't have to
c	must not	should	shouldn't
d	must	have to	must not
e	doesn't have to	has to	must not
f	has to	must not	must
g	must not	must	don't have to
h	don't	wouldn't	didn't
i	don't have to	shouldn't	must not
j	must	have to	should

2 Listen and check your answers.

10

LISTENING

1 Listen and complete.

11

a All Francesca's friends are __________.

b Eugenie can keep a __________.

c Eugenie and Francesca both wanted the main __________ in a __________ at school.

d Francesca often sees Bryony on __________.

e Francesca goes to a __________ after school.

2 Listen again and circle the correct answers.

11

a Francesca …
  1 met Bryony at a sports club.
  2 doesn't have a brother.
  3 goes to a school for boys and girls.

b Her friend Eugenie …
  1 doesn't like the other girls in the group.
  2 is not at Francesca's school.
  3 is in a group of six friends.

c Francesca …
  1 sometimes asks Eugenie for advice.
  2 doesn't like telling Eugenie her secrets.
  3 usually tells the whole group her problems.

d Eugenie …
  1 wasn't jealous of Francesca's role in the play.
  2 didn't get a part in the play.
  3 and Francesca think the same things are funny.

e Bryony …
  1 has never met Francesca's new friends.
  2 and Francesca are at different schools.
  3 and Francesca usually meet during the week.

f Hannah …
  1 and Francesca are going to their sports club this weekend.
  2 is at Francesca's school.
  3 and Francesca are doing something together this weekend.

EXTENSION

Underline the correct words to complete the text.

Amanda and I have known each other **a since / for** nearly ten years. We **b met / have met** at primary school, so we **c were / have been** friends since we were six years old. We are both very keen **d for / on** acting, dancing, and playing music. Amanda is a better musician **e than / by** me. In fact, she's the **f best / better** singer I know. She **g must / should** be a professional singer right now, really. Anyway, I know she'll be famous one day. At the moment, we both **h playing / play** in a band called Infinity and she also **i is singing / sings**. I play the drums, but I've **j never sung / never sang** in public. Last summer, we **k played / were playing** at a school concert when there was a power cut. The lights went out and the microphone didn't **l work / worked**. Amanda was as **m cooler / cool** as a professional singer. She said **n a little / a few** words and apologized about the problem. She said something like, "If it's light enough for you to **o see / saw** me, **p I would / I'll** sing." And everybody clapped and she sang **q some / much** songs without a microphone and without her electric guitar. I wouldn't sing in public if you **r pay / paid** me a million dollars! Luckily, I **s don't have to / must not** sing because I'm just the drummer. But next year, **t I'll / I'm** going to learn to play the guitar as well.

VOCABULARY PLUS

Friendship

1

to arrange to meet someone

2

to become friends with someone

3

to fall out with someone

4

to fight with someone

5

to finish with someone

6

to get on with someone

7

to get to know someone

8

to be done with someone

9

to make friends with someone

10

to make up with someone

11

to meet a new person

1 Write the phrasal verbs in the correct column. Then listen and check.

12 🔊

☺	☹
to arrange to meet someone	

2 Match the verbs and the definitions.

a make friends with
b to get to know
c to be done with
d to make up
e to arrange to meet someone
f to fall out with

to invite someone to a place
to stop liking someone
to have an argument with
to learn more about a person
enjoy someone's company
to become friends again after an argument

3 Complete the sentences with the correct preposition.

in on up with (×3)

Have you heard? Emma and Jane fought with each other and now Emma is done ___with___ Jane.

a We're good friends. We really get ________ with each other.

b I don't want to be Paul's friend anymore. I'm going to finish ________ him.

c Lydia and Caroline are friends again. They made ________ with each other last night.

d "Have you ever been ________ a fight with anyone?" "No, never!"

e I'm done ________ Martin. I won't be friends with him anymore.

4 Answer the questions for you. Write in full sentences. Use phrasal verbs from activity 1.

a Do you sometimes fall out with your family?

____

b Do you always make up with your friends after arguing?

____

c Have you ever been done with someone?

____

5

FOLLOWERS OF FASHION

VOCABULARY 1

Style Adjectives

1 Complete adjectives a-f with vowels. Then match them with pictures 1-6.

a [6] t __i__ g h t

b [ ] s p ___ r t y

c [ ] l ___ ___ s ___

d [ ] ___ l d - f ___ s h ___ ___ n ___ d

e [ ] g l ___ m ___ r ___ ___ s

f [ ] f ___ r m ___ l

1

2

3

4

5

6

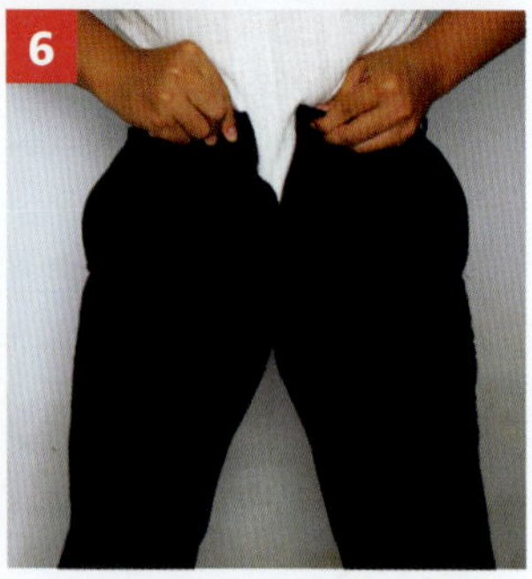

2 Match the columns to make adjectives.

a	cas	[ ]	ventional
b	col	[ ]	practical
c	com	[ ]	dy
d	con	[ ]	fortable
e	fash	[ ]	ual
f	im	[ ]	ionable
g	tren	[ ]	orful

3 Complete the sentences with the style adjectives in the box.

> colorful comfortable ~~fashionable~~ formal loose old-fashioned tight

She's very interested in fashion. All her clothes are very __fashionable__.

a Those jeans are too ______________. She needs a bigger size.

b He's very ______________. He even wears a tie on weekends.

c You can walk all day in these shoes. They are really ______________.

d His shirt was covered in big blue, red, green, and yellow flowers. It was very ______________.

e These shoes are one size too big. They are too ______________ for me.

f At the costume party he wore one of those ______________ striped swimsuits from the 1920s that cover the top part of the body as well.

4 Match the descriptions with the style adjectives in the box.

> casual conventional glamorous impractical ~~sporty~~ trendy

He works at a gym so he often wears a track suit and sneakers. __sporty__

a She was wearing a long silk dress and diamond earrings. She looked like a movie star. ______________

b That's my father in the suit and white shirt with a blue tie. He works in a bank. ______________

c She was wearing a long skirt and high heels on her bike. And she didn't have a helmet on. ______________

d She's always very fashionable. Today she's wearing denim shorts with suede ankle boots. ______________

e Adam is the guy in jeans and a pale blue sweater. ______________

GRAMMAR 1

Relative Pronouns

1 Underline the correct words.

Mary Quant was a fashion designer **which** / **who** became famous in London in the sixties.

- **a** The 1960s was the time **where** / **when** miniskirts first became fashionable.
- **b** The store **which** / **where** I bought this jacket is on Maple Street.
- **c** I know a girl **which** / **who** is a successful fashion model.
- **d** Why don't you wear those shoes **that** / **who** you bought last week?
- **e** I didn't like those people **which** / **that** we met in the park.
- **f** Let's go to that museum **who** / **which** has antique clothes on display.

2 Match the sentence beginnings with the endings.

- **a** [3] My friend has a cat
- **b** [ ] That's the girl
- **c** [ ] Do you remember that day
- **d** [ ] Are you the person
- **e** [ ] Can I see the dress
- **f** [ ] Let's go to that store
- **g** [ ] I don't like people

1. when we both wore the same clothes?
2. who smiled at you in the park.
3. that loves watching TV.
4. where you got your jacket.
5. who always show off.
6. that you wore to the party?
7. that I spoke to on the phone?

3 Complete the text using *which*, *who*, *where*, or *when*.

A friend of mine ___who___ is studying fashion design recently had to create clothes from unusual materials. One material **a** ______ she used was plastic trash bags. She made clothes with them **b** ______ looked really expensive. There were other students in her course **c** ______ made amazing skirts and dresses out of newspaper **d** ______ they folded into pleats. My friend asked me to wear one of her creations on the day **e** ______ her teachers were coming to see her work. I agreed but I didn't realize it was a really big deal. I went to the college **f** ______ there was a room full of photographers. I found my friend and she took me to the back **g** ______ there was a changing room. I put on the black plastic dress **h** ______ she had made and **i** ______ looked amazing on me. Then I had to walk down the catwalk **j** ______ there were lots of other models and loads of photographers who took pictures of me. I enjoyed it, especially at the end **k** ______ a woman from a modeling agency offered me some paid work. But the best bit was **l** ______ I took off the plastic dress. It looked great but it was very hot under those bright lights!

4 Join the sentences using *who*, *which*, *where*, or *when*.

I have some fashion magazines. They're from the sixties.

I have some fashion magazines which are from the sixties.

- **a** There's a man outside. He wants to see you.

  ______

- **b** There's a store on Santee Street. You can get two pairs of shoes for $30.

  ______

- **c** I can't wait for the summer. We can wear shorts and sandals.

  ______

- **d** I have a friend. She always makes her own clothes.

  ______

- **e** There's a bookstore on my street. You can look at books and have a coffee.

  ______

- **f** I have a dress of my grandmother's. It looks great on me.

  ______

5 Choose the correct alternative.

a Is that the store ______ you got your boots?

1 who **2** where **3** that

b There was a famous boutique in London in the 1960s ______ a minidress cost only £5.

1 that **2** where **3** who

c The baby ______ is crying is my sister.

1 who **2** which **3** when

d The book ______ won the Pulitzer prize is getting an illustrated edition.

1 which **2** where **3** when

e He does yoga in the same studio ______ I do Tai Chi.

1 which **2** where **3** who

f Nicki met the singer ______ performed last week at the Opera House!

1 which **2** where **3** who

g Bertrand finished college on the day ______ his daughter was born.

1 when **2** where **3** who

h In a year ______ platform heels are back in fashion, nothing can surprise me anymore!

1 who **2** which **3** when

6 Check the sentences in which the relative pronoun *which*, *who*, or *that* can be omitted.

a ☐ This is the money **that** I will use to pay the electrician.

b ☐ He mentioned the article **that** his professor wrote on the issue.

c ☐ What's the fashion model **who** you saw at the store wearing?

d ☐ She is holding the umbrella **which** I found in her house.

e ☐ My brother is the boy **who** always wears blue jeans.

7 Underline the correct words to complete the text.

My two friends Maxine and Leonie have very different styles. I don't see Leonie during the week anymore because now she's at the school **a when / where** my cousins study. But we still hang out on weekends. And that's **b where / when** I notice their different styles.

Maxine's style is a little trendy and comfortable. She often wears a loose T-shirt and blue jeans. And she has a pair of sneakers **c which / who** look great with her jeans. If we're going dancing or to a party, she still wears jeans, but she sometimes puts on a glamorous top, for example a black one **d which / who** is made of silk with silver touches. School is the only place **e when / where** Maxine usually has her long pink hair in a pony tail, because everywhere else she wears it loose.

While Maxine nearly always wears jeans or pants, Leonie loves dresses, skirts, and overalls. She is the friend **f which / that** was wearing beautiful yellow overalls at my birthday party last year. And her clothes are always colorful. She loves colorful clothes so she spends a lot of time mending the ones **g which / where** she buys in thrift stores. She has one amazing pink coat **h where / that** belonged to her older sister that is so charming.

While Maxine looks very trendy and comfortable, Leonie always looks colorful and cool. But one thing is for certain, both Maxine and Leonie are really stylish in different ways!

VOCABULARY 2

Phrasal Verbs: Clothes

1 Order the letters and write the phrasal verbs. Then match them with the pictures.

a [5] k a t e f o f ____take off____
b [ ] e v i g y a w a ________
c [ ] t u p n o ________
d [ ] u p t w a y a ________
e [ ] t e g t o n i ________
f [ ] w o r t h y a a w ________

2 Underline the correct words.

I need to **go with** / **look for** a new top to wear to Jodie's party.

a I think these jeans will fit you. Why don't you **try them on** / **wear them out**?

b At the summer sales she managed to **look for** / **pick up** a designer handbag for half price.

c These boots are so strong and well made that it takes years to **wear them out** / **try them on**.

d I'm not sure if the blue shoes **go with** / **look for** your black jacket.

e When you don't know what to buy, you can ask the sales clerk to **pick up something** / **pick something out** for you.

3 Match the sentences a-f with the responses 1-6.

a [3] It's cold.
b [ ] Do you think this sweater will fit me?
c [ ] It's hot in here.
d [ ] Do you like my sweater?
e [ ] This sweater has holes in it.
f [ ] I want a cashmere sweater.

1 Take your sweater off.
2 Throw it away.
3 Put your sweater on.
4 Try it on.
5 Try to pick one up during the sales.
6 Yes, it goes well with your jeans.

4 Complete the sentences with the phrasal verbs in the box.

get into	give away	~~look for~~
pick out	put away	wear out

Let's go shopping. I need to ____look for____ a new jacket.

a If you don't like those clothes any more, ________ them ________ or take them to a thrift store.

b Can I ________ some earrings for you to wear with that dress?

c Do you get rid of your clothes when you're bored with them or do you keep them until you ________ them ________?

d I will have to buy some bigger clothes. I can't ________ this dress any more.

e There are clothes all over the floor. Can you ________ them ________?

GRAMMAR 2

some, any, no Compounds

1 Match the questions with the answers.

a [3] What would you like for your birthday?
b [ ] Where's Krasnodar?
c [ ] What kind of hotel would you like to stay at?
d [ ] What's your town like?
e [ ] Who's your best friend?
f [ ] What should I wear in Moscow in winter?

1 Someone from my primary school.
2 Something very warm.
3 Something expensive.
4 Somewhere with a pool.
5 Somewhere in Russia.
6 It's OK, but there's nowhere to go in the evenings.

2 Underline the correct words.

I've grown taller. **Something** / **Nothing** fits me now.

a I'm bored. There's **anything** / **nothing** to do in this town and **anywhere** / **nowhere** to go.
b "Where should we eat?" "**Anywhere** / **Nowhere** – you choose!"
c Let's find **anywhere** / **somewhere** nice for a picnic.
d You're annoyed about **anything** / **something**. Please tell me the problem.
e **No one** / **Someone** liked the movie. We all left early.
f I don't have **anything** / **nothing** to wear to the party.
g There's **anyone** / **someone** at the door. Please can you go and open it?
h There isn't **someone** / **anyone** outside. I think it was a cat.

3 Complete the dialogue with the correct *some*, *no*, or *any* compounds.

Eva Is there ___anywhere___ to buy a present for my parents?
Kate What kind of thing do you want?
Eva **a** ____________ nice for the house, I think.
Kate You can't get **b** ____________ nice in this area.
Eva I don't mind going downtown.
Kate There's **c** ____________ really good for kitchen things on Katy Freeway, it's not too far from where we are. I bought **d** ____________ there last week.
Eva Really? What was it?
Kate **e** ____________ very exciting. It was just something cheap and useful.
Eva What?
Kate It was **f** ____________ to keep food in, in the fridge.
Eva You mean a plastic container?
Kate Yes. My mom asked me to buy her one.
Eva Oh. Do they have **g** ____________ more interesting than plastic food containers in this appliance store?
Kate Yes. They have lovely plates and bowls and really expensive glasses.

4 Complete the sentences so they are true for you. Use *some*, *no*, or *any* compounds.

My best friend is ___someone who lives on my street___.

a I grew up ____________.
b If I could travel ____________ in Europe, I would choose ____________.
c ____________ that I love to eat is ____________.
d If I could meet ____________ in the world, I would love to meet ____________.

GRAMMAR CHECK

1 Read the text and circle the correct answers.

Ding dong. The front doorbell rings.

Luke There's someone at the door.
Dan Don't answer it. It **a** ______ someone annoying **b** ______ wants to sell us something.
Luke OK, **c** ______ a look out of the window.
Dan Don't let them see you looking.

Luke looks out of the window.

Luke **d** ______. I can't see **e** ______.
Dan Are you sure?
Luke Quite sure. There's **f** ______ there.
Dan Perhaps they're **g** ______ in the garden. Or perhaps they've gone around the back of the house and they **h** ______ at the back door.

Knock knock. There's a knock at the back door.

Luke Yes. There's **i** ______ at the back door. It's a tall girl carrying a guitar case **j** ______ too big for her.
Dan Oh, that's Marianne.
Luke Why does she have such an enormous guitar?
Dan She **k** ______ in the school band, and that's a double bass, not a guitar!

	A	B	C
a	is	(might be)	is being
b	who	which	he
c	I'm taking	I'm going to take	I'll take
d	I'm not	I won't	I don't
e	no one	someone	anyone
f	someone	anyone	no one
g	anywhere	somewhere	nowhere
h	knocked	're going to knock	're knocking
i	someone	no one	anyone
j	when it's	it's	that's
k	's going to play	'll play	's playing

2 Listen and check your answers.
13

LISTENING

1 Listen to a radio show where four teenagers talk about clothes and fashion. Circle T for *true*, F for *false*, or DS for *doesn't say*.
14

a Georgia wears the same style of clothes every day. **T / F / DS**

b Georgia always feels aggressive. **T / F / DS**

c Daniel never wears sneakers. **T / F / DS**

d Daniel works after school to pay for his clothes. **T / F / DS**

e Serena often wears cheap clothes. **T / F / DS**

f Serena doesn't have any designer clothes. **T / F / DS**

g Serena's blue velvet pants cost her $200. **T / F / DS**

h Tim has a few different clothing styles. **T / F / DS**

i Tim has expensive jeans. **T / F / DS**

j He never wears natural materials like wool and cotton. **T / F / DS**

2 Listen again and write Georgia, Daniel, Serena, or Tim next to each statement.
14

a Fashion's great because there are no rules.
____

b I can't afford new designer clothes but I sometimes get them secondhand.
____

c I express my feelings through my clothes.
____

d I might look the same every day but I'm never a mess.
____

e I spend a lot more than most people on my clothes.
____

f If it's not practical and comfortable, it's not for me.
____

g Shopping is about picking up bargains.
____

h I would never wear cheap shoes!
____

EXTENSION

Underline the correct words to complete the text.

a Anyone / Someone who thinks our interest in fashion and beauty is **b somewhere / something** new is mistaken. Beauty treatments and make up have been around **c since / for** thousands of years. The ancient Egyptians **d used / were using** ground minerals to make colored eye shadows and powders. And Queen Cleopatra **e was taking / used to take** baths in milk and honey.

f Everywhere / Anywhere in the world people decorate their bodies and faces in order to look more beautiful. But there are quite a lot of beauty practices **g where / which** seem unusual for people in the West. For example, in Kenya, Masai girls **h think / are thinking** long ears are beautiful. So they **i are stretching / stretch** their ears with heavy weights.

A lot of beauty practices are painful. In China they **j have stopped / stopped** binding girls' feet now. Until the middle of the 20th century, older women **k were putting / used to put** tight cloth around the feet of three-year-old girls and break the bones in their feet so that they would have small feet. It **l hurt / was hurting** a lot and the girls **m have grown / grew** up with deformed feet, unable to walk normally.

And what painful things **n do we do / we do** in the West in the name of beauty? Well, **o I'm standing / I stand** outside a tattoo parlor at the moment and a few men and women **p go / are going** into it. That's one painful beauty practice **q when / that** people are happy to pay for in the West. **r Will there be / Is there being** a time when people won't suffer to be beautiful? I don't think so!

VOCABULARY PLUS

Clothes and Accessories

1  _______________

2  _______________

3  _____tie_____

4  _______________

5 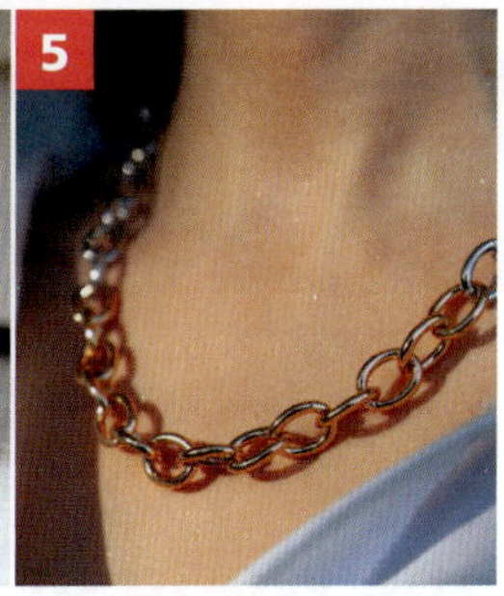 _______________

6  _______________

7  _______________

8  _______________

9  _______________

10  _______________

1 Label the pictures with the words in the box. Then listen and repeat.

15

belt	pocket
button	sleeve
collar	slippers
laces	~~tie~~
necklace	zipper

2 Underline the correct words.

You look very stylish today. I like your **tie** / **slippers**.

a These jeans are too loose. I need a **belt** / **collar**.

b Hang on! I need to tie the **laces** / **sleeve** on my sneakers.

c I lost my keys because there was a hole in my **zipper** / **pocket**.

d Don't do up the top **button** / **necklace** on your shirt.

e Oh no! The **collar** / **zipper** is broken and I can't close my pants.

3 Complete the definitions with the correct words.

A _____pocket_____ is a small bag in your clothes that holds small objects.

a Things you put on your feet to keep warm: _______________.

b Men often wear a _______________ under their collar.

c The _______________ is the part of a coat, jacket, or shirt that goes round your neck.

d A _______________ is a piece of jewelry you wear around your neck.

e The _______________ is the part of a shirt, jacket, or dress that covers your arm.

4 Answer the questions for you. Write full sentences.

a What do you keep in your pockets?

____

b Do you prefer jeans with buttons or a zipper?

____

c How often do you wear a belt?

____

d Do you wear slippers at home?

____

6

WORK AND MONEY

VOCABULARY 1

The World of Work

1 Complete the words with the vowels.

b _o_ n _u_ s

a c __ n d __ t __ __ n s

b __ p p l __ c __ t __ __ n f __ r m

c j __ b __ d v __ r t __ s __ m __ n t

d p __ y r __ __ s __

e __ x p __ n s __ s

f p r __ m __ t __ __ n

g w __ r k __ x p __ r __ __ n c __

2 Find eight work and money words in the wordsnake.

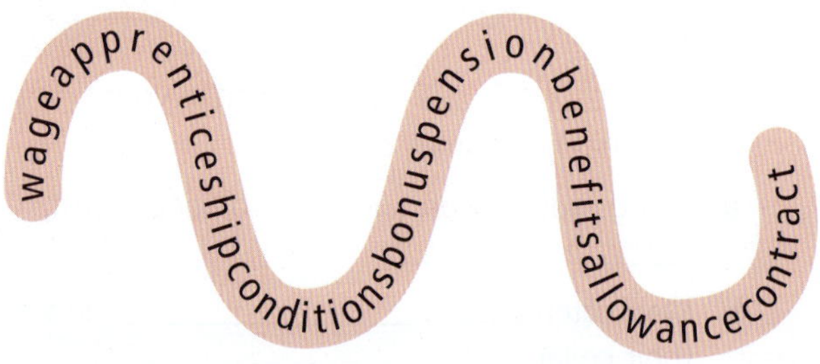

3 Imagine you are looking for a new job. Put these events in the correct order.

a ☐ application form

b ☐ contract

c ☐ interview

d 1 job advertisement

e ☐ promotion

f ☐ wage

4 Underline the correct words.

My older sister has to fill in her qualifications and experience on the **job advertisement** / **application form**.

a I want to train to be a plumber so when I am older I will have to do an **apprenticeship** / **application form**.

b As a waiter, his **pay raise** / **wage** isn't great but he gets tips from some customers.

c Let's go out for a meal to celebrate. My Dad's boss has given him a **pay raise** / **benefits** of $3,000 a year.

d When my mother goes abroad for her job, she gets a daily **apprenticeship** / **allowance** to cover her food, transportation, and hotel.

e The salary is OK but the **expenses** / **conditions** aren't great at my uncle's job. He only gets ten days of vacation a year and he has to work on Saturdays.

5 Complete the sentences with the words in the box.

allowance benefits bonus ~~contract~~ pension promotion wage work experience

I have a new job. They've sent me the ____contract____ so now I must sign it and send it back.

a My father has to use his own car at his job but he gets an ____________ for gasoline.

b My grandfather retired a few years ago but he has plenty of money for vacations because he gets a good ____________.

c Her starting ____________ at the travel company is $1,500 a month but she gets a ____________ if she sells lots of vacation packages.

d My cousin got a ____________ last week. He's going to be senior sales manager now.

e The salary isn't very good at that company but the ____________ are excellent. There are long vacations and free flights all around the world.

f I want to be a journalist, so I'm getting ____________ at a local newspaper.

GRAMMAR 1

First and Second Conditionals

1 Underline the correct words.

If you **will apply** / **apply** for this job, I'm sure you will get it.

- **a** My father **wears** / **will wear** a suit if they call him for an interview.
- **b** If my sister gets an application form, **will you help** / **do you help** her fill it out?
- **c** He will lose his job if he **won't stop** / **doesn't stop** being late for work.
- **d** If they **will offer** / **offer** her a job, will she take it?
- **e** You **don't regret** / **won't regret** it if you go and work for them.
- **f** If she **doesn't get** / **won't get** that job, she will be very disappointed.

2 Complete the sentences using the first conditional.

If you ___don't work___ (not work) harder, you ___won't pass___ (not pass) your exams.

- **a** If you ________________ (not pass) your exams, you ________________ (not get) a job.
- **b** If you ________________ (not get) a job, you ________________ (not earn) any money.
- **c** If you ________________ (not earn) any money, you ________________ (not have) enough money for a vacation.
- **d** If you ________________ (not have) enough money for travel, we ________________ (not be able) to go away together.

3 Complete the advertisements using *if* and the first conditional.

Workwise Employment Agency

We can find you your dream job!

If you need a job, we'll find you one today!

____

____

you (need) a job, we (find) you one today!

a The Knocky 221 Smartphone Makes Life Easier!

____

____

____

you (buy) one today / we (give) you $20 of free talk time!

b Akiko XL Laptop

Light, easy, and fun to use!

____

____

____

you (want) to work on the move, you (love) this!

c Student Supersaver Account

The best bank account for young people

____

____

____

you (open) an account with us today, we (give) a free cell phone!

d Traveler Watches

Smart, stylish, accurate

____

____

____

you (like) good design, you (want) one of these!

4 Order the words to make second conditional sentences.

$5000, / had / how / If / it / spend / would / you / you ?

If you had $5000, how would you spend it?

a do / If / president, / the / were / what / would / you / you ?

____

b a / buy / house / I / I'd / if / lottery / my / new / parents / the / won

____

c a rock star / any / choose / could / I / I'd be / If / in the world, / job

____

d buy / cost / didn't / I / If / one / so much, / those laptops / would !

____

e a job, / didn't / father / bored / have / he / If / very / my / be / would

____

5 Complete the sentences using the second conditional.

If she (know) the answer, she (tell) us.

If she knew the answer, she would tell us.

a He (not be) so poor if he (not waste) all his money on expensive restaurants.

____

b If I (be) you, I (not lend) him any money.

____

c He (not work) for that company if he (can) get a job somewhere else.

____

d If I (have) enough money, I (start) my own design company.

____

e You (not like) it if you (lose) your job.

____

6 Match the sentence beginnings with the endings to make first or second conditional sentences.

a [6] If your sister doesn't apply for the job,

b [ ] If they offered him more money,

c [ ] What would your father say

d [ ] If I forget,

e [ ] Will you ask for help

f [ ] If he left his job tomorrow,

1 how would he pay for his apartment?

2 if I offered you a job?

3 if you have a problem?

4 will you please remind me?

5 would he stay at the job?

6 she won't get it.

7 Complete the dialogue using the first or second conditional.

Rose Let's do the quiz in this magazine.

Lila No, I'm busy.

Rose Please. If you ____do____ (do) it with me, I **a** _______________ (help) you with your math homework.

Lila Fine. It's a deal.

Rose Here's the first question. What **b** _______________ (you do) if you **c** _______________ (see) a ghost?

Lila That's ridiculous. I don't believe in ghosts.

Rose Wait. **d** _______________ (you scream)? **e** _______________ (you call) the police? Or **f** _______________ (you faint)?

Lila I can't choose any of those answers. What's the next question in this silly quiz?

Rose What **g** _______________ (you do) if you **h** _______________ (find) $500 in the street? **i** _______________ (you keep) it, **j** _______________ (you take) it to the police, or **k** _______________ (you give) it to charity?

Lila I'm pretty honest so I **l** _______________ (not keep) it. I **m** _______________ (take) it to the police, probably.

Rose Me, too. Next question. If you **n** _______________ (have) to parachute from a plane, swim with sharks or lie on a bed of hot coals, which **o** _______________ (you do)?

Lila I don't know and I don't care.

Rose If you **p** _______________ (not answer), I **q** _______________ (not help) you with your homework. Remember the deal?

Lila I don't care. I'll do my homework without your help, thanks.

8 Complete the sentences for you. Use the first or second conditional.

If I had a magic carpet,

I would fly to India to see the Taj Mahal.

a If I do well on the exams this summer,

_______________.

b If I went to the fancy dress party,

_______________.

c If the weather is nice this weekend,

_______________.

d If I won the lottery,

_______________.

VOCABULARY 2

Work Verbs

1 Complete the phrases with the verbs in the box.

apply be earn fill out ~~have~~ have

___have___ an interview

a ________________ a salary

b ________________ unemployed

c ________________ a full-time job

d ________________ an application form

e ________________ for a job

2 Order the letters to make phrases.

m a l i c p e n s e x e s

claim expenses

a k r o w t r a p - m i e t

____

b t e g a b o j

____

c e g t a n o s i n e p

____

d s o l e a o b j

____

e n i g s a c a n c r o t t

____

3 Match the sentence beginnings with the endings.

a [2] He should get a haircut before he has

b [ ] She decided to work

c [ ] It took her three hours to fill out

d [ ] If your cousin is late for work every day, he'll

e [ ] Make sure your uncle understands everything before

f [ ] They are accountants so they both

1 earn a good salary.

2 an interview.

3 lose his job.

4 part-time after having her second baby.

5 this application form.

6 he signs the contract.

4 Complete the sentences with the words in the box.

apply claim earn fill out ~~full-time~~ get get have lose sign unemployed work

He was only working 12 hours a week but now he has a ___full-time___ job and works a 40-hour week.

a There's an advertisement for a store assistant at the Surf Shack. Why doesn't your sister ________________ for it? Look, I picked up the application form for her to ________________.

b It isn't easy to ________________ a job at the moment – more than two million people are ________________.

c When my aunt retires from the police force, she will ________________ good pension.

d She had to buy a train ticket for a work trip with her own money so now she needs to ________________ expenses.

e I'm free on Tuesday and Thursday afternoons because I only ________________ part-time now.

f Here's a pen. Can you ________________ the contract, please?

g She loves being a cook but she doesn't ________________ a very good salary.

h When they close the car factory, my brother will ________________ his job.

i Your cousin looks really smart. Is he about to ________________ an interview?

GRAMMAR 2

Gerunds and Infinitives

1 **Complete the sentences using the gerund form of the verbs in the box.**

clean get up learn read ~~see~~ sleep surf swim

Are you looking forward to ___seeing___ your American cousins again?

a Have you finished ______ *War and Peace* yet?

b What time did you finish ______ your bedroom?

c I don't enjoy ______ in cold water.

d ______ the internet is fun but you can waste a lot of time.

e I'm not looking forward to ______ at 5am on Monday.

f My sister really enjoys ______ languages.

g ______ takes up about one third of our lives!

2 **Match the sentence beginnings with the endings. Then change the verbs in parentheses to gerunds.**

a [4] I am looking forward to

b [ ] I'm always hungry and I enjoy

c [ ] When will you finish

d [ ] All children look forward to

e [ ] I haven't finished

f [ ] My sister spends a lot of time

1 ______ (eat) more than cooking.

2 ______ (look) in her mirror.

3 ______ (read) this wonderful book yet.

4 ___starting___ (start) my new job next week.

5 ______ (write) that essay?

6 ______ (open) their Christmas presents.

3 **Complete the sentences using the infinitive form of the verbs in parentheses.**

I can't afford ___to buy___ (buy) another pair of shoes.

a They've decided ______ (go) camping together.

b Would you like ______ (see) my application form?

c When did you learn ______ (speak) Russian?

d She doesn't want ______ (move) to a new house.

e We've arranged ______ (meet) at 7pm.

f I'm applying ______ (join) the police force.

4 **Complete the text using the infinitive or gerund form of the verbs in parentheses.**

Dear Felicity,
I'm really looking forward to ___seeing___ (see) you next week. I've decided **a** ______ (come) by bus because I can't afford **b** ______ (get) the train. Have you finished **c** ______ (make) the costumes for your school play? How much time have you spent so far **d** ______ (work) on them? I'd like **e** ______ (help) with our school play too. I really enjoy **f** ______ (paint) and I'm also learning **g** ______ (make) things out of wood, so maybe I can apply **h** ______ (be) one of the set builders. Do you want **i** ______ (come) and stay with us in August? Mom says she's going to be near your house in Hereford and she can arrange **j** ______ (pick) you up.
Bye for now,
Angie

5 **Complete the sentences for you, your friends or your family.**

___My brother___ really enjoys ___writing songs___.

a One day I would like ______.

b I am looking forward to ______.

c At the moment I am learning ______.

d My friend has decided ______.

e I can't afford ______.

f ______ spends a lot of time ______.

g I've arranged ______.

GRAMMAR CHECK

1 Read the text and circle the correct answers.

I am looking forward to **a** ______ high school. I've applied **b** ______ to college in Canada. If I got a scholarship, my parents **c** ______ have to pay the fees. But they still couldn't afford **d** ______ all my living costs there. So if they **e** ______ me a place, I'll need to get a vacation job in the summer before I go. I would like **f** ______ a job as a lifeguard at the beach. I've learned **g** ______ people in the water and I've spent a lot of time **h** ______ a training course on artificial respiration. So I **i** ______ what to do if somebody **j** ______ into trouble while I was on duty.

	A	B	C
a	leave	(leaving)	I leave
b	for go	for going	to go
c	won't	wouldn't	don't
d	to pay	paying	pay
e	are offering	will offer	offer
f	to get	getting	if getting
g	saving	to save	my saving
h	doing	to doing	to do
i	would know	knew	have known
j	will get	got	gets

2 Listen and check your answers.
16

LISTENING

1 Listen and write T for *true*, F for *false*, or DK for *don't know.*
17

a ☐ Children under 14 can legally get a job doing "light work."

b ☐ Most employers don't give work to people younger than 15.

c ☐ More boys than girls get paid to deliver newspapers.

d ☐ The rules about working hours change when you are 16.

e ☐ Employers have to pay the minimum wage to people younger than 16.

f ☐ Fruit picking is better paid than store work.

2 Listen again and answer the questions.
17

a Name three of the jobs the speaker says someone under 15 might realistically get.

____

____

____

b How many hours a week can schoolchildren under 16 work during the school term?

____

____

c What's the latest time they can stop working?

____

____

d What's the maximum time people under 16 can work per week during the holidays?

____

____

e Is the maximum time 16- and 17-year olds can work per week limited by law?

____

____

EXTENSION

Underline the correct words.

Do you know **a somebody which / anybody who** chose their career when he or she was very young? Melissa Thornton **b has decided / decided** to become a vet when she was 7. "I **c have grown up / grew up** on a farm and I **d used to help / was helping** my parents to look after the animals. I remember the day **e when / where** I thought, "I'm **f being / going to be** a vet when I grow up." I was seven years old and we had a horse which had **g something / anything** wrong with its leg. While the vet **h has checked / was checking** its leg, I watched her very carefully. This incident **i made up / makes up** my mind about my future career." When she was 16, Melissa **j was spending / spent** two weeks during her summer vacation helping in a veterinary office. "It was very helpful and I **k learned / have learned** a lot about a vet's life and work." She is now in her last year of secondary school and **l has applied / was applying** for a place at Edinburgh University to study veterinary medicine. "They **m were offering / have offered** me a place but I won't be able to go there if I **n don't / won't** get three As in my exams. **o I work / I'm working** really hard at the moment. It would be terrible if **p I'll get / I got** two As and a B instead of three As. If I **q got / get** my grades, I'm going to spend a month in Ghana as a volunteer with local vets. Apparently, **r we're visiting / we'll visit** farms and **s I'm learning / I'll learn** about vaccinations. What an amazing experience before I start college!"

VOCABULARY PLUS

In the Office

1 
2 
3 
4 
5 

6 
7 
8 
9 
10 

1 Label the pictures with the words in the box. Then listen and repeat.

18))

calendar	guillotine
desk diary	hole punch
drawers	paper shredder
file	photocopier
filing cabinet	safe

2 Read the definitions and write the correct words.

The part of your desk where you can keep small objects and papers.
drawers

a A secure place where you can keep money and important documents.

b An object that makes holes in paper.

c A machine that makes copies.

d A piece of office furniture where you can file away papers.

e A machine with a sharp blade to cut paper.

3 Circle the correct words.

My mom keeps all the information about her clients in a _____.

1 filing cabinet **3** guillotine
2 paper shredder

a I have a _____ on my wall so I don't forget my friends' birthdays.
1 file **3** calendar
2 safe

b I'm not sure if I'm free on that date. I'll look in my _____.
1 hole punch **3** safe
2 desk diary

c The information in that letter is confidential. Please destroy it after reading with the _____.
1 hole punch **3** paper shredder
2 photocopier

d I have some _____ under my desk for my pens, pencils, etc.
1 drawers **3** desk diaries
2 calendars

e We have a different _____ for all our school subjects.
1 guillotine **3** hole punch
2 file

f My aunt keeps her jewelry in a _____.
1 drawers **3** safe
2 guillotine

7

CRIME DOESN'T PAY

VOCABULARY 1

Crime Verbs

1 Match the beginnings with the endings to make crime-related phrases.

a	catch	[ ]	a crime
b	commit	[ ]	clues
c	go to	[ ]	a fine
d	go on	[a]	a thief
e	do	[ ]	prison
f	look for	[ ]	trial
g	pay	[ ]	community service

2 Order the letters to complete the crime-related phrases.

investigate a ___crime___ m e r i c

a be ____________ o n c e n i n t

b be ____________ u g l i t y

c ____________ a suspect s t a r e r

d ____________ a crime l o v e s

e ____________ a suspect s t o n i q u e

f ____________ someone c e s s p u t

3 Match the definitions with the words in the box.

> clues community service crime fine guilty innocent ~~prison~~ suspect thief trial

place where criminals are locked up: ___prison___

a illegal action: ____________

b adjective for a person who has done nothing wrong: ____________

c money paid by someone who breaks the law: ____________

d someone who steals: ____________

e the legal process which finds out if someone is guilty or innocent: ____________

f things that give the police information about a criminal: ____________

g adjective for a person who has broken the law: ____________

h useful work that a criminal does as a punishment: ____________

i person that the police think is a criminal: ____________

4 Complete the sentences with the words in the box.

> arrest catch commit go to prison ~~investigate~~ pay a fine question solve suspect

She is the detective and it is her job to ___investigate___ this crime.

a The police want to ____________ him about his activities on the night of April 23.

b Why did the murderer ____________ these terrible crimes?

c The bank robbers will ____________ for a long time.

d There were no clues, so the police couldn't ____________ the crime.

e When the police ____________ someone of a crime, they ____________ the person and take him or her to the police station for questioning.

f She drove away very fast and the police couldn't ____________ her.

g If you park your car illegally, you might have to ____________.

GRAMMAR 1

Modals of Deduction and Possibility

1 Order the words to make sentences.

after / be / journey / long / must / tired / You / your
You must be tired after your long journey.

a after / be / big bowls / can't / cereal / hungry / of / She / three / eating

______

b be / email / fraud / internet / might / of / some kind / This

______

c a / be / girl / could / model / over there / That

______

d problem / be / to / a solution / might not / this / There

______

e after / be / can't / hours of / sleep / tired / 12 / You

______

f have / the / must / thief / through / window / The / open / climbed

______

g our class / I / in / may / Russian / somebody / speak / think

______

2 Complete the sentences using *must be* or *can't be*.

He has an unusual accent. He ___must be___ foreign.

a He's had three car accidents this year so he ______ a good driver.

b He's just broken that car window. He ______ a thief.

c She always says horrible things about her friends so she ______ a nice person.

d Somebody has just stolen his passport so he ______ at the police station now.

e They started playing tennis in the hot sun two hours ago. They ______ thirsty.

f This dictionary has my name in it so it ______ yours.

3 Underline the correct options.

The living room window is broken. There **can't** / **might** be a thief in there.

a They found the money and jewelry in her pockets. She **can't** / **must** be the thief.

b Her face is very red. She **could** / **can't** be guilty or she **could** / **must** just be hot!

c Don't try to catch the man because he **might** / **might not** have a knife and he **may** / **can't** be dangerous.

d The house is dark. They **must** / **can't** be out.

e Ask Andrew because he **can't** / **might** know the answer.

f He has a private plane so he **must** / **could** be a smuggler.

g The cat hasn't eaten for two days so I think it **can't** / **could** be sick.

4 Match statements a-h with responses 1-8. Then complete the responses with *must* or *can't*.

a [3] He hasn't slept for three days.
b [ ] It's freezing in this house.
c [ ] I don't have any money.
d [ ] Alex is in Australia at the moment.
e [ ] I haven't had anything to eat all day.
f [ ] Let's try the new restaurant on Second Avenue.
g [ ] It's illegal to park there.
h [ ] There's nothing to eat in this house.

1 He ______ be. I saw him in the mall an hour ago.

2 There ______ be some bread in the cabinet.

3 He ___must___ be exhausted, poor man.

4 It ______ be good. There's never anybody eating there.

5 The heating ______ be broken again.

6 It ______ be. Everybody always parks there.

7 That ______ be right. I gave you $30 yesterday.

8 You ______ be very hungry.

5 Rewrite the sentences using the words in parentheses.

He speaks English without an accent so he's almost certainly American. (must)

He speaks English without an accent so he must be American.

a She never smiles so I'm sure she isn't happy. (can't)

b He lives on the same road as Jill so perhaps he knows her. (might)

c I don't recognize this music but it's possibly Beethoven. (could)

d The police have arrested our neighbor. He is almost certainly a suspect. (must)

e Don't walk up those old stairs because they are possibly not strong enough. (might not)

f Don't go near that dog because it's possibly aggressive. (may)

6 Rewrite the sentences using *must*, *can't*, *might*, or *might not*.

This thing isn't moving – it's almost certainly dead.

This thing isn't moving – it must be dead.

a It's definitely not a spider – it only has six legs.

b Well, in that case it's definitely an insect.

c It's definitely not an insect because it doesn't have any wings.

d Not all insects have wings so it is possibly an insect.

e Maybe it's some kind of beetle.

f Let's ask Alan – he will possibly know.

g But Alan is possibly not in at the moment.

h I have a wildlife book and it possibly has a picture of a creature like this.

7 Look at the pictures and write sentences. Use *must be*, *might be*, and *can't be*.

acting in a movie ~~cold~~
hot lost thirsty

It can't be cold.

a

b

c

d

asleep and dreaming real
somebody playing a trick

e

f

g

VOCABULARY 2

Crimes and Criminals

1 Complete the words with the vowels.

th __e__ ft

a m ___ rd ___ r

b p ___ ckp ___ ck ___ t ___ ng

c k ___ dn ___ pp ___ ng

d v ___ nd ___ l ___ sm

e r ___ bb ___ ry

2 Write the missing words for crimes or criminals.

crime	criminal
murder	murderer
a kidnapping	
b	robber
c pickpocketing	
d theft	
e	vandal

3 Find five criminals in the wordsnake.

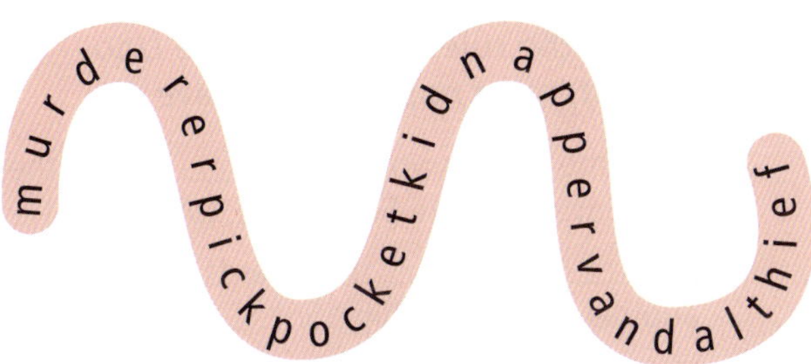

4 Match the news stories with the words in the box.

kidnapping ~~pickpocketing~~ robbery theft vandalism

The man stole a boy's cell phone from his pocket.
pickpocketing

a They drove the boy away in a car and then asked his parents for money.

____

b A group of men stole $50,000 from the bank on 45th Street this morning.

____

c Teachers are concerned about the amount of graffiti at the school.

____

d The woman stole a laptop computer from the office.

____

5 Complete the sentences with the words in the box.

kidnapping pickpocketing ~~robbery~~ theft vandalism

There was a bank ___robbery___ here last week. The robbers stole $5 million.

a Keep your bag shut. It's very crowded here and that's when a lot of ______________ happens.

b She got arrested for ______________. She stole clothes from a department store.

c There's a lot of ______________ in this town. Last week some people spray-painted the swings in the park.

d He went to prison for ______________ last year after taking a child from its parents.

GRAMMAR 2

Review: *must / must not*

1 Match the sentence beginnings with the endings.

a [2] In case you witness a crime,
b [ ] To have access to this email account,
c [ ] In order to board the aircraft,
d [ ] To enter the country,
e [ ] If you want to do research in the rain forest,
f [ ] To win the game *Risk*,

1 you must go through customs first.
2 you must inform the authorities.
3 you must accomplish your strategy.
4 you must get the yellow fever vaccine.
5 you must add two-factor verification of passwords.
6 you must not be carrying any flammable items.

2 Complete the sentences below with *must* or *must not.*

a You ______________ leave all electronic items at the door to enter this bank.
b You ______________ learn English if you want to survive in today's globalized world.
c You ______________ speak other languages in English class.
d You ______________ wear your seatbelt if you're a passenger in a car.
e You ______________ enter the classroom after the class has started.
f You ______________ smile when you get your picture taken.
g You ______________ copy off your friend's test.
h You ______________ use a baby car seat to carry toddlers in the car.
i You ______________ play your music loud after 10pm.
j You ______________ use your cell phone during the test.

3 Choose the correct alternative.

a We ________ turn off our cell phones in the classroom.
1 must
2 must not
3 don't have to

b We ________ act like robots in class, but we sure have to behave well.
1 must
2 must not
3 don't have to

c We ________ wear a uniform at our school, so I can wear dresses if I want to.
1 must
2 must not
3 don't have to

d However, we ________ follow a dress code, so I can't wear a very short dress.
1 must
2 must not
3 don't have to

e If we are too sick to remain in school, we ________ officially sign out at the main office.
1 must
2 must not
3 don't have to

4 Complete the rules for card game *Uno* with *must, must not,* or *don't have to.*

a To be the winner, you ____________ be the first player to score 500 points. [obligation]
b You ____________ trade cards with another player. [prohibition]
c If the previous player plays the skip card, you ____________ skip your turn. [obligation]
d You ____________ play your Wild card if you have other cards in hand. [not an obligation]
e A player who plays his or her next-to-last card ____________ call "Uno" as a warning to the other players. [obligation]
f If you draw a card from the deck, you ____________ discard it. [prohibition]
g When drawing from the deck, you ____________ either play or keep that card. [obligation]

GRAMMAR CHECK

1 Read the text and circle the correct answers.

"Well, one thing is for sure," Detective Mactaggart said slowly, "the thief **a** ________ be a woman." "How can you be so sure of that?" Morgan, his assistant, asked. "Because he's left a footprint outside the window and it's very big," Mactaggart answered. "The criminal **b** ________ be a woman with very large feet," his assistant suggested. "I suppose that's possible," Mactaggart agreed. "Anyway, this man or woman with big feet must **c** ________ red hair," he said suddenly. "Really? What tells you that?" Morgan asked. "Well, there's a red hair here on the carpet," said Mactaggart. "That **d** ________ be a human hair," Morgan said. "The criminal **e** ________ have a dog with red hair." "No. It's definitely a human hair," the detective said putting down his magnifying glass. "And what about that open locker there?" said Detective Mactaggart. "It **f** ________ someone with really good burglar skills." "Well, the proprietors **g** ________ a bit forgetful and left it just like that," said the assistant. "All right, all right, let's call it a day. It's too dusty in here anyway," said Detective Mactaggart.

	A	B	C
a	mustn't	(can't)	shouldn't
b	can	must	could
c	have	to have	having
d	could not	might not	must not
e	might	must	can't
f	can't be	might be	must be
g	must be	may be	can't be

2 Listen and check your answers.
19

LISTENING

1 Listen and order 1-7. Be careful! Two events did not happen.
20

a ☐ Anti-trafficking officers started watching the man secretly.

b ☐ Anti-trafficking officers stopped the man and opened his suitcase.

c ☐ One of the animals bit an officer's hand.

d ☐ Someone drugged baby mammals and put them in flat cages.

e ☐ The baby mammals yawned.

f ☐ The man bought endangered baby mammals on the black market.

g ☐ The man tried to smuggle snakes and turtles to China and Vietnam.

h ☐ The man went to Bangkok airport, in Thailand.

i ☐ They found endangered animals.

2 Listen again and write T for *true*, F for *false*, or DK for *don't know*.
20

a ☐ The man had just one suitcase full of animals.

b ☐ Some of the animals were dead.

c ☐ The man was on a plane when the officers arrested him.

d ☐ The man has never smuggled snakes or lizards to China.

e ☐ Leopards and panthers go for almost the same price on the black market in Bangkok and Dubai.

f ☐ There is a lot of wildlife trafficking in Thailand.

g ☐ The authorities in Thailand don't often catch people smuggling a large number of mammals.

EXTENSION

Underline the correct options to complete the text.

Someone's toy tiger **a has started / started** a big police operation in Hampshire, England, last week and stopped play at a nearby cricket ground and golf club. The police **b received / have received** calls from members of the public on Saturday about a white tiger **c who / which** was "hiding in a field" near Hedge End. Armed police **d stood / stand** near the field while a helicopter prepared to take thermal images of it from above. Animal experts from nearby Marwell Zoo **e were also standing / have also stood** ready to provide help.

Golfers at a nearby golf club were told to stay indoors and cricket players at the Rose Bowl **f were stopping / stopped** their game for 20 minutes while the police **g were investigating / have investigated**.

The police officers **h saw / have seen** that the "wild animal" was not moving and the people in the helicopter didn't **i detected / detect** body heat. Then the tiger **j was falling / fell** onto its side as a rush of air from the helicopter knocked it over. At that stage, the team realized the tiger was a life-size toy. Here are some comments from people who read about the incident.

"It was very realistic. If you **k see / saw** it, you **l 'd be / were** scared."

"When I saw the tiger, I said 'it **m mustn't / can't** be real.'"

"It **n would / will** be funny if the police closed the road for a toy tiger."

"I'm never **o forgetting / going to forget** this story."

"I haven't laughed this much **p for / since** a very long time. It's the funniest news story **q I'm ever hearing / I've ever heard**."

VOCABULARY PLUS

Breaking the Law

1 
2 
3 
4 
5 

6 

7 
8 
9 

10 

1 Label the pictures with the words in the box. Then listen and repeat.

21

animal smuggling	indictment
break into	hack
file a police report	press charges
fraud	smash a window
get away	witness a crime

2 Complete the definitions with the correct options form activity 1.

If you ___hack___ something, you illegally access someone's computer, system, or online accounts.

- **a** If you ______________, you officially register the crime you've suffered or witnessed.
- **b** If you receive an ______________, you are accused of a crime.
- **c** If you ______________, you see a crime taking place.
- **d** If you ______________, you break the glass into small pieces.
- **e** If you ______________ a building, you enter a place by force in order to steal.

3 The expressions in bold are wrong. Write the correct ones using the correct verb form.

The burglars stole my mom's jewelry when they **got away** our house.
broke into

- **a** The thieves ran out of the bank and **pressed charges** in a fast car.
  ____
- **b** He was indicted for **animal smuggling** when he pretended to be someone else.
  ____
- **c** Vandals **broke into** the windows and stole the furniture.
  ____
- **d** The bank robbers **smashed** the bank's security network before breaking in.
  ____

4 Answer the questions for you. Write full sentences.

- **a** Have you ever witnessed a crime?
  ____
- **b** What would you do if you saw someone breaking into a building?
  ____

8

COMMUNICATE

ABC VOCABULARY 1

The Written Word

1 Find six communication words in the word snake. Use the left-over letters in the boxes to make another communication word.

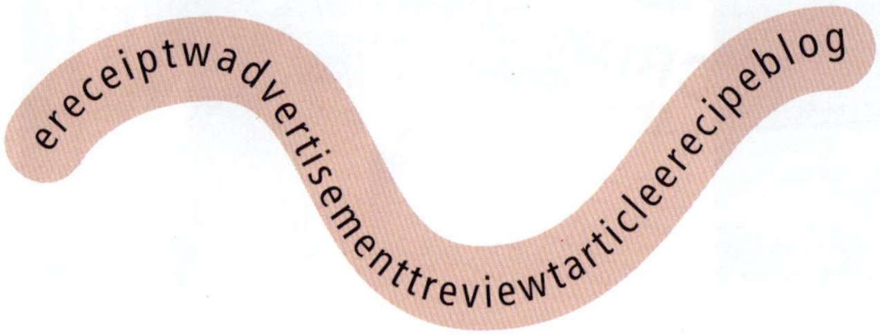

☐ ☐ ☐ ☐ ☐

2 Complete the communication words with the vowels.

b l _o_ g

a t r ___ v ___ l g ___ ___ d ___

b c ___ r t ___ ___ n

c d ___ c t ___ ___ n ___ r y ___ n t r y

d ___ n s t r ___ c t ___ ___ n m ___ n u ___ l

e l ___ b ___ l

f q ___ ___ t ___

3 Underline the correct words.

I read a **travel guide** / **review** of the new Elizabeth Olsen movie.

a I'm keeping the **recipe** / **receipt** for my new bag because I might take it back to the store and exchange it.

b I saw a funny **advertisement** / **article** for a new kind of lemonade. I'm going to try it soon.

c There's a really funny **quote** / **cartoon** in the paper. It's a picture of a cat saying to its human owner, "I'm going out. Do you need any mice?"

d I read an interesting **dictionary entry** / **article** about global warming.

e I have a **blog** / **recipe** about food. I write new posts every week.

4 Match the definitions with the words in the box.

article dictionary entry label quote recipe travel guide ~~tweet~~

information posted online in very few words; the maximum number of letters or characters is 280: _tweet_

a piece of writing in a newspaper or magazine: ___________

b a book providing information about a place: ___________

c a small piece of paper, on a bottle for example, or a small piece of material on clothes, that gives information: ___________

d information given to explain the meaning of a word or phrase: ___________

e a text that explains how to prepare a dish, as an apple pie or a carrot soup: ___________

f the exact words which someone said: ___________

5 Complete the sentences with the words in the box.

advertisement article ~~blog~~ instruction manual receipt recipe travel guide

Let's go online and read her _blog_ so we can see what she's up to at the moment.

a There are hardly any ___________s or interesting ___________s about food in *Let's Cook* magazine. It's full of ___________s for fridges, cooktops, and kitchen equipment.

b Here's your change. Your ___________ for the shirt is in the bag.

c I want to see all the best things in Seville when I go there in the summer. I've already bought a ___________.

d Can you help me install my new printer? The ___________ is incomprehensible!

GRAMMAR 1

Tense and Form Review

1 Complete the sentences with the time expressions in the box.

~~always~~ at the moment just last year next week since tomorrow two weeks ago while

My sister ___always___ sends me postcards from France.

a I spent three months in California ________.

b I got a text message from Fran ________.

c Dave hasn't called ________ Friday.

d We're going to meet one day ________.

e Joey is lying in bed ________.

f I was working ________ you were lying in bed.

g You've ________ sat on my glasses!

h I'm playing soccer at two o'clock ________.

2 Match the sentence beginnings with the endings.

a I don't [5]

b He used to be a designer but now [ ]

c She read the article while she [ ]

d At the moment Ellie is [ ]

e He didn't find [ ]

f You've never [ ]

g I'll send you [ ]

h She's going to [ ]

i We're meeting at Stacey's house [ ]

1 a text message later today.

2 at four o'clock tomorrow.

3 he writes movie reviews.

4 was waiting for the train.

5 read the cartoons in newspapers.

6 reply to the job advertisement.

7 that recipe on a website.

8 writing a letter to her cousin.

9 written an instruction manual.

3 Underline the correct form of the verbs.

Hello, readers and welcome to my travel blog!

a I write / I'm writing this from a youth hostel in Sweden. It's a lovely day and the sun **b is shining / shines**. It **c doesn't shine / isn't shining** every day, though. In fact, it **d is raining / rains** quite often. I can see the beach from my window. It's only eight o'clock in the morning so people **e aren't swimming / don't swim** yet. **f I'm having / I have** a great time here. I have a great routine. Every day **g I'm getting up / I get up** at seven. Then I **h go / am going** for a run and I **i watch / am watching** the birds on the seashore. I **j begin / 'm beginning** to know the names of quite a lot of these birds.

After my run, I **k am sitting / sit down** with my Swedish books. Yes, guys, I **l 'm learning / learn** Swedish. I **m don't know / am not knowing** many words yet. "Tack" is a very useful word, though. It **n is meaning / means** "thank you". I **o am loving / love** the food here. Swedish people **p eat / are eating** a lot of raw and pickled fish. In fact, I **q 'm eating / eat** raw fish right now for my breakfast!

4 Complete the sentences with the correct form of the verbs in parentheses. Use the simple past, past progressive or present perfect.

She ___hasn't answered___ (not answer) my email yet.

a I got a text message from Jan while I ________ (talk) to my mom.

b Where is Tom? We ________ (not hear) from him in months.

c They ________ (have) their own computers since they were 12.

d I ________ (not read) her blog yesterday, but I ________ (listen) to her podcast last week.

e My mom ________ (just join) TikTok. She ________ (spend) an hour watching videos yesterday.

f She ________ (write) a tweet at 6am yesterday.

5 Complete the text with the correct form of the verbs in parentheses.

Maggie Wright is a cartoonist. She ___has worked___ (work) for Laugh Magazine for two years. She **a** ________ (start) drawing funny pictures when she was 14.
"I **b** ________ (go) to all my classes, but often I couldn't concentrate on the lessons so I **c** ________ (begin) to draw penguins. While I **d** ________ (draw), I **e** ________ (start) to invent characters for them. I **f** ________ (stop) drawing penguins now, but I **g** ________ (keep) all my first drawings."
At 18, Maggie **h** ________ (go) to art college where she **i** ________ (learn) a lot about illustration. "I **j** ________ (work) very hard there and I **k** ________ (develop) my own personal style."

6 Underline the correct words.

Laura Do you want to come to Hyde Park with me and Izzie? The forecast says it's **a going to be / being** lovely and sunny tomorrow. **b We'll have / We're having** a picnic by the lake at two o'clock.

Claire I can't. **c I'll play / I'm playing** tennis in the club tournament all day. It's crazy because I know **d I won't win / I'm not winning**.

Laura Why do you say that?

Claire Because I'm sure Yasmin **e is winning / will win** again.

Laura Do you feel like going to the movies on Sunday afternoon? There's a movie with Emma Stone. I'm sure **f you'll / you're** going to like it.

Claire No, thanks. **g I'm going to / I'll stay** at home. I need to work on my new blog. **h I'll / I'm going to** put some new pictures on it.

Laura New pictures? What are they of?

Claire **i You'll / You're going to** see when you check the blog! Hey! Is that a new camera?

Laura Yes. I'm **j going to take / taking** lots of pictures in the park. I think **k I'll share / I'm sharing** some of them to you if they're nice.

7 Complete the sentences about you and your friends.

I always ___check my emails before I go to bed___.

a My friend usually ________.

b At the moment, I'm ________.

c Last year my friend ________.

d While I was ________.

e While my friend ________.

f Tomorrow I'm ________.

g One day ________.

h I've never ________.

VOCABULARY 2

Adjectives with *-able* and *-ible*

1 Complete the adjectives with the vowels. Then write their opposites.

r _e_ _a_ s _o_ n _a_ b l _e_

unreasonable

a r ___ s p ___ n s ___ b l ___

____

b v ___ s ___ b l ___

____

c r ___ l ___ ___ b l ___

____

d ___ c c ___ p t ___ b l ___

____

e f l ___ x ___ b l ___

____

f b ___ ___ r ___ b l ___

____

2 Underline the correct words.

People say the Great Wall of China is **reasonable** / **visible** from space.

a He is very **bearable** / **reliable**. If he says he'll do something, he does it.

b She didn't have any problems moving to New York. She is very **acceptable** / **flexible**.

c My tooth hurts, but it's **bearable** / **responsible**. I can wait until tomorrow to see the dentist.

d He is very mature and **responsible** / **acceptable**. He works hard at school and has a part-time job.

e Jenny wouldn't help her brother with his homework because she was watching TV – she's so **responsible** / **unreasonable**!

f Will it be **bearable** / **acceptable** to wear jeans to their dinner party or will I have to wear something more formal?

3 Complete the sentences with the negative form of the correct adjectives.

He doesn't like traveling and foreign food. He is totally _inflexible_.
(responsible / reliable / flexible)

a I'm going to go crazy if that noise doesn't stop. It really is ______________.
(reasonable / bearable / reliable)

b You can see the trees moving, but the wind itself is ______________.
(responsible / acceptable / visible)

c He adopted a dog, but he doesn't look after it or take it for walks. He is completely ______________.
(flexible / responsible / bearable)

d She was supposed to bring food to the party, but she forgot. She really is ______________.
(reasonable / responsible / reliable)

4 Complete the sentences with one of the adjectives or opposites from activity 1.

She'll be here on time. She's never late. She's very _reliable_.

a You can't go for a walk in the forest in those high heels. Don't be so ______________.

b When Superkid puts on his magic coat, you can't see him. He's ______________.

c Take me to the hospital now. This pain is ______________.

d Here are your tickets and passport. You are ______________ for them now, not me.

e A ______________ person like you will have no problems when you go and live in Australia.

f It's ______________ to send text messages during a family dinner.

GRAMMAR 2

Tense and Form Review: Questions

1 Order the words to make questions. Then match the verbs with tenses and forms a-h.

a about / is / she / talking / What ? [1]
What is she talking about?

b Amanda, / have / how / I / known / long / you ? [ ]

______

c in / Do / go / vacation / on / they / usually / July ? [ ]

______

d back / did / from / get / he / France / When ? [ ]

______

e Are / going / jeans / party / to / to Tonya's / you / those / wear ? [ ]

______

f keys / leave / the / they / will / Where ? [ ]

______

g an / artist / become / her / made / What ? [ ]

______

h airport / drove / Scott / the / to / Who ? [ ]

______

1 present progressive
2 future
3 simple past
4 present perfect
5 *be going to* for future
6 simple present

2 Match the question beginnings with the endings.

a What were you doing [3]
b Have you [ ]
c When will [ ]
d Are you [ ]
e What are [ ]

1 ever lost your cell phone?
2 going to get in touch with her?
3 when he walked into the room?
4 you give me an answer?
5 you writing on your blog?

3 Read each sentence. Then write questions in the simple past or past progressive.

Liza fell off her bike yesterday.
(go / fast?) Was she going fast?
(get hurt?) Did she get hurt?

a (Where / it / happen?)
______

b I saw Kate and Andy at the beach. (When exactly / see them?)
______

c (they swim / or lie in the sun?)
______

d (speak / to them?)
______

e A man stole my cell phone on the bus. (he / sit / next to you?)
______

f (what / he / look like?)
______

g (go / to the police?)
______

4 Complete the dialogue with the correct form of the verbs and the words in parentheses.

James Where did you meet (you meet) Ed?
Thomas In a movie.
James Really? **a** ______ (he act) in it?
Thomas Yes, and so was I.
James Wow! **b** ______ (you be) in a lot of movies?
Thomas Three so far. That was my first.
James **c** ______ (it be) his first, too?
Thomas No, it wasn't. **d** ______ (he work) in TV and movies since he was eight.
James **e** ______ (you be) in any more productions together?
Thomas I hope so. We've both just done auditions for a movie called *Midnight*.
James When **f** ______ (you know) if you've got the part?
Thomas Tomorrow at 10am!
James **g** ______ (you celebrate) if you get the part?
Thomas Definitely!

GRAMMAR CHECK

1 Read the text and circle the correct answers.

Communication **a** ______ very easy. We **b** ______ in touch with people thousands of miles away. We **c** ______ to be in our homes near a telephone to do this. At the moment, 18-year-old Dave Roberts **d** ______ around Asia on his gap year. Mostly he **e** ______ in touch with friends and family by text messages. But last week he **f** ______ Google Meet to talk to his grandmother on her birthday. "My granddaughter Tess **g** ______ her tablet to me and there was Dave on the screen. He **h** ______ on a beautiful white beach. He **i** ______ to me for about fifty minutes, and **j** ______ again at six tomorrow evening. Tess and Dave's father **k** ______ me a tablet. **l** ______ speaking to my friends in Australia and sharing pictures with them."

	A	B	C
a	became	becomes	has become
b	are staying	stay	have stayed
c	don't need	aren't needing	didn't need
d	was traveling	travels	is traveling
e	stayed	is staying	stays
f	was using	used	has used
g	brought	was bringing	has brought
h	sat	has sat	was sitting
i	spoke	was speaking	has spoken
j	will call	is calling	calls
k	will get	are going to get	gets
l	I'll enjoy	I'm enjoying	I enjoyed

2 Listen and check your answers. 22

LISTENING

1 Listen and answer the questions. 23

a How long does Mark spend online?

______

b How long does Angie spend online?

______

c How long does Dan spend online?

______

d Who uses the internet mainly for entertainment?

______

e Who uses it for research?

______

f Who uses it for communication?

______

2 Listen again and answer the questions. 23

a How long did Mark use to spend online?

______

b Why did he read about the nuclear disaster in Fukushima?

______

c When did he decide to reduce his internet use?

______

d What does Angie use Instagram for? (three things)

______

______

e What does she write a blog about?

______

f Why does Dan like virtual reality games?

______

______

g What video did Dan upload to YouTube?

______

EXTENSION

Underline the correct words to complete the text.

SMARTPHONE NEWS

A smartphone expert **a is asking / was asked** why **b sales are / are sales** still increasing.

He said that sales **c have increased / is increasing** by 19% last year because people **d have bought / were buying** new and more modern models. He added that now people **e didn't just want / hasn't just wanted** high-res cameras on their phones. They want to create with their phones.

Young people **f which / who** are good with technology **g are encouraged / are encouraging** by some tech companies to develop apps for smartphones. Fourteen-year-old Luke Firth from New York said: "At the moment **h I develop / I'm developing** a game about an alien. It's fun, but it's tiring, and my mom **i isn't liking / doesn't like** me working on it. But if I **j sell / will sell** it to a game company, **k I'll make / I made** a lot of money. I **l would have / have** perfected it by now if I didn't have to spend so much time at school."

So what **m is being next big thing / will be the next big thing** in smartphone technology? Experts **n already developed / have already developed** technology **o which / who** turns your hand into a touchscreen. A user's hand **p is filmed / is filming** by the smartphone camera and the information **q has sent / is sent** is processed by the phone. So in the future, smartphones **r will be left / are left** in the pocket or bag and users **s is making / will send** texts from the palm of their hand. But who would buy this technology if it **t became / will become** available? Drivers? Cyclists? Who **u knows / does know**?

VOCABULARY PLUS

The Newspaper

1

______

2

______

3

______

4

______

5

______

6

______

7

______

8

______

9

______

10

______

1 Label the pictures above with the words in the box. Then listen and repeat.

24))

caption	headline
cartoon	horoscope
classified ads	letters to the editor
crossword	sports pages
gossip columns	weather report

2 Underline the correct words.

The drawings in these **cartoons** / **crosswords** are really good.

a I always read the **headlines** / **gossip** first to see what the most important news is.

b My dad often reads out the clues to the **weather report** / **crossword** while we're having breakfast.

c If you want to know who won the game, read the **letters to the editor page** / **sports pages**.

d When my sister wanted to buy a second-hand car, she looked at the **captions** / **classified ads**.

e I like reading the **gossip columns** / **horoscope** to find out what famous people are doing.

3 Match extracts a-f with the newspaper sections in activity 1.

FIRE HITS THE CITY [1]

a Dear editor, I think the new mall ... [ ]

b TV star George Smith has just gotten divorced again. [ ]

c Matt Baker scored the winning goal. [ ]

d Gemini: money will come your way today. [ ]

e Tomorrow will be cloudy with rain in the east. [ ]

f 5 across: a female horse. [ ]

4 Complete the sentences for you. Try to use words from activity 1.

a My favorite part of the newspaper is ______.

b I never read the ______.

c My parents usually read the ______, but I prefer the ______.

WORDLIST

PHONETIC CHART

25 **VOWELS AND DIPHTHONGS**

/ɪ/ p**i**g	/e/ br**ea**d	/u/ l**o**se	/aɪ/ **I**
/i/ sh**e**	/ɜr/ c**ur**ly	/ə/ act**o**r	/ɔɪ/ t**oy**
/æ/ c**a**t	/ɔ/ b**a**ll	/ʌ/ s**u**nny	/aʊ/ m**ou**ntain
/ɑ/ **a**rm	/ʊ/ g**oo**d	/eɪ/ US**A**	/oʊ/ b**oa**t

26 **CONSONANTS**

/p/ **p**otato	/tʃ/ **ch**air	/s/ **S**pain	/n/ **n**ewsstand
/b/ **b**lue	/dʒ/ fri**dg**e	/z/ ea**s**y	/ŋ/ spri**ng**
/t/ **t**axi	/f/ **f**inish	/ʃ/ **sh**ower	/l/ **l**ake
/d/ **d**rama	/v/ **v**erb	/ʒ/ televi**s**ion	/r/ **r**ead
/k/ **c**arrot	/θ/ ba**th**room	/h/ **h**i	/j/ **y**esterday
/g/ **g**randpa	/ð/ **th**ere	/m/ **m**outh	/w/ **w**ater

27 A

a few /ə fju/

a lot of /ə lɑt əv/

acceptable (adj) /ək'septəb(ə)l/

adaptable (adj) /ə'dæptəb(ə)l/

agree about /ə'gri ə'baʊt/

agree with /ə'gri wɪð/

allowance (n) /ə'laʊəns/

amazing (adj) /ə'meɪzɪŋ/

American Sign Language /ə'merɪkən saɪn 'læŋgwɪdʒ/

animal migration (n) /'ænɪm(ə)l maɪ'greɪʃ(ə)n/

animal smuggler (n) /'ænɪm(ə)l 'smʌg(ə)lər/

animal smuggling (n) /'ænɪm(ə)l 'smʌg(ə)lɪŋ/

any (adv) /'eni/

application form (n) /ˌæplɪ'keɪʃ(ə)n fɔrm/

apply for a job /ə'plaɪ fər ə dʒɑb/

apprenticeship (n) /ə'prentɪsˌʃɪp/

architecture (n) /'ɑrkɪˌtektʃər/

argue about /'ɑrˌgju ə'baʊt/

argue with /'ɑrˌgju wɪð/

arrest a suspect /ə'rest ə sə'spekt/

arrive early /ə'raɪv 'ɜrli/

article (n) /'ɑrtɪk(ə)l/

awful (adj) /'ɔf(ə)l/

28 B

bad (adj) /bæd/

be charged /bi tʃɑː(r)dʒd/

be guilty /bi 'gɪlti/

be innocent /bi 'ɪnəs(ə)nt/

be late /bi leɪt/

be polite /bi pə'laɪt/

be rude /bi rud/

be unemployed /bi ˌʌnɪm'plɔɪd/

bearable (adj) /'berəb(ə)l/

become rich /bɪ'kʌm rɪtʃ/

being friendly /'biɪŋ 'fren(d)li/

belt (n) /belt/

benefits (n) /'benəfɪts/

big (adj) /bɪg/

blog (n) /blɔg/

boiling (adj) /'bɔɪlɪŋ/

bonus (n) /'boʊnəs/

break into /breɪk 'ɪntu/

bring a present /brɪŋ ə 'prezənt/

business (n) /ˈbɪznəs/

button (n) /ˈbʌt(ə)n/

buy a guidebook /baɪ ə ˈgaɪdˌbʊk/

Buy Nothing Day (n) /baɪ ˈnʌθɪŋ deɪ/

buy souvenirs /baɪ suvəˈnɪrz/

29)) **C**

can't /kænt/

caption (n) /ˈkæpʃ(ə)n/

cartoon (n) /kɑrˈtun/

casual (adj) /ˈkæʒuəl/

catch a thief /kætʃ ə θif/

change schools /tʃeɪndʒ skulz/

claim expenses /kleɪm ɪkˈspɛnsəz/

cold (adj) /koʊld/

colorful (adj) /ˈkʌlərf(ə)l/

come back home /kʌm bæk hoʊm/

comfortable (adj) /ˈkʌmfərtəb(ə)l/

commit a crime /kəˈmɪt ə kraɪm/

compost food scraps /ˈkɑmˌpoʊst fud skræps/

conditions (n) /kənˈdɪʃ(ə)nz/

contract (n) /ˈkɑnˌtrækt/

conventional (adj) /kənˈvenʃ(ə)nəl/

crossword (n) /ˈkrɔsˌwɜrd/

cut (n) /kʌt/

30)) **D**

delighted (adj) /dɪˈlaɪtəd/

depend on /dɪˈpend ɑn/

dictionary entry (n) /ˈdɪkʃəˌneri ˈentri/

do community service /du kəˈmjunəti ˈsɜrvɪs/

do the washing up /du ði ˈwɑʃɪŋ ʌp/

dream about /drim əˈbaʊt/

drop out of college /drɑp aʊt əv ˈkɑlɪdʒ/

31)) **E**

earn a wage /ɜrn ə weɪdʒ/

electric vehicle (n) /ɪˈlektrɪk ˈviɪk(ə)l/

engineering (n) /ˌendʒɪˈnirɪŋ/

enormous (adj) /ɪˈnɔrməs/

exhausted (adj) /ɪgˈzɔstəd/

expenses (n) / ɪkˈspɛnsəz/

32)) **F**

fashionable (adj) /ˈfæʃ(ə)nəb(ə)l/

file (n) /faɪl/

fill out an application form /fɪl aʊt æn ˌæplɪˈkeɪʃ(ə)n fɔrm/

flexible (adj) /ˈfleksəb(ə)l/

folk music (n) /foʊk ˈmjuzɪk/

formal (adj) /ˈfɔrm(ə)l/

fraud (n) /frɔd/

freezing (adj) /ˈfrizɪŋ/

33)) **G**

garbage (n) /ˈgɑrbɪdʒ/

get a pension /get ə ˈpenʃ(ə)n/

get into /get ˈɪntu/

get into trouble /get ˈɪntu ˈtrʌb(ə)l/

get off a bus /get ɔf ə bʌs/

get on a train /get ɑn ə treɪn/

give advice /gɪv ədˈvaɪs/

give away /gɪv əˈweɪ/

give customers advice /gɪv ˈkʌstəmərz ədˈvaɪs/

give presents /gɪv ˈprezənts/

glamourous (adj) /ˈglæm(ə)rəs/

go abroad /goʊ əˈbrɔd/

go for a job interview /goʊ fɔr ə dʒɑb ˈɪntərˌvju/

go on trial /goʊ ɔn ˈtraɪəl/

go to prison /goʊ tu ˈprɪz(ə)n/

go with /goʊ wɪð/

good (adj) /gʊd/

graffiti (n) /grəˈfiti/

guillotine (n) /ˈgɪləˌtin/ or /ˈgɪjəˌtin/

34)) **H**

happy (adj) /ˈhæpi/

have a full-time job /hæv ə fʊl taɪm dʒɑb/

have adventures /hæv ædˈventʃərz/

have an accident /hæv æn ˈæksɪdənt/

have an argument /hæv æn ˈɑrgjəmənt/

have an interview /hæv æn ˈɪntərˌvju/

have fun /hæv fʌn/

headline (n) /ˈhedˌlaɪn/

35 I

immigrant (n) /ˈɪmɪgrənt/

immigration (n) /ˌɪmɪˈgreɪʃ(ə)n/

impractical (adj) /ɪmˈpræktɪk(ə)l/

inflexible (adj) /ɪnˈfleksəb(ə)l/

install solar panels /ɪnˈstɔl ˈsoʊlər ˈpænəlz/

instruction manual (n) /ɪnˈstrʌkʃ(ə)n ˈmænjuəl/

insulate windows /ˈɪnsəˌleɪt ˈwɪndoʊz/

interrupt a conversation /ˌɪntəˈrʌpt ə ˌkɑnvərˈseɪʃ(ə)n/

investigate a crime /ɪnˈvestɪˌgeɪt ə kraɪm/

invisible (adj) /ɪnˈvɪzəb(ə)l/

irresponsible (adj) /ˌɪrɪˈspɑnsəb(ə)l/

isn't true /ˈɪz(ə)nt tru/

it is possible /ɪt ɪz ˈpɑsəb(ə)l/

36 J

job advertisement (n) /dʒɑb ædˈvɜrtɪsmənt/

jump a line /dʒʌmp eɪ laɪn/

37 K

kidnapper (n) /ˈkɪdˌnæpər/

kidnapping (v) /ˈkɪdˌnæpɪŋ/

38 L

label (n) /ˈleɪb(ə)l/

law (n) /lɔ/

listen to /ˈlɪs(ə)n tu/

look for /lʊk fɔr/

look for clues /lʊk fɔr kluz/

look forward to /lʊk ˈfɔrwərd tu/

loose (adj) /lus/

lose a job /luz ə dʒɑb/

39 M

make a playlist /meɪk ə ˈpleɪˌlɪst/

make coffee /meɪk ˈkɑfi/

make new friends /meɪk nu frɛndz/

many (adv) /ˈmeni/

meet people /mit ˈpip(ə)l/

mend old clothes /mend oʊld kloʊðz/

might /maɪt/

misinform (v) /ˌmɪsɪnˈfɔrm/

misplace (v) /ˌmɪsˈpleɪs/

misunderstand (v) /ˌmɪsʌndərˈstænd/

move /muv/

much (adv) /mʌtʃ/

murder (n) /ˈmɜrdər/

murderer (n) /ˈmɜrdərər/

must /mʌst/

40 O

old-fashioned (adj) /oʊld ˈfæʃənd/

one by one /wʌn baɪ wʌn/

overcrowd (v) /ˌoʊvərˈkraʊd/

overeat (v) /ˌoʊvərˈit/

overpopulate (v) /ˌoʊvərˈpɑpjəleɪt/

41 P

pack a suitcase /pæk ə ˈsutˌkeɪs/

participate in /pɑrˈtɪsɪˌpeɪt ɪn/

part-time job /pɑrt taɪm dʒɑb/

pay a fine /peɪ ə faɪn/

pay raise (n) /peɪ reɪz/

pension (n) /ˈpenʃ(ə)n/

pick out /pɪk aʊt/

pick up /pɪk ʌp/

pickpocket (n) /ˈpɪkˌpɑkɪt/

pickpocketing (v) /ˈpɪkˌpɑkətɪŋ/

plan a journey /plæn ə ˈdʒɜrni/

play music at a party /pleɪ ˈmjuzɪk æt ə ˈpɑrti/

pocket (n) /ˈpɑkɪt/

poem (n) /ˈpoʊəm/

point at someone /pɔɪnt æt ˈsʌmwʌn/

press charges /pres ˈtʃɑrdʒəz/

prom night /pram naɪt/

promotion (n) /prə'moʊʃ(ə)n/

protest song (n) /'proʊˌtest sɔŋ/

punishment (n) /'pʌnɪʃmənt/

put away /pʊt ə'weɪ/

put on /pʊt ɔn/

42 Q

question a suspect /'kwestʃ(ə)n ə sə'spekt/

questionnaire (n) /ˌkwestʃə'ner/

quote (n) /kwoʊt/

43 R

reasonable (adj) /'riz(ə)nəb(ə)l/

receipt (n) /rɪ'sit/

receive advice /rɪ'siv əd'vaɪs/

receive presents /rɪ'siv 'prezənts/

recipe (n) /'resəpi/

recycle packaging /ri'saɪk(ə)l 'pækɪdʒɪŋ/

reliable (adj) /rɪ'laɪəb(ə)l/

reorganize (v) /ri'ɔrgəˌnaɪz/

replace (v) /rɪ'pleɪs/

replay (v) /'riˌpleɪ/

responsible (adj) /rɪ'spansəb(ə)l/

retire (v) /rɪ'taɪr/

review (n) /rɪ'vju/

ride a bike /raɪd ə baɪk/

robber (n) /'rabər/

robbery (n) /'rabəri/

44 S

safe (n) /seɪf/

sailor (n) /'seɪlər/

save water /seɪv 'wɔtər/

sell clothes /sel kloʊðz/

send postcards /send 'poʊstˌkardz/

serve customers /sɜrv 'kʌstəmərz/

set off /set ɔf/

settle down /'set(ə)l daʊn/

shake hands /ʃeɪk hændz/

share car journeys /ʃer kar 'ʤɜrniz/

sign a contract /saɪn ə 'kanˌtrækt/

small (adj) /smɔl/

snap your fingers /snæp jʊr 'fɪŋgərz/

solve a crime /salv ə kraɪm/

some (adv) /sʌm/

spend money /spend 'mʌni/

spend time /spend taɪm/

sporty (adj) /'spɔrti/

start your own business /start jʊr oʊn 'bɪznəs/

still (adv) /stɪl/

suspect someone /sə'spekt 'sʌmwʌn/

45 T

take a gap year /teɪk ə gæp jɪr/

take off /teɪk ɔf/

take off your shoes /teɪk ɔf jʊr ʃuz/

talk to /tɔk tu/

tell jokes /tel dʒoʊks/

tell lies /tel laɪz/

tell the truth /tel ði truθ/

terrifying (adj) /'terəˌfaɪɪŋ/

theft (n) /θeft/

thief (n) /θif/

throw away /θroʊ ə'weɪ/

tight (adj) /taɪt/

tiny (adj) /'taɪni/

tired (adj) /'taɪrd/

to arrange to meet someone /tu ə'reɪndʒ tu mit 'sʌmwʌn/

to get to know someone /tu get tu nəʊ 'sʌmwʌn/

to make friends with someone /tu meɪk frendz wɪð 'sʌmwʌn/

to meet a new person /tu mit ə nu 'pɜrs(ə)n/

trash-free /træʃ fri/

travel by public transport /'træv(ə)l baɪ 'pʌblɪk træns'pɔrt/

travel guide (n) /'træv(ə)l gaɪd/

trendy (adj) /'trendi/

try on /traɪ ɔn/

turn off lights /tɜrn ɔf laɪts/

tweet (n) /twit/

46 U

unacceptable (adj) /ˌʌnək'septəb(ə)l/

unbearable (adj) /ən'bɛrəbəl/

undercook (v) /əndər'kʊk/

underestimate (v) /ˌʌndər'estɪˌmeɪt/

underpay (v) /ˌʌndər'peɪ/

underuse (v) /ˌʌndər'juz/

unreasonable (adj) /ən'riznəbəl/

unreliable (adj) /ˌʌnrɪ'laɪəb(ə)l/

use rechargeable batteries /juz ri'ʧɑrʤəbəl 'bætəriz/

47 V

vandal (n) /'vænd(ə)l/

vandalism (n) /'vænd(ə)lˌɪzəm/

visible (adj) /'vɪzəb(ə)l/

48 W

wage (n) /weɪdʒ/

wait for /weɪt fɔr/

wear out /wer aʊt/

went /went/

witness a crime /'wɪtnəs ə kraɪm/

work experience (n) /wɜrk ɪk'spɪriəns/

work part-time /wɜrk pɑrt taɪm/

worry about /'wʌri ə'baʊt/

would /wʊd/

Based on *InstaEnglish* and *Motivate*
© Macmillan Education Brasil 2019 and Macmillan Education Limited 2013
Written by Patrick Howarth, Patricia Reilly, and Olivia Johnston
Grammar, Speaking, and *Culture* pages adapted by Gisele Marçon Bastos Périgo and Thelma de Carvalho Guimarães
Vocabulary, Reading, and *Writing* pages adapted by Thelma de Carvalho Guimarães
Digital Literacy and *Global Citizenship* pages created by Thelma de Carvalho Guimarães

Director of Languages Brazil: Patricia Souza De Luccia
Publishing Manager and Field Researcher: Patricia Muradas
Content Creation Coordinator: Cristina do Vale
Art Coordinator: Jean Aranha
Lead Editor: Gabriel França
Content Editors: Gabriel França, Tatiana Martins Santana, Viviane Kirmeliene
Digital Editors: Deborah Stafussi, Elaine Lins
Editorial Assistant: Arali Lobo Gomes, Carolina Araujo de Melo, Daniela Alves, Fernanda Kumagai, Nayra Simões, Roberta Somera
Editorial Intern: Pedro Improta
Art Assistant: Jacqueline Alves
Art Intern: Victor Augusto Amorim
Editorial Apprentice: Beatriz Jacinto
Graphic Production: Alexandra L. S. de Carvalho, Thais Mendes P. Galvão
Proofreaders: Ana Lucia Mendes Reis, Andréa Vidal, Catia de Almeida, Edward Willson, James Taylor, Rhennan Santos
Design Concept: Martha Tadaieski
Page Makeup: Figurattiva Editorial
Photo Research: Marcia Sato
Illustrations: StormCreative Studio
Image Processing: Jacqueline Alves, Jean Aranha, Victor Augusto Amorim
Extra Interactive Activities Content Development: Daniela Alves
Cover Concept: Jean Aranha
Cover photography: torwai/iStockphoto/Getty Images
Audio: Argila
Video: Desenredo

We would like to dedicate this book to teachers all over Brazil. We would also like to thank our clients and teachers who have helped us make this book better with their many rich contributions and feedback straight from the classroom!

The authors, adaptor and publishers would like to thank the following for permission to reproduce the photographic material:
p. 10: Stéphane ROCHON/iStockphoto/Getty Image; Peter Schaefer/iStockphoto/Getty Image. p. 12: Mary Evans/Imageplus; Glasshouse Images/Easypix Brasil; British Library; Mary Evans/Imageplus. p. 14: Hubert Boesl/picture-alliance/dpa/Imageplus. p. 15: Luciano_Marques/iStockphoto/Getty Image; Bobex-73/iStockphoto/Getty Image. p. 16: FG Trade/iStockphoto/Getty Image. p. 17: Evgeniia Siiankovskaia/iStockphoto/Getty Image; MicroStockHub/iStockphoto/Getty Image. p. 18: AJ_Watt/iStockphoto/Getty Image; Voyagerix/iStockphoto/Getty Image; freemixer/iStockphoto/Getty Image; Daniel Kloe/iStockphoto/Getty Image; FG Trade/iStockphoto/Getty Image; Vladimir Vladimirov/iStockphoto/Getty Image. p. 19: Stígur Már Karlsson/Heimsmyndir/iStockphoto/Getty Image; Igor Alecsander/iStockphoto/Getty Image; gustavofrazao/iStockphoto/Getty Image; kate_sept2004/iStockphoto/Getty Image. p. 21: Craig Lambert/iStockphoto/Getty Image; PerfectStills/iStockphoto/Getty Image; sharply_done/iStockphoto/Getty Image. p. 23: Tomas Kozak/iStockphoto/Getty Image; SeventyFour/iStockphoto/Getty Image. p. 24: Khosrork/iStockphoto/Getty Image. p. 25: Halfpoint/iStockphoto/Getty Image; PeopleImages/iStockphoto/Getty Image; frantic00/iStockphoto/Getty Image; Jovanmandic/iStockphoto/Getty Image; Prostock-Studio/iStockphoto/Getty Image; Robert Daly/iStockphoto/Getty Image; Akintevs/iStockphoto/Getty Image; Suphaporn/iStockphoto/Getty Image;AaronAmat/iStockphoto/Getty Image; kali9/iStockphoto/Getty Image; triloks/iStockphoto/Getty Image; Ridofranz/iStockphoto/Getty Image; FG Trade/iStockphoto/Getty Image; monkeybusinessimages/iStockphoto/Getty Image; skynesher/iStockphoto/Getty Image; sturti/iStockphoto/Getty Image; Prostock-Studio/iStockphoto/Getty Image; NickyLloyd/iStockphoto/Getty Image; Hispanolistic/iStockphoto/Getty Image; Caiaimage/Sam Edwards/iStockphoto/Getty Image; skynesher/iStockphoto/Getty Image; g-stockstudio/iStockphoto/Getty Image; LeoPatrizi/iStockphoto/Getty Image; PeopleImages/iStockphoto/Getty Image; Ugur Karakoc/iStockphoto/Getty Image; AJ_Watt/iStockphoto/Getty Image. p. 26: piola666/iStockphoto/Getty Image. p. 28: Fly_dragonfly/iStockphoto/Getty Image; martin-dm/iStockphoto/Getty Image; MesquitaFMS/iStockphoto/Getty Image; FluxFactory/iStockphoto/Getty Image. p. 29: Jessica Nabongo. p. 31: SrdjanPav/iStockphoto/Getty Image; rusm/iStockphoto/Getty Image; jacoblund/iStockphoto/Getty Image. p. 32: FG Trade/iStockphoto/Getty Image; nessaflame/iStockphoto/Getty Image; Sean Pavone/iStockphoto/Getty Image. p. 33: duncan1890/iStockphoto/Getty Image; duncan1890/iStockphoto/Getty Image. p. 34: borchee/iStockphoto/Getty Image; South_agency/iStockphoto/Getty Image; grandriver/iStockphoto/Getty Image; MesquitaFMS/iStockphoto/Getty Image; Michael Ver Sprill/iStockphoto/Getty Image; tatyana_tomsickova/iStockphoto/Getty Image; DieterMeyrl/iStockphoto/Getty Image; verbaska_studio/iStockphoto/Getty Image; Mironmax Studio/iStockphoto/Getty Image; Sofir/iStockphoto/Getty Image; andreibanderas/iStockphoto/Getty Image; Tom Hevezi / AP Photo / Imageplus. p. 35: Stephen Barnes/iStockphoto/Getty Image; BrettCharlton/iStockphoto/Getty Image; cullenphotos/iStockphoto/Getty Image; Gfed/iStockphoto/Getty Image; DCrane08/iStockphoto/Getty Image; Michael Zeigler/iStockphoto/Getty Image; ThamKC/iStockphoto/Getty Image; IakovKalinin/iStockphoto/Getty Image; UnitedPhotoStudio1/iStockphoto/Getty Image. p. 37: BrasilNut1/iStockphoto/Getty Image. p. 39: AzmanL/iStockphoto/Getty Image; ljubaphoto/iStockphoto/Getty Image. p. 40: Rudolf Ernst/iStockphoto/Getty Image. p. 41: gradyreese/iStockphoto/Getty Image; MesquitaFMS/iStockphoto/Getty Image; LeoPatrizi/iStockphoto/Getty Image; monkeybusinessimages/iStockphoto/Getty Image; Roman Tiraspolsky/iStockphoto/Getty Image; Kar-Tr/iStockphoto/Getty Image; FatCamera/iStockphoto/Getty Image; FG Trade/iStockphoto/Getty Image; martin-dm/iStockphoto/Getty Image; michaelpuche/iStockphoto/Getty Image; seb_ra/iStockphoto/Getty Image; izusek/iStockphoto/Getty Image; borchee/iStockphoto/Getty Image; Vadym Plysiuk/iStockphoto/Getty Image; Mironmax Studio/iStockphoto/Getty Image; filmfoto/iStockphoto/Getty Image; Michael Ver Sprill/iStockphoto/Getty Image; South_agency/iStockphoto/Getty Image; Borislav/iStockphoto/Getty Image; tatyana_tomsickova/iStockphoto/Getty Image; stanley45/iStockphoto/Getty Image; nensuria/iStockphoto/Getty Image; verbaska_studio/iStockphoto/Getty Image; grandriver/iStockphoto/Getty Image; RyersonClark/iStockphoto/Getty Image; digitalskillet/iStockphoto/Getty Image; Pheelings Media/iStockphoto/Getty Image; Anastasiia Shavshyna/iStockphoto/Getty Image. p. 48: Petmal/iStockphoto/Getty Image. p. 50: torwai/iStockphoto/Getty Image; montiannoowong/iStockphoto/Getty Image; JulPo/iStockphoto/Getty Image; izusek/iStockphoto/Getty Image. p. 51: pixdeluxe/iStockphoto/Getty Image. p. 53: Chalabala/iStockphoto/Getty Image. p. 54: LightFieldStudios/iStockphoto/Getty Image. p. 55: Scharfsinn86/iStockphoto/Getty Image; PlargueDoctor//iStockphoto/Getty Image. p. 56: alvarez/iStockphoto/Getty Image; denozy/iStockphoto/Getty Image; Deagreez/iStockphoto/Getty Image; SIphotography/iStockphoto/Getty Image; sharonotai/iStockphoto/Getty Image; Poravute/iStockphoto/Getty Image; VictorHuang/iStockphoto/Getty Image; Srdjanns74/iStockphoto/Getty Image; everydayplus/iStockphoto/Getty Image. p. 57: undrey/iStockphoto/Getty Image. p. 61: South_agency/iStockphoto/Getty Image. p. 62: Hung_Chung_Chih/iStockphoto/Getty Image. p. 63: BanksPhotos/iStockphoto/Getty Image; cruphoto/iStockphoto/Getty Image; Image Source/iStockphoto/Getty Image; simonapilolla/iStockphoto/Getty Image; Rawpixel/iStockphoto/Getty Image; PIKSEL/iStockphoto/Getty Image; Dorin_S/iStockphoto/Getty Image; eggeeggjiew/iStockphoto/Getty Image; Pekic/iStockphoto/Getty Image; william87/iStockphoto/Getty Image; NiKita Filippov/iStockphoto/Getty Image; LewisTsePuiLung/iStockphoto/Getty Image; alexandr6868/iStockphoto/Getty Image; SIphotography/iStockphoto/Getty Image; RyanJLane/iStockphoto/Getty Image; Bulat Silvia/iStockphoto/Getty Image; a_lis/iStockphoto/Getty Image; Mingirov/iStockphoto/Getty Image; Kostikova/iStockphoto/Getty Image; yunava1/iStockphoto/Getty Image; KatarzynaBialasiewicz/iStockphoto/Getty Image; KatarzynaBialasiewicz/iStockphoto/Getty Image; pmmart/iStockphoto/Getty Image; SIphotography/iStockphoto/Getty Image; Topp_Yimgrimm/iStockphoto/Getty Image. p. 64: martin-dm/iStockphoto/Getty Image. p. 66: PeopleImages/iStockphoto/Getty Image; supersizer/iStockphoto/Getty Image; Sergey Nazarov/iStockphoto/Getty Image; maruco/iStockphoto/Getty Image; Antonio_Diaz/iStockphoto/Getty Image; Boogich/iStockphoto/Getty Image; skynesher/iStockphoto/Getty Image. p. 67: Nastasic/iStockphoto/Getty Image; Patrick Chu/iStockphoto/Getty Image. p. 68: nito100/iStockphoto/Getty Image; staticnak1983/iStockphoto/Getty Image. p. 69: helgakhorimarko/iStockphoto/Getty Image. p. 70: adamkaz/iStockphoto/Getty Image. p. 71: FG Trade/iStockphoto/Getty Image; travelview/iStockphoto/Getty Image. p. 72: LordHenriVoton/iStockphoto/Getty Image; AsiaVision/iStockphoto/Getty Image; miodrag ignjatovic/iStockphoto/Getty Image; jacoblund/iStockphoto/Getty Image; fizkes/iStockphoto/Getty Image; jacoblund/iStockphoto/Getty Image. p. 73: Ridofranz/iStockphoto/Getty Image; shironosov/iStockphoto/Getty Image; Estradaanton/iStockphoto/Getty Image; AntonioGuillem/iStockphoto/Getty Image; AntonioGuillem/iStockphoto/Getty Image; Igor Alecsander/iStockphoto/Getty Image; VioletaStoimenova/iStockphoto/Getty Image; g-stockstudio/iStockphoto/Getty Image; SDI Productions/iStockphoto/Getty Image; Estradaanton/iStockphoto/Getty Image. p. 74: SDI Productions/iStockphoto/Getty Image; Valeriy_G/iStockphoto/Getty Image; JohnnyGreig/iStockphoto/Getty Image. p. 77: insemar/iStockphoto/Getty Image. p. 78: FG Trade/iStockphoto/Getty Image. p. 79: CREATISTA/iStockphoto/Getty Image; ajr_images/iStockphoto/Getty Image; DaniloAndjus/iStockphoto/Getty Image; Image Source/iStockphoto/Getty Image; supersizer/iStockphoto/Getty Image; vm/iStockphoto/Getty Image; Boogich/iStockphoto/Getty Image; kali9/iStockphoto/Getty Image; Antonio_Diaz/iStockphoto/Getty Image; Sergey Nazarov/iStockphoto/Getty Image; ferrantraite/iStockphoto/Getty Image; maruco/iStockphoto/Getty Image; jacoblund/iStockphoto/Getty Image; fizkes/iStockphoto/Getty Image; jacoblund/iStockphoto/Getty Image; AsiaVision/iStockphoto/Getty Image; milla1974/iStockphoto/Getty Image; miodrag ignjatovic/iStockphoto/Getty Image; jacoblund/iStockphoto/Getty Image; Wavebreakmedia/iStockphoto/Getty Image. p. 80: NATALIA KHIMICH/iStockphoto/Getty Image; santypan/iStockphoto/Getty Image; milindri/iStockphoto/Getty Image; KatarzynaBialasiewicz/iStockphoto/Getty Image; Imgorthand/iStockphoto/Getty Image; imtmphoto/iStockphoto/Getty Image; karandaev/iStockphoto/Getty Image; Image Source/iStockphoto/Getty Image. p. 81: FluxFactory/iStockphoto/Getty Image; LeoPatrizi/iStockphoto/Getty Image; Wavebreakmedia/iStockphoto/Getty Image; Ridofranz/iStockphoto/Getty Image; nortonrsx/iStockphoto/Getty Image; Koldunova_Anna/iStockphoto/Getty Image; Group4 Studio/iStockphoto/Getty Image. p. 85: uniquepixel/iStockphoto/Getty Image. p. 86: melitas/iStockphoto/Getty Image; RapidEye/iStockphoto/Getty Image; Motortion/iStockphoto/Getty Image; ngupakarti/iStockphoto/Getty Image; ONYXprj/iStockphoto/Getty Image. p. 88: Goran Jakus Photography/iStockphoto/Getty Image. p. 90: Dan Rentea/iStockphoto/Getty Image; Orbon Alija/iStockphoto/Getty Image; izusek/iStockphoto/Getty Image; binabina/iStockphoto/Getty Image; PeopleImages/iStockphoto/Getty Image. p. 91: filborg/iStockphoto/Getty Image; MStudioImages/iStockphoto/Getty Image. p. 92: Joel Carillet/iStockphoto/Getty Image. p. 93: Evan Agostini/Invision/AP Photo/Imageplus; grinvalds/iStockphoto/Getty Image; AnastasiaRasstrigina/iStockphoto/Getty Image. p. 94: kali9/iStockphoto/Getty Image; fourseasons/iStockphoto/Getty Image; Prostock-Studio/iStockphoto/Getty Image; bernardbodo/iStockphoto/Getty Image. p. 95: JENNIFER E. WOLF/iStockphoto/Getty Image; Paepaestockphoto/iStockphoto/Getty Image; Matteo Guedia/iStockphoto/Getty Image. p. 96: Juanmonino/iStockphoto/Getty Image; wdstock/iStockphoto/Getty Image; chokja/iStockphoto/Getty Image; ljubaphoto/iStockphoto/Getty Image; Marilyn Nieves/iStockphoto/Getty Image; mixetto/iStockphoto/Getty Image; Oleksandra Polishchuk/iStockphoto/Getty Image; Photology1971/iStockphoto/Getty Image; Prostock-Studio/iStockphoto/Getty Image;

FG Trade/iStockphoto/Getty Image; marekuliasz/iStockphoto/Getty Image; SawitreeLyaon/iStockphoto/Getty Image; Drazen Zigic/iStockphoto/Getty Image; NinaMalyna/iStockphoto/Getty Image; ALEKSANDR STRELNIKOV/iStockphoto/Getty Image; AleksandarNakic/iStockphoto/Getty Image. p. 99: krblokhin/iStockphoto/Getty Image; Justin Ng / Avalon / ZUMA Press / Imageplus. p. 102: Portra/iStockphoto/Getty Image. p. 103: izusek/iStockphoto/Getty Image; Tadeush89/iStockphoto/Getty Image; kool99/iStockphoto/Getty Image; Dan Rentea/iStockphoto/Getty Image; MStudioImages/iStockphoto/Getty Image; Prensis/iStockphoto/Getty Image; michaeljung/iStockphoto/Getty Image; iprogressman/iStockphoto/Getty Image; Orbon Alija/iStockphoto/Getty Image; Prostock-Studio/iStockphoto/Getty Image; istockphotoluis/iStockphoto/Getty Image; Willrow_Hood/iStockphoto/Getty Image; insta_photos/iStockphoto/Getty Image; NinaMalyna/iStockphoto/Getty Image; ljubaphoto/iStockphoto/Getty Image; chokja/iStockphoto/Getty Image; Prostock-Studio/iStockphoto/Getty Image; Marilyn Nieves/iStockphoto/Getty Image; mixetto/iStockphoto/Getty Image; marekuliasz/iStockphoto/Getty Image; SawitreeLyaon/iStockphoto/Getty Image; Drazen Zigic/iStockphoto/Getty Image; Oleksandra Polishchuk/iStockphoto/Getty Image; Photology1971/iStockphoto/Getty Image; FG Trade/iStockphoto/Getty Image. p. 104: FG Trade/iStockphoto/Getty Image. p. 107: Sladic/iStockphoto/Getty Image; superjoseph/iStockphoto/Getty Image. p. 119: shironosov/iStockphoto/Getty Image. p. 120: Jasmina007/iStockphoto/Getty Image; Hispanolistic/iStockphoto/Getty Image; WillSelarep/iStockphoto/Getty Image; AfricaImages/iStockphoto/Getty Image; istockphotoluis/iStockphoto/Getty Image; Harbucks/iStockphoto/Getty Image; PeopleImages/iStockphoto/Getty Image. p. 121: FG Trade/iStockphoto/Getty Image; fizkes/iStockphoto/Getty Image; RyanJLane/iStockphoto/Getty Image; dobok/iStockphoto/Getty Image; CiydemImages/iStockphoto/Getty Image; dragana991/iStockphoto/Getty Image; MNStudio/iStockphoto/Getty Image; Inside Creative House/iStockphoto/Getty Image. p. 126: AlessandroPhoto/iStockphoto/Getty Image. p. 128: puhimec/iStockphoto/Getty Image; Rafa Jodar/iStockphoto/Getty Image; shironosov/iStockphoto/Getty Image; djedzura/iStockphoto/Getty Image; ftwitty/iStockphoto/Getty Image. p. 129: vslko/iStockphoto/Getty Image; Capuski/iStockphoto/Getty Image; RichLegg/iStockphoto/Getty Image. p. 130: Chet_W/iStockphoto/Getty Image; Sergii Batechenkov/iStockphoto/Getty Image; Antagain/iStockphoto/Getty Image; allanswart/iStockphoto/Getty Image; turk_stock_photographer/iStockphoto/Getty Image; Roman Stavila/iStockphoto/Getty Image. p. 131: FrankvandenBergh/iStockphoto/Getty Image; KatarzynaBialasiewicz/iStockphoto/Getty Image; Black Lollipop/iStockphoto/Getty Image. p. 132: Prostock-Studio/iStockphoto/Getty Image. p. 133: peerapong boriboon/iStockphoto/Getty Image; Black_Kira/iStockphoto/Getty Image. p. 134: jacoblund/iStockphoto/Getty Image; tzahiV/iStockphoto/Getty Image; AntonioGuillem/iStockphoto/Getty Image; Andrii Lysenko/iStockphoto/Getty Image; StellarStock/iStockphoto/Getty Image; jacoblund/iStockphoto/Getty Image; Prapat Aowsakorn/iStockphoto/Getty Image; Nikolay Chekalin/iStockphoto/Getty Image; Animaflora/iStockphoto/Getty Image; monkeybusinessimages/iStockphoto/Getty Image; ruizluquepaz/iStockphoto/Getty Image. p. 135: cnythzl/iStockphoto/Getty Image. p. 137: ampueroleonardo/iStockphoto/Getty Image; FerreiraSilva/iStockphoto/Getty Image; kickers/iStockphoto/Getty Image. p. 139: RealPeopleGroup/iStockphoto/Getty Image; AaronAmat/iStockphoto/Getty Image; South_agency/iStockphoto/Getty Image. p. 140: Drazen_/iStockphoto/Getty Image. p. 141: puhimec/iStockphoto/Getty Image; djedzura/iStockphoto/Getty Image; Ilya Ginzburg/iStockphoto/Getty Image; gorodenkoff/iStockphoto/Getty Image; jacoblund/iStockphoto/Getty Image; avid_creative/iStockphoto/Getty Image; gorodenkoff/iStockphoto/Getty Image; SDI Productions/iStockphoto/Getty Image; ftwitty/iStockphoto/Getty Image; FOTOKITA/iStockphoto/Getty Image; zoka74/iStockphoto/Getty Image; shironosov/iStockphoto/Getty Image; gorodenkoff/iStockphoto/Getty Image; stocknshares/iStockphoto/Getty Image; Olivier Le Moal/iStockphoto/Getty Image; PeopleImages/iStockphoto/Getty Image; fpphotobank/iStockphoto/Getty Image; StellarStock/iStockphoto/Getty Image; Prapat Aowsakorn/iStockphoto/Getty Image; imagedepotpro/iStockphoto/Getty Image; PeopleImages/iStockphoto/Getty Image; South_agency/iStockphoto/Getty Image; jacoblund/iStockphoto/Getty Image; monkeybusinessimages/iStockphoto/Getty Image; eclipse_images/iStockphoto/Getty Image; Nikolay Chekalin/iStockphoto/Getty Image; innovatedcaptures/iStockphoto/Getty Image; Animaflora/iStockphoto/Getty Image; Andrii Lysenko/iStockphoto/Getty Image; Hispanolistic/iStockphoto/Getty Image; simonkr/iStockphoto/Getty Image. p. 142: Tzido/iStockphoto/Getty Image; sefa ozel/iStockphoto/Getty Image. p. 144: mikimad/iStockphoto/Getty Image; Tanya_F/iStockphoto/Getty Image. p. 145: Willy Sanjuan / Invision / AP Photo / Imageplus. p. 146: peshkov/iStockphoto/Getty Image. p. 147: Natsuo0729/iStockphoto/Getty Image; Filip_Krstic/iStockphoto/Getty Image; mikolajn/iStockphoto/Getty Image. p. 148: cokada/iStockphoto/Getty Image; Neustockimages/iStockphoto/Getty Image; joshblake/iStockphoto/Getty Image. p. 149: Juan Carlos Martinez de Maya/iStockphoto/Getty Image. p. 150: 4x6/iStockphoto/Getty Image. p. 152: 3bugsmom/iStockphoto/Getty Image. p. 155: gorodenkoff/iStockphoto/Getty Image; supersizer/iStockphoto/Getty Image. p. 156: monkeybusinessimages/iStockphoto/Getty Image. p. 157: Alexey Surgay/iStockphoto; 20lbsPerception/iStockphoto/Getty Image; MarioGuti/iStockphoto/Getty Image; scyther5/iStockphoto/Getty Image; andrewgenn/iStockphoto/Getty Image; alexsl/iStockphoto/Getty Image; monkeybusinessimages/iStockphoto/Getty Image; robas/iStockphoto/Getty Image; ZavgSG/iStockphoto/Getty Image; Liudmila Chernetska/iStockphoto/Getty Image; ugurhan/iStockphoto/Getty Image; pavlen/iStockphoto/Getty Image; wsphotos/iStockphoto/Getty Image; thitiwat tapingkae/iStockphoto/Getty Image; AzriSuratmin/iStockphoto/Getty Image; zhz_akey/iStockphoto/Getty Image; Thierry Hebbelinck/iStockphoto/Getty Image; RazvanDP/iStockphoto/Getty Image; Dean Mitchell/iStockphoto/Getty Image; Drazen Zigic/iStockphoto/Getty Image; AndreyPopov/iStockphoto/Getty Image; PeopleImages/iStockphoto/Getty Image; Prostock-Studio/iStockphoto/Getty Image; sumnersgraphicsinc/iStockphoto/Getty Image; Francesco Marzovillo/iStockphoto/Getty Image. p. 158: andresr/iStockphoto/Getty Image; Hispanolistic/iStockphoto/Getty Image; miodrag ignjatovic/iStockphoto/Getty Image; urbazon/iStockphoto/Getty Image; artursfoto/iStockphoto/Getty Image; ABEMOS/iStockphoto/Getty Image; ImageKit/iStockphoto/Getty Image. p. 159: dolgachov/iStockphoto/Getty Image; ljubaphoto/iStockphoto/Getty Image; KatarzynaBialasiewicz/iStockphoto/Getty Image; RichLegg/iStockphoto/Getty Image; D-Keine/iStockphoto/Getty Image; vernonwiley/iStockphoto/Getty Image; PerfectVectors/iStockphoto/Getty Image; AndreyPopov/iStockphoto/Getty Image. p. 160: Neustockimages/iStockphoto/Getty Image; Jacob Wackerhausen/iStockphoto/Getty Image; AntonioGuillem/iStockphoto/Getty Image. p. 163: EvilWata/iStockphoto/Getty Image. p. 164: Vadim Sazhniev/iStockphoto/Getty Image; a/iStockphoto/Getty Image. p. 165: SiberianArt/iStockphoto/Getty Image; lemono/iStockphoto/Getty Image; Alina Vovk/iStockphoto/Getty Image; Bulgakova Kristina/iStockphoto/Getty Image; Anna_Isaeva/iStockphoto/Getty Image; invincible_bulldog/iStockphoto/Getty Image. p. 170: JohnnyGreig/iStockphoto/Getty Image. p. 171: nattrass/iStockphoto/Getty Image. p. 172: RetroAtelier/iStockphoto/Getty Image. p. 175: Eva-Katalin/iStockphoto/Getty Image; Serbek/iStockphoto/Getty Image. p. 176: Lucy Pemoni / AP Photo / Imageplus. p. 177: Anton Vierietin/iStockphoto/Getty Image; mactrunk/iStockphoto/Getty Image; Charday Penn/iStockphoto/Getty Image; bluegame/iStockphoto/Getty Image; StefaNikolic/iStockphoto/Getty Image; Michał Chodyra/iStockphoto/Getty Image; ridvan_celik/iStockphoto/Getty Image; insjoy/iStockphoto/Getty Image; SolStock/iStockphoto/Getty Image; AnnaStills/iStockphoto/Getty Image. p. 187: CasarsaGuru/iStockphoto/Getty Image. p. 188: fotoVoyager/iStockphoto/Getty Image. p. 191: jacoblund/iStockphoto/Getty Image; monkeybusinessimages/iStockphoto/Getty Image. p. 192: Damocean/iStockphoto/Getty Image. p. 193: Eerik/iStockphoto/Getty Image; GalapagosFrame/iStockphoto/Getty Image; Evelin Elmest/iStockphoto/Getty Image; Sunnybeach/iStockphoto/Getty Image; VukasS/iStockphoto/Getty Image; heibaihui/iStockphoto/Getty Image; Tomy Ardiansyah/iStockphoto/Getty Image; AVR/iStockphoto/Getty Image; andreusK/iStockphoto/Getty Image; vtorous/iStockphoto/Getty Image. p. 194: AdamGregor/iStockphoto/Getty Image; Drazen_/iStockphoto/Getty Image; SolStock/iStockphoto/Getty Image; giovanna-fotos/iStockphoto/Getty Image; PCH-Vector/iStockphoto/Getty Image; hxyume/iStockphoto/Getty Image; kali9/iStockphoto/Getty Image. p. 195: monkeybusinessimages/iStockphoto/Getty Image; Hispanolistic/iStockphoto/Getty Image; xavierarnau/iStockphoto/Getty Image. p. 197: FamVeld/iStockphoto/Getty Image. p. 200: vgajic/iStockphoto/Getty Image. p. 201: AndreyPopov/iStockphoto/Getty Image; XtockImages/iStockphoto/Getty Image; fizkes/iStockphoto/Getty Image; Halfpoint/iStockphoto/Getty Image; Prostock-Studio/iStockphoto/Getty Image; AntonioGuillem/iStockphoto/Getty Image; MarijaRadovic/iStockphoto/Getty Image; Xavier Lorenzo/iStockphoto/Getty Image; Cecilie_Arcurs/iStockphoto/Getty Image; jacoblund/iStockphoto/Getty Image; blackCAT/iStockphoto/Getty Image. p. 210: Rawpixel/iStockphoto/Getty Image. p. 211: clubfoto/iStockphoto/Getty Image. p. 213: DMEPhotography/iStockphoto/Getty Image. p. 215: Aleksandr Zhurilo/iStockphoto/Getty Image; pixelfit/iStockphoto/Getty Image. p. 216: RgStudio/iStockphoto/Getty Image. p. 217: Fahroni/iStockphoto/Getty Image; fermate/iStockphoto/Getty Image; Jeliva/iStockphoto/Getty Image; undefined undefined/iStockphoto/Getty Image; bancha singchai/iStockphoto/Getty Image; anna avdeeva/iStockphoto/Getty Image; limpido/iStockphoto/Getty Image; simpson33/iStockphoto/Getty Image; piyaphun/iStockphoto/Getty Image; cyano66/iStockphoto/Getty Image. p. 218: Kira-Yan/iStockphoto/Getty Image. p. 220: Koldunova_Anna/iStockphoto/Getty Image; Sergey Khakimullin/iStockphoto/Getty Image. p. 221: Jun/iStockphoto/Getty Image. p. 223: Kutsuks/iStockphoto/Getty Image; RHJ/iStockphoto/Getty Image. p. 224: JamesBrey/iStockphoto/Getty Image. p. 225: KatarzynaBialasiewicz/iStockphoto/Getty Image; sanjeri/iStockphoto/Getty Image; Business/iStockphoto/Getty Image; acilo/iStockphoto/Getty Image; Wavebreakmedia/iStockphoto/Getty Image; Svitlana Hulko/iStockphoto/Getty Image; BrianAJackson/iStockphoto/Getty Image; KLH49/iStockphoto/Getty Image; karenfoleyphotography/iStockphoto/Getty Image; mb-fotos/iStockphoto/Getty Image. p. 228: Denis Pobytov/iStockphoto/Getty Image. p. 229: guruXOOX/iStockphoto/Getty Image; AaronAmat/iStockphoto/Getty Image. p. 231: SDI Productions/iStockphoto/Getty Image; gorodenkoff/iStockphoto/Getty Image. p. 232: Igor Alecsander/iStockphoto/Getty Image. p. 233: Zerbor/iStockphoto/Getty Image; Liliboas/iStockphoto/Getty Image; tagphoto/iStockphoto/Getty Image; Devonyu/iStockphoto/Getty Image; andrewgenn/iStockphoto/Getty Image; Maurice Savage/Alamy/Fotoarena; claudiodivizia/Deposit Photos/Imageplus; bgblue/iStockphoto/Getty Images; littleny/iStockphoto/Getty Images; bedobedo/Deposit Photos/Imageplus.

Catalogação na Publicação (CIP)
(BENITEZ Catalogação Ass. Editorial, MS, Brasil)

R675i Reilly, Patricia
2.ed. InstaEnglish 2nd edition level 3 : student's book and workbook / Patricia Reilly ... [et al.]. – 2.ed. – São Paulo : Macmillan Education do Brasil, 2022.
240 p.; il.; 21 x 29,7 cm.

ISBN : 978-65-5752-107-6

1. Língua inglesa (Ensino fundamental).
I. Reilly, Patricia. II. Título. III. Série.

07-2022/87 CDD 372.652

Índice para catálogo sistemático:
1. Língua inglesa : Ensino fundamental 372.652
Bibliotecária : Aline Graziele Benitez CRB-1/3129

MACMILLAN EDUCATION BRASIL
Av. Brigadeiro Faria Lima, 1.309, 2º Andar
Jd. Paulistano – São Paulo – SP – 01452-002
www.macmillan.com.br
Customer Service: [55] (11) 4613-2278
0800 16 88 77

MISTO
Papel | Apoiando o manejo florestal responsável
FSC® C103020

Impresso no Brasil, EGB, 09 2025